Persuasion and Influence in American Life

Eighth Edition

Gary C. Woodward
College of New Jersey

Robert E. Denton, Jr.
Virginia Polytechnic Institute and State University

WAVELAND
PRESS, INC.
Long Grove, Illinois

For information about this book, contact:
   Waveland Press, Inc.
   4180 IL Route 83, Suite 101
   Long Grove, IL 60047-9580
   (847) 634-0081
   info@waveland.com
   www.waveland.com

10-digit ISBN 1-4786-3612-2
13-digit ISBN 978-1-4786-3612-0

Printed in the United States of America

7 6 5 4 3 2 1

To Our Parents

Contents

PART III
Persuasion Settings

Preface

A recent survey of psychology textbooks found that most present more definitive conclusions about key psychological concepts than is justified by the available research. The researchers who reviewed the books noted that the authors may be "unconsciously prone to overcompensating by overstating the conclusiveness of psychological research and understating its limitations or theoretical controversies."[1]

This observation about texts that simplify too much is important because, like many works in the humanities and social sciences, *Persuasion and Influence in American Life* is intended to answer big questions related to how persons conduct themselves when urged to change. Indeed, some of the ideas surveyed in these pages have been adopted by major figures in behavioral psychology. But while it is the nature of a textbook to offer firm theories and models, we attempt to acknowledge real-world doubts that give exceptions and qualifications their due. To do any less is would be to ignore the multiplicity of ways individuals understand the world.

A student in a persuasion course questioned why so much time was spent studying the many forms of resistance that audiences use to disarm persuasive appeals. If resistance is the norm, she asked, why bother at all? How could there be interest in a subject where failure is more likely than success? The best answer is perhaps another question: who ever said that persuasion to sentient and freethinking people should be easy? After all, our species and its tribes are varied and unpredictable. We know that the generalizations we apply to others are, at best, contingent and incomplete. We also understand the complexities of our own relationships and thoughts, which are not always transparent even to ourselves. Because we are innovators and communicators, complication is built into the human experience. Our multitiered lives come with multilayered motivations; we live in ideas as well as spaces. We see and know with words. We detect and judge each other's motivations. And all of these attributes feed into elaborate webs of personal connections and mediated networks. How could predictions of our future thoughts and behaviors be easy?

The mysteries of human action speak to the glorious truth that humans are marvels at surprising each other. It is our birthright as responsive beings to make a path in life that is not a straight line but is full of functional adaptations. If we need evidence, we have the unanticipated results in recent elections in the United States and Britain. Britain's vote to leave the European Union and the election of Donald Trump to the US presidency were surprises to professionals who were reasonably sure they understood the voters. These results were not unlike the unexpected outcomes that happen every day as we pitch ideas to others, only to discover that our enthusiasm has failed to persuade. Sometimes we may only succeed in hardening the attitudes and behaviors that we sought to change.

So while textbooks are supposed to be foundational accounts of what we know, any discipline that tries to anticipate human behavior must be satisfied with understandings that are conditional. We have discovered many of the secrets of the physical world. We can make accurate predictions about the behavior of electrons in a circuit. But we are still enigmas to ourselves. That means simple formulas for inducing others to change rarely exist. Some texts bravely lay out hard rules and strategies; our hope is that we have mostly avoided the false comfort of certainty.

The eighth edition has been reconfigured to be more concise than earlier versions. An important goal was to pare subject areas down to core theories and principles that seem the most durable. This edition has several new features. We include short sidebars in every chapter to make some ideas and issues more personal and vivid. These brief diversions also suggest applications of key ideas to spheres of activity not otherwise addressed in the text. A second feature is content that fully acknowledges the opportunities and challenges posed by social media and different kinds of digital platforms. Messaging on social media creates opportunities for peer-to-peer influence, complicating the dominant older model of persuasion based on more formal audiences. The book closes with a shift in focus that is unique for university-level texts. On the theory of learning by doing, the last chapter takes on the challenge of considering and implementing core strategies for persuasion design, with an emphasis on the construction of short messages common to digital and commercial media in this century. This approach makes this text not only a study of persuasion but also a primer on doing it.

Although this edition was prepared by Gary C. Woodward, the book continues to reflect the scholarship and insights of longtime coauthor, Robert E. Denton Jr. It has also been immeasurably strengthened over the years by our editor and friend at Waveland Press, Carol Rowe, and from many patient students in the theories of persuasion course offered at The College of New Jersey.

 NOTE

1 Jesse Singal, "There's a Problem with a Bunch of Psychology Textbooks," *Science of Us*, January 5, 2017, http://nymag.com/scienceofus/2017/01/theres-a-problem-with-a-bunch-of-psychology-textbooks.html.

1

Persuasion and Influence
Introduction

> All told, persuasion ranges from the bluntest quest of advantage, as in sales promotion or propaganda, through courtship, social etiquette, education, and the sermon, to a "pure" form that delights in the process of appeal for itself alone.[1]
>
> —Kenneth Burke

The crisis began when CNN broadcast the 2013 film *Blackfish*, an 83-minute documentary about a killer whale at SeaWorld Entertainment's aquarium and water park in Orlando. Rarely had a single persuasive message so deeply undermined the financial prospects of a large US corporation. The company would fight for years against the disturbing allegations in what seemed like a minor television documentary. But viewers took note. Word spread, and soon the film was picked up by a Hollywood distributor and released in theaters. Sea World began a campaign of counter-persuasion to try to blunt the bad publicity. Paid messages began to show up in newspapers assuring readers the firm was a good corporate citizen. Then television ads ran nationally offering the promise to change its practices.

The orca, Tilikum, was linked to the deaths of two trainers and a spectator. Former employees noted that the large animal was unpredictable. The documentary also made the broader case that the captivity of large sea mammals like Tilikum was inherently inhumane, slowly driving them to erratic behaviors. The release of *Blackfish* coincided with a noticeable increase in public distrust of live entertainment built around animal acts. SeaWorld Entertainment became one of the most visible targets for Americans newly sensitized to the realities of capturing and maintaining animals for daily performances. The changing tide was fully evident in 2017 when the legendary Ringling Brothers Circus announced that it was closing, having already retired its elephants several years earlier.

Crisis advertising isn't about the short-term goal of selling more tickets or products. The underlying persuasion strategy is more defensive—to reassure general consumers who could drift toward open opposition and also to keep the stock price of the company from tumbling. SeaWorld's stock price fell by 34 percent in 2016; attendance and revenues at the company's parks had both fallen, creating "a corporate failure of epic—even biblical—proportions."[2]

Defensive ads began to appear on several media platforms. An op-ed page advertisement in the *New York Times* carried the headline "Making Better Habitats." Hendrik Nollens, a veterinarian at SeaWorld, wrote the copy.

> SeaWorld's killer whale habitats are among the largest and most advanced in the world. But that's not enough. Here in San Diego, we're set to transform these habitats into dramatically larger, more natural settings. These new habitats will provide all of us—marine experts and visitors alike—with a deeper appreciation and understanding of these magnificent animals.[3]

More ads followed, with a statement to television viewers that the company recognized it needed to change. SeaWorld announced an end to their Orca program, including the capture of new animals and cessation of all Orca shows. Tilikum died in the same year.

SeaWorld may well win back its audiences with a sustained campaign; corporations usually recover from public relations calamities. In addition, many Americans shy away from messages that redefine entertainment preferences as ethical choices. We don't like to give up leisure habits even if we know they come with risks or liabilities. Even so, *Blackfish* is convincing evidence that the long-form documentary must be counted as one of the many significant forms of persuasion available to advocates.

THE NECESSITY AND CHALLENGE OF PERSUASION

Persuasion is usually described as a request for others to agree or yield—outcomes that are not easy to achieve. The Roman statesman Cicero characterized persuasion as "the most difficult of all attainments"[4] He thought that mastery of its various components was beyond the reach of most. The Greek philosopher Aristotle was more optimistic. He believed that the study of persuasion could be systematized, although he also noted that resistance was more the norm than the exception.[5] For both, persuasion was a special subject made more interesting by its tendency to put all forms of human genius and frailty on conspicuous display.

The primary goal of this book is to offer a systematic description and vocabulary for the persuasive process. How do we change deep-seated attitudes? What makes us susceptible to or immune from constant attempts to persuade us to accept ideas, products, and people? How can advocates sometimes cause people to deny their beliefs and accept actions that impose serious hardships? The answers to these questions not only equip us to better adapt to our communication-saturated world but they also reveal some interesting and surprising characteristics of human nature.

There is no single form of persuasion. It occurs in a diverse range of contexts and media from simple exchanges of opinions between friends to elaborate campaigns designed for specific broadcast and internet audiences. Persuaders may be as well financed as the Microsoft Corporation or as resource poor as a single homeowner challenging the decision of a zoning board. The variety of human contacts that call for effective advocacy is nearly endless. Members of a free society cannot escape responsibility for organizing or participating in public persuasion. In our roles as citizens and consumers, we face the necessity of managing a vast array of demands and opportunities.

In the remainder of this chapter we define persuasion and examine several additional case studies. We also offer a set of key baseline propositions about persuasion, which will help explain why it is one of the most cherished of all social skills.

PERSUASION DEFINED

There are two competing but related traditions in defining persuasion. One tradition sees it as an ethically suspect process—a form of *hucksterism*—where advocates create messages with exaggerated claims that ask others to comply for financial gain. Aristotle's teacher, Plato, saw persuasion as little more than a "knack": "a part of a questionable human impulse that isn't admirable at all."[6] Others have similarly defined persuaders as behind-the-scenes "compliance practitioners,"[7] an alarming label that suggests a mastery of *deceptive* manipulation. In a related sense, during and after World War II it was common to describe many kinds of messages using the word "propaganda." The legacy of suspicion reflected in all of these terms remains today in approaches that emphasize that we are likely to be potential victims of messages that cleverly muscle out our better critical instincts.[8] Many in the social sciences have learned to live with the "vulgar contentiousness" they associate with persuasion, sometimes preferring a newer label of "attitude change" that they see as carrying less baggage.[9] They often speak in terms of gaining "compliance," inducing "conformity," engaging in "social influence" or "yielding to social forces."[10]

While we have no quarrel with a cautionary stance toward persuasion, we prefer a point of view that is less prejudiced against persuaders and more conscious of how humans engage in the process of shaping consensus and agreement. The second tradition, the *rhetorical tradition*, is more hopeful. *Rhetoric* is the classical term for *persuasion*, terms that we will use interchangeably in this book. Erwin Bettinghaus and Michael Cody build on the idea of the necessity of rhetoric with their observation that a persuasive situation involves "a conscious attempt by one individual or group to change the attitudes, beliefs, or the behavior of another individual or group of individuals through the transmission of some message."[11] Similarly, Herbert Simons and Jean Jones describe persuasion as communication designed to influence the judgments and actions of others."[12] Along with Rod Hart and Suzanne Daughton,[13] they also emphasize what is sometimes missed by persuasion's critics: that it is a cooperative and *coactive enterprise.*[14] Audiences are more than targets or victims. They are often willing participants in their own persuasion. As Hart and Daughton note, rhetoric

> is a reciprocal or transactive art, because it brings two or more people together in an atmosphere of potential change. By sharing communication, both rhetors and audiences open themselves up to each other's influence. In that sense, communication is not something that is done to others. Rather, it is something that people choose to do to themselves by consenting to communicative contact.[15]

This coactive feature is important to keep it mind. The first tradition assumes that people are objects or victims of persuasion, defenseless against the clever appeals of others. The favored phrase within many persuasion industries is *target audience*. From this perspective, the persuader is sometimes an active agent in search of vulnerable and mostly passive quarry. The task is to find the hapless victim and to land a rhetorical bull's-eye on the most vulnerable part. But while the idea of a target is often useful and sometimes essential, it can let us miss the second tradition of persuasion as a change agent. Change is a necessary feature for societies that must periodically renew themselves to survive. The same can also be applied to individuals. As the late essayist Chris Hitchens once observed, *it isn't always that someone plans something that will change our mind, it's that our mind changes us.*[16] We learn, adapt, and grow.

Daniel O'Keefe makes the unusual decision to decline a "sharp line of definition," noting that any precise meaning sets up boundaries that are partially arbitrary. Despite his reluctance, he describes most persuasion as "a successful intentional effort at influencing another's mental state through communication in a circumstance in which the persuadee has some measure of freedom."[17] We like his insistence on a persuadee's freedom of choice. Although not all theorists agree,[18] we believe that forcing someone to act is *not* the same thing as truly persuading them. In fact, the use of any kind of power advantage—physical, hierarchical or financial—seems contrary to the spirit of authentic persuasion. If an employer orders you to complete what you consider is a meaningless task, you may well comply, but you've hardly been persuaded.

We endorse elements of other characterizations as well. The important qualifier offered by Bettinghaus and Cody that persuasion may affect behavior *as well* as judgments and attitudes is especially relevant. We would resist the urge to reduce persuasion to just behavioral change—what people do rather than what they may think. It is important to remember that persuasion can create internal changes—attitudes—that may not take any outward form. Our behavior may hide important conflicting feelings. For example, an individual's behavior in a certain moment may indicate that they have momentarily given in to another's request. But if underlying attitudes are not changed, their behavior is likely to revert to its original form.

As we have noted, mere **compliance** because of someone's request mostly falls outside of what we consider as a persuasive effect. Sometimes we comply with another's request more out of courtesy than genuine agreement. **Conviction,** however, is a real persuasion effect because it suggests a more unequivocal change of mind. It represents the supreme goal of many persuaders seeking acknowledgement and assent from others.

While persuasion is most apparent when a transformation of some sort occurs within an individual, an exclusive emphasis on change overlooks the pervasive role of communication to *prevent* the erosion of support. As most advertisers know, the most effective persuasive strategies are essentially defensive. It is easier to reassure a listener's faith in what is already accepted than to urge change to something new.

We define persuasion as a process composed of five concurrent dimensions:

1. the coactive process of preparing and presenting
2. verbal or nonverbal messages
3. to autonomous and often receptive individuals and audiences
4. to alter or strengthen
5. their attitudes and/or behaviors.

Our definition emphasizes that persuasion is interactive—an ongoing process that takes place between people. It comes with hopes but no guarantees. One can prepare and present a message, and yet still fail. In true persuasion, as O'Keefe has noted, audiences are **autonomous** and can freely withhold their consent. Individuals and audiences are clearly presented as a target in our definition, but sometimes it is easier to imagine than to know them. We lean heavily on the belief that we can lump individuals together in cohesive groups with demographic and lifestyle similarities (age, sex, income, region of residence, and so on). Traditional media outlets such as television networks often sell their audiences to advertisers based on some of these features. And virtually every music, film and television producer is convinced they know their market. Even so, the concept of the audience rarely works as well in fact as it does in theory. In their study of *The Mass Audience,* James Webster and Patricia Phalen remind us that "audiences are not naturally occurring 'facts,' but social creations. In that sense, they are what we make them."[19]

There are several challenges with this core idea of a known audience. One is the proliferation of media platforms that block a clear view of who is on the receiving end. On the web, audiences turn out to be partly invisible and not very predictable. Even the motives of those who self-select themselves into the same group can be surprisingly diverse. For example, it would be risky to infer much about the audience for content on Snapchat or any of the thousands of sites that stream video and audio content for free. Analysts at most audience research firms would concede that it's extremely difficult to come up with reliable metrics, especially for one-off events. Twitter may theoretically be able to know who sees a president's tweets. But it's less obvious to the rest of us who see the retweets and forwards of them.

> **What Counts As Genuine Persuasion?**
>
> Properly used, persuasion has occurred when an individual freely assents to what another asks. No coercion. No risk of retribution. No organizational advantage has figured in the outcome. Everything else that may look like persuasion is really what should be called compliance-gaining, as when a boss "asks" an employee to work late.
>
> This is not just an academic distinction with little real-world application. The difference actually matters. To fully understand persuasion, we need to know who or what is actually doing the heavy lifting. The use of threats, power or position are all *coercive*, a fact that takes away a receiver's opportunity to truly exercise their own judgment.
>
> This is why we are less interested here in compliance. In communication terms, there's not that much going on. Frequently compliance happens because of an unequal distribution of power. Like shooting animals within a fenced game reserve, getting compliance is often easily done—but in a free society, it is not very sporting.

Another problem is even more daunting. *Structural* changes in our newly dominant media make individual usage far more scattered and fragmented. Aristotle wrote one of the first studies of human communication (*The Rhetoric*, circa 335 BC) with an eye on the challenges of addressing a few hundred citizens within a small city. Today, audiences are sometimes defined in the millions, with messages delivered to them on platforms that increasingly muddle the question of what makes a message public or private. Even popular message aggregators cannot be easily defined by their audiences. The impact of their customizable messaging is difficult to access.

Consider just two snapshots of recent media use:

- Digital devices of various sorts get about ten times more attention than newspapers and magazines. Most of these devices are accessing the web, where the average time spent on a single page is under a minute.

- Among US teens who will shape future discourse, texting has become a time-consuming preoccupation, with an average of 60 separate messages daily plus six hours of visiting social media sites.[20]

Usage patterns like these hint at the challenges of defining audiences. Does our dependence on digital devices with imagistic platforms (graphical interfaces loaded onto virtually all digital devices) disallow the kind of thinking required for successful message design? Put another way, if modern life is built around visual riffs in space-restricted media such as YouTube or Twitter, is there any chance to create a series of appeals whose effects can be measured? Even with these problems there is value in the assumption that audiences are knowable.

FIVE INTRODUCTORY SETTINGS

This section discusses specific cases that suggest the breadth of our study. They are useful in setting the stage for the study of persuasion and for considering several additional questions posed by our definition.

Door to Door

Political *canvassing* is a tradition in many Western democracies. In its simplest form, supporters of a political candidate or a cause knock on the doors of their neighbors or residents in nearby communities. The goal is to make a brief personal connection with a homeowner and to serve as a surrogate for the cause—whatever or whoever it is. The election of President Obama in 2008 and 2012 owed a great deal to a ground game that included many volunteers going door to door. In 2016 the unusual insurgent Trump campaign was the exception, not using an extensive ground game. Even so, it's important to remember that most of the candidates who run for the roughly 510,000 elective offices in the United States have won in part because of their own canvassing efforts. Think of members of a local school board or city council. By the time they are elected, the candidates have met most or many of their neighbors.

The process of canvassing *can* be disconcerting. Some homeowners are suspicious of any solicitation. Others refuse to come to the door. But some are open to hearing a canvasser's pitch. The general rule for an effective political campaign is to persuade six percent of the people approached to make a commitment to support the cause.

The usual rule for canvassing is for the canvasser to explain what they are supporting but not get into long exchanges with the homeowner. But a study in California found that transgender individuals were surprisingly successful in persuading their contacts to reconsider their initial suspicions. The levels of support exhibited by the contacts were rated on the canvassing group's scale of 1 at the low end up to 10.

> After a long day of canvassing . . . tired but exuberant volunteers returned for a debriefing. One canvasser stood up and spoke of moving a man to a seven from a three. Another—tattooed student identifies as gender nonconforming—proudly recalled persuading a voter "who clearly had no experience with anyone who identified as being outside the gender binary. He said I blew his mind,

and that he would never forget the conversation we had!" Meg Riley, a 60-year-old Unitarian Universalist minister from Minnesota who volunteers with a racial-justice group, recounted her eventful day. Her second conversation, she said, was with a black man in his 50s who was a seven on the 10-point scale. The man's daughter, though, would have none of it: She practically pushed him out of the way to tell Riley they were a 10. "I'm with Black Lives Matter, and I know a lot of trans people," the woman told Riley. We're a 10! This family is a 10!"[21]

Finding Converts

Every year about 30,000 men and women between the ages and 18 and 21 pass through a well-manicured collection of low buildings that adjoin the Provo campus of Brigham Young University. The Missionary Training Center of The Church of Jesus Christ of Latter-day Saints (LDS) lies at the base of Utah's Wasatch Mountains and runs what is perhaps one of the largest missionary training schools on the globe. The specific goal of the center is to prepare recruits to proselytize for converts in the United States and overseas. Future missionaries spend up to twelve weeks honing their foreign language skills, studying the Book of Mormon and the Bible, and getting ready for the rigors of 10-hour days trying to ingratiate themselves with strangers in distant locales. It's all part of the church's tradition of encouraging young members to devote two years to finding new converts.

All male Mormons over 18 are asked to serve on a mission, and about half do. Women who are at least 21 can also join the ranks; they do so, but in smaller numbers.[22] After they leave the center, individuals are assigned a partner who will be their constant companion for the duration of the mission. Young men in white button-down shirts, pressed slacks, and conservative haircuts easily stand out from their surroundings. They may end up in Baltimore, Manila, or Sao Paulo. But they look like they could have just walked out of the pages of your grandparent's high school yearbook. Missionaries call potential converts "investigators," in recognition of the fact that conversion is not necessarily a sudden thing. The logic is that the more people learn, the more willing they may be to explore the church by attending services or meetings.

The *Student Manual* at the Missionary Training Center sees the task of winning converts in terms of the biblical admonitions to go out and serve as witnesses for the faith. Missionaries teach the two primary works in the Mormon canon with the hope that some of these scriptures will be compelling. The church also emphasizes the classic persuasion idea that you should physically embody what you advocate, a principle that echoes back to ancient rhetorics that urged persuaders to show in their own demeanor the values they espouse.[23] Missionaries are taught to be positive, always courteous, and to approach every person as a potential new friend. Earnestness is the order of the day. Missionaries also talk up the importance of family, and they communicate with the unambiguous certainty of a committed believer.

One researcher studying these advocates estimates that in the thousands of contacts a single member makes in each year, he or she will convert only about four to seven people.[24] That is a success rate of one percent or less. Jonathan Hoy went through the experience and remembers even fewer converts but still found his limited success worth the effort. He spoke with almost 10,000 people during his 22-

month stint in Ohio and Greece. He especially remembers a young woman in Athens who converted after spending time studying various scriptures from *The Book of Mormon.* "I saw it change her life," he said. "That's what keeps me going."[25]

The low rates of conversion obscure the crucial role that this rite of passage has on the missionaries themselves. Sometimes the greatest effect a message has is on the *persuader.* This is the important process of **self-persuasion** that usually occurs with advocates. While these missionaries come back with limited success in turning large numbers toward the church, they themselves have become committed activists for their faith.[26]

Doubt and Influence in the Jury Room

Graham Burnett's account of his time spent with eleven other jurors deciding the fate of a murder suspect in New York City provides multiple examples of small and large moments of persuasion.[27] To be sure, the jury room is not a common scene for persuasion. Most criminal cases are plea-bargained rather than decided by a jury. If a trial takes place, the jury is assumed to be objective in evaluating the presentations of the prosecution and the defense before reaching a collective and unanimous decision about guilt or innocence.

The trial Burnett heard was unusual. A man dressed as a woman had lured the defendant to his apartment in Greenwich Village, promising sex. A scuffle ensued, and the victim ended up with multiple and fatal stab wounds. The prosecution argued a simple case of murder. The man coaxed into entering the apartment claimed self-defense. When he tried to leave, the seducer had pulled a knife and a deadly fight began.

The basic facts were not in dispute, but there was little convincing evidence supporting a *reason* for the deadly scuffle. Did the victim bait potential lovers and then aggressively pursue them? Had the two men known each other before? The jury was instructed to decide between a verdict of second degree murder or a lesser charge of manslaughter if they found the defendant guilty. If they believed his story that he had acted in self-defense and found him innocent, he would be released.

As an academic historian, Burnett was used to looking at the details of events. Throughout the trial and deliberations, he kept a diary of observations that became the basis of his book. One of his first impressions was the arrogance of the prosecution. The more the lead attorney for the state spoke, the less Burnett liked him and his message. The defendant—poor but soft spoken—was treated with contempt. The prosecutor used a badgering, sarcastic, and belligerent tone during cross examination to get the defendant to change his story—which he politely but firmly refused to do. Burnett remarked: "So egregious did I find the whole performance that . . . I felt a deep desire to see the prosecutor lose the case."[28] How did that opinion affect his thinking? By the time Burnett and his colleagues were sent to the jury room, he had privately committed himself to a complete acquittal, or at least a hung jury. The aggressive hostility of the prosecution had unintentionally boomeranged.

In the first long day of deliberations the jury was divided and confused. Individual members who had formed an opinion tried to convince others of the defendant's guilt or innocence. People sometimes paired off into groups of two or three, working to weaken the resistance of others. A few retreated to the lavatory in the jury room to compare notes out of earshot of the others. It was a process that would take four days and test everyone's endurance.

Despite his quasi-neutral status as foreman, Burnett at times found himself engineering the defeat of some views and actively promoting others. Weaving his comments around the constant ebb and flow of discussion, he found ways to isolate jurors he believed were taking the jury down endless black holes. At one point when it appeared that the group edged closer to a "not guilty" verdict, Burnett collected ballots in a way that made it easy for others to know the vote of a potential holdout. "I placed it, consciously and more or less conspicuously, at the bottom of the pile. I wanted the full dismay of the room to land on her if she had voted for a conviction."[29]

After three days of deliberations, the stalemate was broken by the sudden eloquence of one of the jurors. Burnett had stereotyped the former bull-riding cowboy who now sold vacuum cleaners as a typical working-class male, but the man's fluency broke through an impasse. He noted that he believed the defendant had done something very wrong but "I've been asked to apply the law. Justice belongs to God; men only have the law. Justice is perfect, but the law can only be careful."[30] Burnett heard another juror, almost sobbing, say that she agreed. For the first time Burnett saw the pathway the jury would eventually follow in reaching a not-guilty verdict.

Advocating Dangerous Forms of Religion

Successful persuasion involves a receiver's freely given agreement with the pleas or requests of an advocate. One of our basic assumptions is that listeners will weigh messages against their self-interests. If we buy a car, for example, we are likely to weigh the claims made by the sales person against our own views of what we need and can afford. It seems axiomatic that people cannot be easily persuaded to act in harmful or dangerous ways. In our recent past, however, Americans have seen several instances involving mass suicides committed at the apparent request of a strong cult leader: the 1997 suicides of 39 members of the Heaven's Gate Group in California and the fiery immolation of 87 Branch Davidians in Waco, Texas, in 1993. The Davidians died after a long standoff with federal agents. The members of Heaven's Gate willingly dosed themselves with poison in the belief that they would leave their containers and catch a ride on a spaceship behind the Hale-Bopp comet.[31]

Perhaps Americans were most shocked by the deaths of 912 people in 1978 in the remote South American nation of Guyana. How could so many people agree to their own deaths? What kind of influence did Jim Jones, the leader of the American cult in Guyana, possess? Jones was considered unorthodox in his days as a California evangelist, but he shared more similarities than differences with many other groups that mingled politics with religion and social action with antigovernment paranoia. He was especially popular among the poor because his indignation toward exploiters and the rich struck a responsive chord. The mission he established attracted members through activities and services designed to make them feel special and different. Like David Koresh (the leader of the Branch Davidians), Jones was a powerful leader. He used his pulpit to preach not only a religious doctrine but also long diatribes against the secular culture outside. Also like Koresh, Jones grew increasingly strident and isolated.[32] He began to make every issue a personal one and every member a part of his own private crusade. He cultivated a following by cleverly mixing his gospel of social change with carefully orchestrated demonstrations of support. Members were required to give their money and personal allegiance to "The Father."

The remote Guyana village was an unlikely spot for an American religious commune, but Jones must have realized that a leader's control is enhanced though physical isolation. He touted his jungle location as a place free from persecution. "I am preparing a promised land for you in Jonestown," he said. "When you get there all of your tribulations will be over. There will be no need for discipline when you get away from the capitalistic society of America. There you will be able to love and be loved."[33]

According to one member of the People's Temple, the only source of pleasure for Jones "was observing his followers' total devotion to him."[34] He became obsessed with his control over the inhabitants of the new village. Members were publicly beaten and humiliated. Bizarre marathon meetings were held in which he revealed his belief that he was the target of assassination plots. He began preaching with a gun at his side and erupting into tirades when a member tried to leave a meeting, ominous signs of his growing paranoia.

After hearing complaints from members of families that relatives were being held against their wishes, California Congressman Leo Ryan visited the Guyana village with several members of the press. His visit pushed Jones to a deadly state of paranoia and rage. In poor health himself, he calmly planned the demise of his commune and everyone in it. After ordering the assassination of Ryan and several reporters, he persuaded and coaxed almost one thousand people to commit the ultimate act of self-destruction. Many willingly gave doses of a fruit drink laced with poison to themselves and to their children while others were murdered by the bodyguards for Jones. The bizarre final moments were tape recorded.

> So my opinion is that you be kind to children and be kind to seniors and take the potion like they used to take it in ancient Greece, and step over quietly, because we are not committing suicide. It's a revolutionary act. We can't go back, and they won't leave us alone. They're now going back to tell more lies, which means more congressmen. And there's no way, no way, we can survive.[35]

Fighting a Social Media Storm

Several years ago the marketing staff managing the Bud Light brand decided to tinker with the labeling. Building on a campaign running in multiple media and using the slogan, "Up for Whatever," the label on some products was redesigned to include an additional hashtag and bold letter wording that said: "The Perfect Beer for Removing 'No' From Your Vocabulary for the Night." Obviously, the campaign was meant to appear relevant and responsive to quips that fly between users of social media. But since beer drinkers are often younger adults, it might have been expected that a social media backlash could result. And it did. Complaints poured in. Anheuser-Busch-InBev was forced to formally apologize, acknowledging heightened sensitivities about unwanted sexual advances abetted by too much alcohol, especially on college campuses. New York Congresswoman Nita Lowey was one of many Americans to express their displeasure on Twitter. She asked followers to write the company if you agree that the "Up for Whatever" "campaign should promote responsible—not reckless—drinking." Her hashtag was #NoMeansNo. In a follow-up email to the *New York Times* she noted that "We need responsible companies to help us tackle these serious public health and safety problems, not encourage them." That was enough for an Anheuser representative to admit that "the message missed the mark, and we regret it."[36]

To be sure, this was a small moment in the nation's busy marketing landscape. But it is representative of how quickly a campaign that seeks to tie itself into social media can go off the rails. As a Walmart executive noted at a recent marketing conference, "the customer is in control," meaning that individuals now have the social media power to disrupt a marketing campaigns that might have unfolded 25 years ago with no mechanisms for immediate public rejection.[37] Of course all of this has the effect of making persuasion outcomes even less predictable than they already were.

PERSUASION IN EVERYDAY LIFE

The process of persuasion is embedded in the transactions of daily life. Sociologist Erving Goffman had a remarkable ability for seeing the recurring patterns that emerge as we seek influence in even routine moments of communication. He noted "that when an individual appears before others he will have many motives for trying to control the impression they receive of the situation."[38] We want to be liked and to have our ideas accepted. We want others to show regard for our feelings and for the values that serve as the anchors for our actions. Goffman reminded us that children, teachers, parents, close friends, employees, employers, spouses, lovers, and coworkers all have strategies for projecting their interests to those with whom they come in contact. He referred to such strategies as *impression management*. Since we perform many of these roles simultaneously, we are constantly faced with the imperatives of making our actions and attitudes acceptable to others. Every role we play carries many possible strategies for influencing others. In words, gestures, and small signs, we leave a trail of cues that are meant to guide the responses of our audiences. No moment in the routine events of the day is too small to be devoid of persuasion. Goffman cited George Orwell's hilarious account of the routine strategies of restaurant waiters to make this point.

> It is an instructive sight to see a waiter going into a hotel dining room. As he passes the door a sudden change comes over him. The set of his shoulders alters; all the dirt and hurry and irritation have dropped off in an instant. He glides over the carpet, with a solemn priest-like air. I remember our assistant maitre d'hôtel, a fiery Italian, pausing at the dining room door to address his apprentice who had broken a bottle of wine. . . . "Do you call yourself a waiter, you young bastard? You a waiter! You're not fit to scrub floors in the brothel your mother came from . . ." Then he entered the dining room and sailed across it dish in hand, graceful as a swan. Ten seconds later he was bowing reverently to a customer. And you could not help thinking, as you saw him bow and smile, with that benign smile of the trained waiter, that the customer was put to shame by having such an aristocrat to serve him.[39]

Life is full of such moments. Any novel or film could be studied for all the subtle but significant cues that are performed to elicit acceptance or approval. We read such acts so routinely that we tend to forget how essential they are as oil for the machinery of everyday interaction.

Consider, for example, how the following conventional situations invite the use of various persuasive strategies:

- You have agreed to work with an organization that promotes literacy. They need your help to recruit more volunteers who can teach reading to adults one evening a week. Can you come up with a plan that goes beyond asking your friends?

- There is a rumor that your university is considering cutting financial support for varsity gymnastics. Its goal is to save the costs associated with coaches, travel, and equipment. As a team captain you would like to make a case to save the program. What should you say to academic leaders who have agreed to meet with you?

- A friend you have known since high school seems to have a drinking problem. He drinks heavily on weekends and is increasingly missing meetings and other commitments. You would like him to see a therapist, but you don't want to seem like you are prying.

- As a part-time salesperson paid on commission, every sale increases the amount of your monthly paycheck. You would rather not spend a lot of time with browsers who probably will not make a purchase. What does a motivated buyer look like?

- You have agreed to canvass several neighborhoods on behalf of a candidate for the U.S. House of Representatives. The problem is what to say to members of households as they come to their front doors.

All the cases we have mentioned raise a number of issues that are at the heart of the study of persuasion. They also indicate the range of theories and strategies that inform persuasive analysis and practice. While some theories will be discussed in other chapters, we can offer a few preliminary conclusions here.

Persuasion Is as Much about Sources as Messages

In 350 BC Aristotle expressed what was already a truism: good character—*high ethos*—"may be the most effective means of persuasion" that a person possesses.[40] Messages do not stand alone; consumers weigh both the *credibility* of advocates as well as the *quality* of their messages. The presence of a gay activist on a person's front step has the potential to overcome possible resistance. Personal contact can soften opposition by humanizing a cause. Conversely, the hectoring style of the New York City prosecutor antagonized Burnett and predisposed him to find the defendant innocent. Jim Jones used his popularity to attract followers to his increasingly demented ideas. In each case the process of persuasion makes sense only when we look again at *how* the reputations of specific individuals played to specific audiences. The power of charismatic persuaders such as Jim Jones or the influence of celebrities who voice opinions about political and economic conflicts fascinate us. Research and scholarship have explored how specific traits of advocates affect the process of influence.

Persuasion Is Enormously Difficult

The topic of persuasion is often accompanied with a vocabulary suggesting moments of instant conversion—times when an overwhelming force wipes away any resistance. Plato regularly hinted at the risks of teaching the dark arts of manipulation and seduction.[41] Mid-twentieth century America was consumed with fears of communist *brainwashing, indoctrination,* and *propaganda*—all suggesting rapid and mysterious ways to get people to abandon their beliefs. Even a leader of the powerful Screen Actor's Guild, Ronald Reagan, expressed this view. When he was still in Hollywood the future President noted that the Communist plan for Hollywood was remarkably simple: "to gradually work into the movies the requisite propaganda attitudes . . . to soften the American public's hardening attitude toward Communism."[42] The idea was that leftist screenwriters doing Moscow's bidding would subvert US attitudes from within.[43]

If only persuasion were so easy and predictable. We've just read about a prosecutor who lost his case, LDS missionaries with very low rates of conversion, and marketing efforts that are too clever by half. Earlier we mentioned Aristotle's conclusion that resistance is the norm rather than the exception. Two modern researchers note that "resistance hounds persuasion the way friction frustrates motion."[44] To be sure, we often get the reverse impression. Theater and film frequently need the pivot point of a sudden change in attitude. It's a sure thing that within a two-hour film someone will undergo a significant transformation.[45] But the truth is less dramatic. We are typically hard to move.

Persuasion: The Myth of Easy Influence

The task of trying to alter attitudes or behaviors is often a difficult challenge. And yet Americans have traditionally believed that spellbinders, "brainwashers" and marketing experts know secret pathways to persuasion—a secret back door for finding another person's vulnerabilities.

We would also like to believe that personal transformation happens—Hollywood style—when the strong hand of unexpected experience creates a sudden change of heart. Dramas in three acts typically need the transformation of a character by the end of Act III. At the beginning of the legendary film *Casablanca* (1942) Rick may be the world's greatest cynic. But in the short span of two acts he becomes a patriot. Rapid changes of attitude or behavior are unusual in everyday life, but often a necessity for someone writing a screenplay.

Mormon missionaries soldier on despite low conversion rates; marketing experts sometimes don't know that even their best efforts will create a backlash; and political candidates sometimes discover too late that the uncommitted make the difference between victory and loss. The suffragist Carrie Chapman Catt estimated that to win votes for women there were 56 separate referendum campaigns in the states, along with "480 campaigns to get legislatures to submit suffrage amendments to voters, 47 campaigns to get constitutional conventions to write woman suffrage into state constitutions; 277 campaigns to get state party conventions to include woman suffrage planks, 30 campaigns to include woman suffrage planks in party platforms, and 19 campaigns with 19 successive Congresses."[46] With such evidence of the challenges of persuasion, noting that we resist change is an understatement.

The primary result of resistance is a low degree of change, expressed in persuasion analysis as the *theory of minimal effects*.[47] In a nutshell, many studies of persuasion confirm that even fluent and effective messages usually produce only minor changes in their intended receivers—with the percentage of respondents who comply numbering in single digits. In one meta-analysis of media messages urging health-related changes (i.e., wearing seat belts while driving), Charles Atkin found a success rate of between 5 and 10 percent.[48] These low numbers remind us that a clear majority of people targeted will remain unmoved.

In some ways this is hardly surprising. Change carries significant costs for an individual: sometimes in financial terms, but almost always in the subtle ways that pieces of our identity must be reconstructed to reflect new choices. Consider, for example, how much is psychologically on the line when we urge a friend to accept an addicted label for their behavior of too much drinking. That acknowledgement would not come easily. In short, because persuasion is usually about change, it can create seismic shifts we aren't willing to accept.

Finally, persuasion is difficult because audiences have never been more distracted. Not only do we now spread ourselves thin among various venues and forms of communication, but even in one form of media such as a consumer magazine there is an enormous amount of *clutter*, the advertising industry's word for too many messages competing for attention in the same limited place. Historically, being in the same physical space and in direct communication with the target of a message was the presumed ideal context for successful persuasion.[49] We now assume that media technologies have successfully changed that requirement, and in some ways they have.[50] But researchers generally find that newer ways to reach others (including texting and other social media) have different and mostly weaker direct persuasive effects than is possible in face-to-face communication.[51] Health communication researchers have similarly discovered that a person sitting and watching a videotaped health message is less likely to be compliant with a need to change than a person in face-to-face interaction with a doctor or nurse.[52] That's perhaps no surprise. Even amidst the tsunami of social media and digital devices connecting us, it is still true that *direct interpersonal contact* represents perhaps the optimal chance to produce more than minimal change.

Even Minimal Effects Can Be Important

We can never be indifferent about even small changes in attitude or behavior. In the fields of politics and marketing, for example, if only *six percent* of all buyers of a product or voters on Election Day chose *other* options, enormous changes would follow. Voting margins significantly less than six percent have decided many elections. In 2000 and 2004 the margins of difference at the presidential level were very small. And overall, in our recent past, a six percent change in the popular vote would have denied Bill Clinton, George W. Bush, John F. Kennedy, Richard Nixon, and Donald Trump the presidency.[53] There are many other examples where a six percent shift would create significant shifts. For example, women would be the dominant majority in the Swedish parliament;[54] Miller Lite would be as popular a beer in the United States as Coors Lite;[55] Raisin Bran would replace Honey Nut Cheerios as the top-selling cold cereal;[56] and CNN would be as popular with election-year voters as Fox News.[57]

Persuasion Can Easily Stray toward Deception

The variety of cases we have cited remind us that the study of persuasion both attracts and repels. Few questions are more intriguing than "What makes people change their minds or alter the ways they act?" We have a natural curiosity about the ways we manipulate and influence others and how others do the same to us. Yet through the ages persuasion has sometimes been perceived as the territory of charlatans and grifters. Some of the synonyms attached to persuasion reveal perceptions of its dark side: brainwashing, subversion, mind control, and subliminal persuasion In fiction and in fact, manipulative con artists are villains, whether they are selling cars or duping believers. Persuaders such as Jim Jones remind us that persuasion can succeed for all the wrong reasons. On the other hand, some of the New York jurors were mostly altruistic, doing their best to find the truth in the service of justice. As they debated and argued, their personal inconvenience hardly mattered. At least some became committed to the idea that their deliberations could rescue each other from making mistakes of reasoning that might cost the freedom of the defendant. The leaders of the Civil Rights movement in the crucible of the 1960s magnified this pattern of advocating for justice: people protesting and canvassing who risked a great deal to promote a righteous cause.

Persuasion Outcomes Are Unpredictable

Persuasion is not a field that allows safe predictions. We are still a long way from creating a true science of persuasion. The biologist can predict accurate timetables of progression and regression in cell formation. The student of persuasion deals with the much more volatile effects created by the interaction of a new message with an individual's accumulated personal experiences. To be sure, we can create many appeals, strategies, and theories; but we cannot match the sciences in fully predicting whether our persuasive efforts will work in new situations. Similarly, we have theories that suggest possible cause-and-effect sequences, but we really have no laws of human persuasion that can match the predictive power of the laws of, say, physics. No doubt the prosecutors who addressed Burnett and his jury colleagues *thought* they were persuasive. If only they had known of the unanticipated effects of their methods. Similarly, it is unlikely that Bud Light anticipated that it's "Up for Whatever" labeling would provoke a social media backlash. Persuasion that backfires and pushes members of a target audience away from the action we wanted them to take is said to *boomerang*: a fascinating and very common effect. We will revisit the subject of boomerangs many times in the remainder of this book.

THREE TYPES OF COMMUNICATION

We close with a brief overview of what persuasion is and is *not*. There is good reason to explore forms of communication that fall outside the very permeable boundaries of persuasion. We discover what is unique about the task of urging change on others by also thinking about settings where changing another person's behavior or thinking is *not* a goal.

Just as one can use a prism to refract ordinary light into the primary colors, it is equally possible to break down communication into its three primary motivations of *information giving, expression,* and *persuasion*. Although many complex forms of communication contain elements of all three, their theoretical differences reveal how we sometimes deceive ourselves about our real intentions.[58]

Pure Information

Information giving involves communicating facts, attitudes, or data with minimal interest in whether others accept them. The information is passed on because it might be useful, not because it will alter another person's view of the world. The primary motivation is to be clear. If someone asks for directions from New York City to the center of Philadelphia, an information giver might start by telling them to go through the Lincoln Tunnel and take the New Jersey Turnpike South. The questioner could comment that they dislike the congestion near the tunnel entrance and find the Turnpike too crowded. But the pure information giver will consider her task completed once the recipient indicates that they have received and understood the information. Dislike for the suggested route is not her problem. Reception and understanding are the key goals, not acceptance.

It is trickier to sort out where the pure information line is crossed if you use mobile-phone apps or Google. An address or local information will appear. But many internet platforms have the persuasive slant of favoring businesses and organizations that have paid to be very visible on a searchable list. Even ostensibly informational platforms that get paid by businesses for every click through to their business site are doing something more than just building an information society.

Pure Expression

Pure expression is characterized by a desire to speak one's mind rather than have others agree or disagree, act or not act. We may want to unload our anger, joy, anxieties, or fears merely for the sake of the cathartic release it provides. Hit a finger instead of the nail, and you have pure expression. It feels right to offer a verbal response even if no one is within hearing distance. Expression provides a release, but it is undertaken more for the need it satisfies within us rather than for those who overhear it. Many expressions can make us feel better, such as lecturing the family dog for eating the furniture, cheering on the home team, or delivering a long rant to a patient friend about the injustices inflicted on us. As many bloggers or social media users can attest, giving our inward feelings outward expression can be its own reward. We know that others will see it, but the release of expressing our opinion often matters more to us than subsequent posts about our message.

President Harry Truman was known for his habit of writing angry letters to various people that he never intended to send.[59] He declared that the effect of having written them was enough—perhaps today's equivalent of posts on various online sites and bulletin boards. Pure expression is sometimes egocentric; it is intended to be a report of our state of mind. In this mode we ask little of others beyond their considerable patience and silent acceptance. At other times the expressive efforts of others become surrogates for our own feelings. Film viewers watching Damien Chazell's retro musical hit *La La Land* (2016) sometimes expressed the view that it offered an upbeat world at the very moment they needed it.[60]

Pure Persuasion

Pure persuasion is more complex than either pure information or pure expression. It involves a new and fascinatingly complex dimension: a concern with how our ideas or actions will affect someone else. The persuasive message is constructed to be believed, not merely understood. In the language of attitude research, it wants both *reception* (understanding) as well as *yielding* (acceptance and compliance). A listener could reply, "I understand what you are saying, but I do not accept it." The information giver could be satisfied with that response; the goal of delivering information was achieved. The persuader, however, would be frustrated because the goal of commitment or approval of the message was not achieved.

In real world settings these forms usually overlap. For example, statistics on automobile safety indicate that wearing seat belts saves lives. These numbers are— in a simple sense—pieces of information. It is also easy to imagine a persuader using them with the intention of gaining support for increased fines on individuals who still refuse to wear seat belts. If listeners respond by saying that they understand the statistics, the persuader might ask impatiently, "Yes, but do you accept the action that follows? Will you use your seat belts"

It is also apparent from these somewhat artificial distinctions that a good deal of persuasion occurs under the pretext of information giving. Most of us are far from indifferent to how others accept even simple statements of fact. We want approval and acceptance from those with whom we interact. Information giving is often an interesting deflection of attention away from deeper persuasive intentions.[61] It is reasonable to have a skeptical stance toward news stories, lectures, scientific reports, and entertainment. These are often offered as pure information or diversion. But these benign intentions sometimes mask persuasive objectives. News and entertainment, for example, depend on high circulation or ratings figures. Advertisers and content providers are attracted to big audiences. Larger numbers translate into larger fees and budgets. Professors engage in persuasion. While they want to impart the core ideas of their disciplines, they also "profess." They usually offer data and narratives within their own ethical and value-laden boundaries. When a course is over, the self-contained world created in the classroom may be abandoned by a student, but not until after the last exam.

Does this mean that *all* communication is persuasive? Have the authors fallen into the expert's disease of describing their subject as the inevitable center of the universe? To both questions we give a qualified "no," but it would not take much effort to engage us in a spirited defense of the view that most messages have at least a *latent* persuasive attempt. Persuasion is a far more common process than may at first be evident. We frequently do want our messages to change the way others think, act, and feel. It may be the exception rather than the rule when a communicator feels genuine indifference about whether a message is favorably received.

To be sure, artists create, poets write, and musicians perform in the hope that their work will fall on receptive eyes and ears. But it would be too simplistic to think that their work is primarily for us. Many creative people would continue to do what they do even without an audience. In these contexts, it would be wrong to assume that the prime motivation is total acceptance. Acknowledgment can be enough. Yet it is otherwise for persuasion. *Persuasion exists for an audience.* Fail with them and the persuader will likely experience a sense of failure.

SUMMARY

Kenneth Burke, whose words open this chapter, wrote that the effective persuader needs to be prepared to discard what does not work and constantly search for what does. "So we must keep trying anything and everything," he noted, "improvising, borrowing from others, developing from others, dialectically using one text as comment upon another."[62] In that spirit, this book draws on diverse and sometimes conflicting systems of knowledge, combining rhetorical models with social science research, strategic thinking with idealistic values, tested theories with educated hunches. Sometimes we are concerned that the audiences of persuasion might be misled. At other times we admire the cunning with which an act of influence is performed. If we have a bedrock premise for the book, it is that human behavior is infinitely complex and varied. Individuals do not react in consistent and predictable ways. We all carry our own personalized ballast that allows us to weather challenges to our beliefs in unpredictable ways. The best for which we can strive is a reasonable estimate of an appeal's probable effects on an audience.

Persuasion has its own Greek goddess, Peitho, the companion of the goddess of love, Aphrodite. Peitho was associated with eloquence and the power to persuade.[63] Through the centuries, efforts to discover her secrets have continued, but the goddess sometimes keeps the clearest answers to herself.

QUESTIONS AND PROJECTS FOR FURTHER STUDY

1. If you have done door-to-door canvassing, explain to another person or group what it was like. What person or idea were you selling? How receptive were the citizens you approached? Did any of the people you talked to give some indication that they agreed with your pitch?

2. Some analysts have suggested that Jim Jones was a more effective persuader in the remote jungle in Guyana than he was in the United States. What differences are evident in the two settings that might explain the increased allegiance of his followers in remote Jonestown? How do less dramatic changes in settings (such as moving from home to a college campus) affect individuals?

3. Look at public service announcements prepared by the Truth campaign (http://www.thetruth.com). The campaign receives money from the 1998 tobacco settlement that gave government organizations funds to discourage smoking. The campaign focuses on teens and tries to reach them in their own voice. After sampling some of their videos and materials, write a critique of what you saw using some of the defining features of persuasion cited in the last half of the chapter.

4. Tom McCarthy's film *Spotlight* (2015) documents the real-life story of a group of Boston reporters exploring a church cover-up of pedophiles in local parishes.

Reporters need sources who will go "on the record." View the Oscar-winning film with special attention to how the reporters coax reluctant victims and officials to open up to tell their stories. What different persuasion styles do the reporters played by actors Mark Ruffalo and Rachel McAdams display? Is coercion involved?

5. Strong leadership may bring misery to those who succumb to persuasive efforts—the Jonestown case being one of the most chilling. Identify other examples of destructive persuasion. Identify positive cases that suggest persuasion can be a constructive process. Compare your examples with a friend.

6. Choose some examples of persuasion. Probe the five features of the authors' definition of persuasion. How adequate are they? Does the definition fail to account for certain kinds of persuasion?

7. The authors suggest that persuasion can be contrasted with communication that gives information and with communication that delivers pure expression. Why are these two categories exempt from the impulse to change others? How common are these two forms?

8. The discussion of The Church of Jesus Christ of Latter-day Saints missionaries suggests that the greatest impact they have may be on *themselves*. Explain the idea of self-persuasion. Why is the process of persuading others likely to intensify our own commitment to the persuasion objective?

 ## ADDITIONAL READING

Aristotle, *The Rhetoric* (available in many editions and versions).
Robert Cialdini, *Influence: Science and Practice*, 5th ed. (New York: Pearson, 2009).
Erwin P. Bettinghaus and Michael Cody, *Persuasive Communication*, 5th ed. (New York: Harcourt, 1994).
Erving Goffman, *The Presentation of Self in Everyday Life* (New York: Anchor, 1959).
Rod Hart and Susan Daughton, *Modern Rhetorical Criticism*, 3rd ed. (Boston: Allyn & Bacon, 2005).
Daniel J. O'Keefe, *Persuasion: Theory and Research*, 3rd ed. (Thousand Oaks, CA: Sage, 2015).
Anthony Pratkanis and Elliot Aronson, *The Age of Propaganda*, Revised ed. (New York: Henry Holt and Company, 2002).
James Price Dillard and Lijiang Shen, Eds. *The Sage Handbook of Persuasion*, 2nd ed. (Thousand Oaks, CA: Sage, 2013).

 ## NOTES

[1] Kenneth Burke, *A Rhetoric of Motives* (Berkeley: University of California Press, 1969), p. xiv.

[2] Erika Fry, "Meet the Man Trying to Save SeaWorld from Itself," *Fortune*, September 14, 2016, http://fortune.com/seaworld-orlando-joel-manby/

[3] SeaWorld ad, "Making Better Habitats," *The New York Times*, July 16, 2015, p. A23.

[4] Quoted in Lester Thonssen and A. Craig Baird, *Speech Criticism* (New York: Ronald Press, 1948), p. iv.

[5] Aristotle, *Rhetoric*, trans. W. Rhys Roberts (Mineola, New York: Dover Thrift Editions), Book II, Chapters 12–17.

[6] Plato, *Gorgias* Trans. By Donald Zeyl (Indianapolis: Hackett, 1987) 462e, 463a.

[7] Robert Cialdini, *Influence: Science and Practice*, 5th ed. (New York: Pearson, 2009), p. xi.

[8] See, for example, Anthony Pratkanis and Elliot Aronson, *Age of Propaganda* (New York: Henry Holt, 2002), pp. 1–19.

[9] Nancy Rhodes and David Ewoldsen, "Outcomes of Persuasion: Behavioral, Cognitive and Social," in James Price Dillard and Lijiang Shen (Eds.), *The Sage Handbook of Persuasion*, 2nd ed. (Thousand Oaks, CA: Sage, 2013), pp. 56–61.

[10] Anthony Pratkanis, "Social Influence Analysis: An Index of Tactics," in Anthony Pratkanis (Ed.), *The Science of Social Influence: Advances and Future Progress* (New York: Psychology Press, 2007), p. 17.

[11] Erwin B. Bettinghaus and Michael Cody, *Persuasive Communication*, 5th ed. (New York: Holt, Harcourt, 1994), p. 6.

[12] Herbert W. Simons and Jean Jones, *Persuasion in Society*, 2nd ed. (New York: Routledge, 2011), p. 24.

[13] Roderick Hart and Suzanne Daughton, *Modern Rhetorical Criticism*, 3rd ed. (Boston: Allyn and Bacon, 2005), p. 8.

[14] Herbert W. Simons and Jean Jones, *Persuasion in Society*, 2nd ed. (New York: Routledge, 2011), p. 24.

[15] Hart and Daughton, p. 8.

[16] Christopher Hitchens, *Hitch 22: A Memoir* (New York: Twelve Hachette Book Group, 2010), p. 407.

[17] Daniel J. O'Keefe, *Persuasion: Theory and Research*, 3rd ed. (Thousand Oaks, CA: Sage, 2015), p. 4.

[18] Gerald R. Miller, "On Being Persuaded," in Dillard and Lijiang, p. 73.

[19] James Webster and Patricia Phalen, *The Mass Audience* (Mahwah, NJ: Lawrence Erlbaum, 1997), p. xiii.

[20] Amanda Lenhart, "Teens, Smartphones and Texting," March 19, 2012, *Pew Internet and American Life Project* http://www.pewinternet.org/~/media/Files/Reports/2012/PIP_Teens_Smartphones_and_Texting.pdf

[21] Benoit Denizet-Lewis, "Can We Talk?" *The New York Times Magazine*, April 10, 2016, p. 53.

[22] For a sample of the missionary efforts of two twin sisters, see their YouTube video, http://www.youtube.com/watch?v=s0HcpekX4gk&feature=related

[23] *Missionary Preparation: Student Manual* (Salt Lake City: The Church of Jesus Christ of Latter-day Saints, 2005), 99.

[24] Gustav Niebuhr, "Youthful Optimism Powers Mormon Missionary Engine," *The New York Times,* May 23, 1999, http://www.nytimes.com/1999/05/23/us/youthful-optimism-powers-mormon-missionary-engine.html

[25] Josh Jarman, "God's Salesman," *The Columbus Dispatch*, July 6, 2007, p. 3B.

[26] Gary Shepherd and Gordon Shepherd, *Mormon Passage: A Missionary Chronicle* (Urbana: University of Illinois Press, 1998) p. xii.

[27] D. Graham Burnett, *A Trial by Jury* (New York: Knopf, 2001).

[28] Ibid., pp. 72–73.

[29] Ibid., p. 166.

[30] Ibid., p. 138.

[31] See Barry Bearak, "Odyssey to Suicide," *The New York Times*, April 28, 1997, p. A1.

[32] Comparisons between Jones and Koresh abound. See, for example, Melinda Liu and Todd Barrett, "Hard Lessons in the Ashes," *Newsweek*, May 3, 1993, p. 31.

[33] Jones quoted in Jeannie Mills, *Six Years with God* (New York: Times Books, 1979), p. 317.

[34] Ibid., p. 319.

[35] Jones quoted in James Reston Jr., *Our Father Who Art in Hell* (New York: Times Books, 1981), p. 324.

[36] Stephanie Strom, "Bud Light Label Draws Ire on Social Media," *The New York Times*, April 29, 2015, B3.

[37] Stuart Elliott, "Marketers Chase Evolving Consumer," *The New York Times*, October 7, 2013, B6.

[38] Erving Goffman, *The Presentation of Self in Everyday Life* (New York: Anchor, 1959), p. 15.

[39] Ibid., pp. 121–122.

[40] Aristotle, p. 7.

[41] Plato, "Gorgias" in Patricia Bizzell and Bruce Herzberg (Eds.), *The Rhetorical Tradition*, 2nd ed. (New York: St. Martin's, 2001), pp. 87–138.

[42] Ronald Reagan, *Where's the Rest of Me?* (New York: Karz, 1981), p. 163.

[43] People named as communist sympathizers were blacklisted; many careers were ruined, and the legacy of this troubled period lives on. At the Academy Awards in 1999, screen director Elia Kazan received the lifetime achievement award to the frustration of many of his former friends. Kazan had testified before the House Un-American Activities Committee and had named members of the entertainment industry as members of the Communist Party. For an account of this period see Richard Schickel, *Elia Kazan: A Biography* (New York: Harper Perennial, 2005), pp. xiii–xxxi, 251–272.

[44] Eric Knowles and Jay Linn, "The Importance of Resistance to Persuasion," in Eric Knowles and Jay Linn (Eds.) *Resistance to Persuasion* (Mahwah, NJ: Lawrence Erlbaum, 2004), p. 3.

[45] Among our favorites from classic films: Charlie's sudden inability to resist the urgings of Rose to take huge risks in *The African Queen* (1951), Tracy's sudden discovery in the last 10 minutes of *The Philadelphia Story* (1940) that she really does love Dexter, whom she divorced a few years earlier, or the ease with which Dorothy recruits the scarecrow, the tin man, and the lion for the risky trip down the yellow brick road to meet *The Wizard of Oz* (1939).

[46] Catt quoted in Gail Collins, "My Favorite August," *The New York Times*, August 14, 2010, p. A19.

[47] Minimal effects theory primarily rose out of the work of Elihu Katz and Paul Lazerfield in their book, *Personal Influence: The Part Played by People in the Flow of Mass Communications* (Glencoe, IL: Free Press, 1955). For a modern critique of this thesis and the author's argument that face-to-face persuasion is greater than mass-mediated persuasion, see Jefferson Pooley, "Fifteen Pages that Shook the Field: Personal Influence, Edward Shils, and the Remembered History of Mass Communication Research," in *The Annals of the American Academy of Political and Social Science*, November 2006, pp. 130–157.

[48] Charles Atkin, "Promising Strategies for Media Health Campaigns," in William Crano and Michael Burgoon (Eds.), *Mass Media and Drug Prevention* (Mahwah, NJ: Erlbaum, 2002), pp. 35–64.

[49] See Pooley, 130–157.

[50] See, for example, Rosanna Guadagno and Robert Cialdini, "Online Persuasion and Compliance: Social Influence on the Internet and Beyond," in Yair Amichai-Hamburger (Ed.), *The Social Net: Human Behavior in Cyberspace* (New York: Oxford, 2005), pp. 91–114.

[51] See, for example, Kai Sassenberg, Margarete Boos, and Sven Rabung, "Attitude Change in Face to Face and Computer Mediated Communication," *European Journal of Social Psychology, Vol. 35*, 2005.

[52] Stevenson, F. A., Cox, K., Britten, N. and Dundar, Y., "A Systematic Review of the Research on Communication between Patients and Health Care Professionals about Medicines: The Consequences for Concordance." *Health Expectations*, September 2004, pp. 235–245.

[53] Al Gore and George W. Bush each polled about 48 percent of the electorate in 2000. John Kerry polled 48 percent in 2004, compared to George W. Bush's 50 percent. In 2016 Clinton's popular vote was about two percent above Trump's. The electoral college complicates presidential races somewhat. Even so, in each case a six percent change in favor of the loser would have made them president. 2008 was a rare year: Barack Obama (52.9 percent) would have still beaten John McCain (45.7 percent) in the popular vote even with a six percent shift.

[54] International Parliamentary Union, "Women in National Parliaments," July 31, 2010, http://www.ipu.org/wmn-e/classif.htm

[55] Sales of the Leading Domestic Beer Brands of the United States in 2016 (in million U.S. dollars) *Statista*, https://www.statista.com/statistics/188723/top-domestic-beer-brands-in-the-united-states/

[56] Vince Bamford, "Cold Cereals: Top 10 Best Selling U.S. Brands," Bakery and Snacks.com, March 8, 2016, http://www.bakeryandsnacks.com/Markets/Top-10-best-selling-US-breakfast-cereal-brands-2015

[57] "Old Media Continue to Dominate as a Source of Campaign News," *Pew Center for the People and the Press*, January 18, 2017, https://twitter.com/pewresearch/status/821809468136685570

[58] Assessing persuasive intent is an important question—and extremely difficult. Intentions are rarely as transparent as they may first seem. The sources of personal motivation remain among the most obscure of all human processes, confounding psychologists, philosophers, and rhetoricians. See Bertram Malle, Louis Moses and Dare Baldwin, "Introduction: The Significance of Intentionality," in Bertram Malle, Louis Mowes and Dare Baldwin (Eds.), *Intentions and Intentionality* (Cambridge, MA: MIT Press, 2001), pp. 1–24.

[59] Monte N. Poen (Ed.), *Strictly Personal and Confidential: The Letters Harry Truman Never Mailed*, (Boston: Little, Brown, 1982).

[60] Manohla Dargis, "'La La Land' Makes Musicals Matter Again," *The New York Times*, November 23, 2016, https://www.nytimes.com/2016/11/23/movies/la-la-land-makes-musicals-matter-again.html?action=click&contentCollection=Movies&module=RelatedCoverage&region=EndOfArticle&pgtype=article

[61] Studies in the rhetoric of science sometimes explore the points where knowledge and socially generated values intersect. See, for example, Simons, pp. 307–326, and Alan Gross, "The Origin of Species: Evolution Taxonomy as an Example of the Rhetoric of Science," in Herbert Simons (Ed.), *The Rhetorical Turn* (Chicago: University of Chicago Press, 1990), pp. 91–115.

[62] Burke quoted in Kermit Lansner, "Burke, Burke, the Lurk," in William Rueckert (Ed.), *Critical Responses to Kenneth Burke* (Minneapolis, University of Minnesota Press, 1969), pp. 261–262.

[63] R. G. A. Buxton, *Persuasion in Greek Tragedy: A Study of Peitho* (New York: Cambridge University Press, 1982).

PART I

Origins of Persuasive Practice

2

The Advocate in an Open Society

> Free speech, free press, free religion, the right of free assembly,
> yes, the right of petition. . . . Well, they are still radical ideas.[1]
>
> —Lyndon Johnson

The idea of persuasion naturally aligns with freedom of expression. The presence of rigorous discussion is a key measure of how truly free members of a society are. In this chapter we explore the intimate link between democracy and persuasion. We will briefly trace both ideas back to their Western roots in the Mediterranean, and we will examine the practical limits on persuasion that currently exist in the open society we inhabit.

SUBDUING ADVOCACY IN A ONE-PARTY STATE

We associate life in the United States with personal freedom, individualism, and the robust public discussion of committed advocates. Conversely, suppressing an individual's rights to public advocacy is associated with authoritarian regimes marked by intimidation and censorship. While such threats may seem distant, we need to remind ourselves that all individuals do not enjoy the same freedoms of speech and choice, whether a girl forced out of school in Afghanistan or an American journalist detained by a foreign government.

From a Western perspective, we assume that we have the right to influence others, just as they have the right to persuade us. We routinely believe that everyone has the option to make claims on our loyalties: to encourage us to vote for a candidate, to speak out against a foreign policy decision of our government, to join or not join a church, synagogue, or mosque. Rights of expression come with the possibility to praise, criticize, solicit, or peacefully resist. They also imply the right to be left alone: to live, work, and play without the intrusive surveillance of governments or organizations.[2] If we reduce persuasion to a set of strategies for getting our way, we ignore the stake we have in the idea of democracy as a contract with other citizens to honor unfettered advocacy.

It is easier to see the centrality of persuasion in our civil life by looking in places where advocacy is suppressed. No single nation provides such an interesting collection of contradictory impulses as modern China, with its unlikely combination of a modern consumer society within a repressive political culture. China is an economic miracle. Infrastructure improvements in mass transit, roads, and economic development often surpass what civic leaders in the United States can even dream about. The centers of cities that many Americans barely know—Guangzhou, for example—rival the skylines of Chicago or San Francisco. In one generation China hopes to create livable cities for over 600 million of its citizens, with Starbucks, McDonald's, and luxury shopping centers nearly as widespread as they are in the United States. Not surprisingly, a dramatic rise in television commercials pitching a broad range of products and services promotes the consumer society that the nation needs to sustain its growth. Yet this economic expansion exists within a repressive political structure. YouTube, Wikipedia, Facebook, Google, Instagram, and Twitter are banned, as is the *New York Times*, the BBC, and other media sources in the West.[3] Apple has agreed to not sell virtual private network (VPN) apps that would allow phone users to bypass their internet censorship wall.[4]

Official government outlets such as the *People's Daily* and China Central Television remain powerful. Sometimes the political corruption of local officials will get significant coverage but never the national party and its leaders. Government censors closely manage any reports about major disasters like the sinking of a cruise ship in the Yangtze River or the collapse of the stock market.[5]

Every media outlet—from advertising agencies to internet providers—must observe repressive rules against criticism of top leaders. And nearly all churches, nongovernmental organizations, media outlets, university researchers, and organizations must defer to official bureaucracies that expect a party line of compliance and praise. It is a crime to distribute material that "disturbs social order," "preaches the teachings of evil cults," harms the "honor" of China, or "incites subversion."[6] *Subversion* is the official term for intellectual lawlessness. Essentially, any public criticism of the party or a top leader amounts to a treasonous act.

Individuals jeopardize their liberty if they engage in public dissent. For example, Tan Zuoren, an environmental and human rights activist in Sichuan, was sentenced to five years in prison for publicizing the names of children who died during the Sichuan earthquake in May 2008. He also sought to make public an independent report on the collapse of school buildings during the quake. His alleged crime was "inciting subversion of state power."[7]. Government regulations also affect businesses. Under laws enacted by the Chinese government, copy stores in Tibet must obtain a license to operate, and they must keep a log of all clients and what they sought to copy. Even a report on the environment may be rejected for copying.[8] The fear is that Tibetans chafing under Chinese rule would make photocopies of statements hostile to the People's Republic of China. "Basically, the main purpose is to instill fear into people's hearts," noted a Tibetan activist.[9] As Amnesty International observed in 2016, China's crackdown on open advocacy is unrelenting. The government continues to pass "sweeping laws in the name of 'national security.'"[10]

The dilemma for China and other authoritarian states is that its repression thwarts the natural cleansing power of civil political opposition. That power is real: *criticism is the self-correcting mechanism of change that a state needs to survive.* Politicians in multiparty systems understand that limits on the free flow of information and persuasion are dangerous. When one party is dominant, it might be tempting to try to limit the opposition. But electoral politics are a constant reminder that it is important to preserve freedoms for the days when a majority party becomes the minority. For these reasons, most residents of democracies are likely to be tolerant of social and religious comment.

This is what it means to live in an ***open society***. Open systems accept the idea that advocates will produce ideas that occasionally offend or challenge mainstream beliefs. Liberal democracies believe that a culture is often enriched by this process. "What is freedom of expression?" asked Salman Rushdie. The British

Official Dissent Channels

In 2016 the *New York Times* published a front-page article detailing a memo of dissent signed by 51 senior State Department officials stating that current White House policies to contain the Syrian civil war were not working. Most readers were left with the impression of a State Department in disarray: an agency riddled with complaints that had spilled into the open. But that was not quite the story. From at least one perspective, the *Times* buried the real lead.

Prior to the Trump administration, memos of dissent were encouraged by the State Department. The *dissent channel* was part of a long-established tradition of allowing members of the agency to voice concerns about US policy without worrying that their opinions would negatively impact their careers. Secretary of State William Rogers originated the idea during the Vietnam War to aid the policy review process by encouraging more input from staff in the field.

Although the 2016 memo of dissent was leaked to the press, the Obama administration didn't react publicly as if anything dysfunctional had happened. The concerns were noted, but the signers were not condemned or disciplined. Other agencies, including the CIA, have similar mechanisms: teams that present counterarguments to planned courses of action.

Of course, the press loves to report on bureaucracies at war with themselves. But a marketplace of competing ideas is an inherently noble thing. Peaceful dissent can save an organization or a nation from taking actions that will fail.

writer, who was once put under a death threat by Iranian clerics for writing a supposedly blasphemous novel, noted that "without the freedom to challenge, even to satirize all orthodoxies," freedom "ceases to exist."[11]

WEIGHING THE VALUE OF PUBLIC OPINION

Humankind has long struggled with the question of how much conformity should be forced on individuals living within groups. Since humans are by nature social, and since living together requires common rules (i.e., whether to drive on the left or the right side of the road, whether criticizing others will be a crime, whether children shall be required to attend school), governments have always sought to impose laws and policies that civilize daily life. Even so, most Western states value the ideal of individual freedom, but always with exceptions. Those who have minimized the role of dissent and vigorous public debate as positive forces for self-rule have sometimes had distinguished allies, such as the Greek philosopher Plato, who spent part of his adult life at his Academy on the edge of Athens arguing that democratic states were ultimately bound to fail. He thought ordinary people were frequently incapable of making decisions about their communities because they lacked the intelligence and thorough training necessary for decision making. Democracies were likely to be governed by mobs unable to separate rhetoric from reason.[12] Plato believed that few citizens can discriminate between the thoughtful judgments of the well-trained leader—described in *The Republic* as the philosopher king—and the irrational pandering of the well-trained persuader. Because democratic leaders are elected by the people, they would pander to citizen fears and fantasies rather than focus on the needs of the nation. The leader chosen by popular vote would substitute flattery of the mob in place of true wisdom. To Plato, leaders guided by public opinion were bound to be as misguided as teachers who let their pupils decide what should be taught.

Plato's view did not go unchallenged. A prolonged debate over the wisdom of democracy developed between him and other teachers who traveled through the city-democracies along the coasts of Greece, Sicily, and Italy. He was deeply troubled by the activities of these independent tutors, whom affluent parents hired to educate their male children. (The enlightenment of the Hellenic world ended short of including women, slaves, and the impoverished as full citizens—even in democratic Athens.) Among the first tutors was Corax, who taught public speaking skills to citizens who needed to improve their persuasive abilities in legal and political settings. Plato scorned Corax and other itinerant teachers, who were collectively known as **Sophists**. He disliked them partly because they worked outside of the prestigious intellectual center of Athens and partly because these teachers taught the techniques of persuasion. His aversion to the Sophists was so strong that he named some of the weak-thinking characters in his dialogues after several of them. It is a tribute to Plato's prestige that the term *sophistic* still survives as a label of scorn for people who play too loosely with truth and fact.

In a famous dialogue against the practice of teaching persuasion, Plato writes parts for his own honored teacher, Socrates, and his democratically inclined opposite, Gorgias. In the dialogue, Gorgias is portrayed as superficial and illogical. He is no match for Socrates's superior wisdom and is supposed to be an object lesson about the false delusions of would-be leaders.[13] If there was an ideal form of communication, Plato noted, it ought to replicate the kind of selflessness we would expect in two lovers: neither of whom would presumably seek to harm or mislead the other.[14]

The real Gorgias was born in Sicily but taught and gave performances in many cities, including Olympia, Delphi, and Athens.[15] Like all Sophists, he taught many different subjects, but always the art of persuasion. "A special feature of his displays was to invite miscellaneous questions from the audience and give impromptu replies."[16] To his credit, "he saw the power of persuasion as paramount in every field, in the study of nature and other philosophical subjects no less than in the law-courts or the political arena."[17] Like many of his contemporaries, Gorgias played to the public. He believed that the freedom to speak in defense of opinions and beliefs required skill in knowing how to hold an audience's attention and how to shape their attitudes.[18]

Man Is the Measure of All Things

For the Sophists and for democracies in general, normative attitudes are everything. Our beliefs and aspirations are as important to us as hard truths. Perhaps the clearest statement to that effect came from Protagoras, who offered a convenient declaration that could serve as a seven-word definition of democracy: "Man is the measure of all things."[19] In matters that affect the collective welfare of a society, the *people*—not Gods or rulers—should be left with the power to judge what is just, true, and fair for themselves.

The concept has multiple implications. It is often interpreted to assert that there are no natural or fixed guidelines for conduct. The rules we live by cannot be gleaned from divine sources, only from ourselves. Or, as one scholar put it, "nothing exists save but what each of us perceives and knows."[20] This idea is not a license to trash unwelcome but valid claims of scientific knowledge. Instead, it acknowledges our natural tendencies to be interpreters rather than photographic collectors of experiences. We not only see but also frequently judge.

The phrase has two practical implications for persuaders. First, it implies that many issues that spark public persuasion are about preferences rather than truths or ultimate answers. The Sophists made the commonsense observation that most answers to complex problems cannot be rendered totally false or useless for all people at all times. In a decision as trivial as which brand of soap to buy, or as important as a decision to speak against a coworker's proposal, the final choice is personal and unique to our situation. Sophists reflected the very modern idea of *intersubjectivity of knowledge*—that in most realms of human affairs agreement with others is a crucial tipping point.

Second, the phrase is a refreshing reminder that persuaders must have faith in the good sense of an audience to locate both the wisdom and the puffery that comes with public discussion. Aristotle echoed this view. He began his persuasion text by stating a belief in the ultimate soundness of public opinion formed by exposure to various points of view. Persuasion, he noted, "is useful because things that are true and things that are just have a natural tendency to prevail over their opposites."[21] We have carried the idea forward in the frequently expressed principle that the arc of history bends toward truth. In closed societies where decisions are reserved for the few, there will be hostility to competition from others or unofficial explanations of events. The totalitarian leader can be expected to claim that a variety of viewpoints will confuse and bewilder the ordinary public. The democrat, in contrast, shares a faith in the value of self-government and the belief that the public can find its own best answers if given the benefit of extended discussion.

Individual Freedom and the American Experience

While the Greek intellectual tradition had considerable influence in colonial America, most of the thinkers in the New World were more directly swayed by a belief in individual rights that had its roots in the French Enlightenment of Jean-Jacques Rousseau and British intellectuals such as John Milton and John Locke. From these European origins the colonists acquired a belief in the natural rights of humans—freedoms given eloquent expression in the Bill of Rights and the Declaration of Independence.[22]

Citizens of the colonies also had the more practical goal of establishing local democratic governments to replace the frequently indifferent colonial administrations. They wanted to be able to confront those who were legislating decisions and taxes—an impossibility when the seat of authority was in London. After the War of Independence, they designed independent states and adapted many legal principles and values from the European governments they had known. They attempted to secure for themselves what England had provided for its own citizens: local control with direct access to the legislative process and the right to raise and spend their own revenues.

They had additional pragmatic reasons for breaking with England. Many families had come to the New World years earlier as religious dissidents, most notably Baptists, Quakers, and Catholics. Liberty to practice a religion different from that of one's neighbor was a means of self-protection. By establishing a confederation of states to replace rule by a monarchy, the newly independent Americans (with the enormous exceptions of women and those enslaved as property) attempted to assure that decisions affecting their lives would be subject to public discussion rather than private dictate.

The actual task of inventing a government in the late 1780s was not as easy. The founders of what would become the United States had to deal with one of the questions that divided Plato and the Sophists: how strong a role should persuasion and public opinion play in setting policy? Among the most eloquent voices was Thomas Jefferson's. The unofficial philosopher of American independence was strongly opposed to a centralized federal government; he believed in the inherent wisdom of the common citizen. Along with John Adams, whom he eventually defeated for the presidency, he also shared an aversion to formal political parties.[23]

Other founders such as James Madison and Alexander Hamilton had a general distaste for the power of unbridled persuasion: a legacy we are now burdened with institutions such as the Electoral College and the US Senate. If the Senate were true to the idea of full democratic representation, California would have 136 senators to Wyoming's 2.[24] Some founders feared that the turbulence and contention of pure democracies could produce factions—their code word for angry citizens who might form political parties that could upset a government of independent thinkers. "So strong is this propensity of mankind to fall into mutual animosities," noted Madison, "that where no substantial occasion presents itself, the most frivolous and fanciful distinctions have been sufficient to kindle unfriendly passions."[25] How right he was. Today's highly partisan and dysfunctional Congress is not what most of the founders sought.[26]

Would these early leaders opt for a pure democracy, or a republic of representatives buffered from the explosive impulses of a persuadable crowd? Jefferson included the words, "all men are created equal" in the Declaration of Independence, but few of his colleagues were willing to accept the idea of a full democracy. So the colonists settled on a safer alternative that provided a layer of insulation between the supposedly unpredictable passions of ordinary citizens and the cooler reasoning of those who would run the government. They formed a republic, not strictly a government of the people, but a government of representatives who would be elected to act *for* the people. Only the members of Congress could vote for a president, and citizen voting was restricted to white male landowners. The Constitution was intended as much to protect wealth and property as to insure the natural rights of the citizens who had waged war against the British.

The Bill of Rights was written to allay concerns that the Constitution lacked sufficient protections for individual rights. Ratified by the states on December 15, 1791, it included ten amendments to the Constitution. The First Amendment protects the right to freedom of religion and freedom of expression from government interference. The Supreme Court interprets the extent of the protections.

The First Amendment

Congress shall make no law respecting an establishment of religion, or prohibiting the free exercise thereof; or abridging the freedom of speech, or of the press; or the right of the people peaceably to assemble, and to petition the Government for a redress of grievances.

The fear that freedom of expression could combine with pure democracy to produce unwanted change was very real among the designers of the new government. They believed in public persuasion, but only to a point. Most were less certain than Jefferson, who wrote that "government degenerates when trusted to the rulers of the people alone."[27] In times of conflict with other nations, such as the undeclared naval war against France in 1798 (the Quasi War), even advocates of personal freedom like President John Adams supported the Alien and Sedition Acts. As in contemporary China, the acts made it a crime to utter or write scandalous or malicious statements against the government.[28]

Given the natural impulse to ignore or restrict ideas we don't like, it's important to remember that an open society is not only marked by a tolerance for differences but also by the desire to see differences translated into constructive and peaceful change. The result is that new and sometimes unpopular ideas are given the chance to be heard, making government only one of a competing array of voices. Supreme Court Justice Oliver Wendell Holmes clearly summarized the social necessity for freedom of expression in 1919, noting that free societies should offer a marketplace of ideas:

> The ultimate good desired is better reached by free trade in ideas—that the best test of truth is the power of the thought to get itself accepted in the competition of the market.[29]

In the best of circumstances, the process of public debate gives people the chance to be more than cogs in someone else's wheel.

THE TECHNOLOGICAL PUSH TOWARD OPENNESS

Single-party dictatorships in East Germany, Poland, and elsewhere disintegrated in 1989—fascinating examples of transformations created in part by technology that ignores political borders. Eastern Europeans exposed to frequent doses of broadcast and videotaped television grew steadily more impatient with the slow pace of political and economic change in their countries. Inevitably, the growing tides of electronic information swamped efforts by the old regimes to control it. Images of Western materialism planted the seeds of dissolution first in Europe, followed 25 years later by popular uprisings propelled by social media in many Middle Eastern nations.[30]

Though the conventional view is that the internet alone has destabilized top-down governments, it is easy to overestimate its power in revolutions.[31] Even given their ability to undermine official voices at critical moments of political change, many believe that new media have yet to fully deliver on the promise of redistributing the power to publicize ideas.

The success of the 2016 campaign of Donald Trump first against the Republican Party and then against Hillary Clinton suggests that social media can indeed undermine more traditional media pathways to influence. Trump used Twitter to bypass journalists, while also capturing their interest in what he said. But knowledgeable observers in the United States also note that the increasing commercial dominance of most internet portals by more mainstream media means that we can overestimate the power of social media as agents for change. The merger of Time-Warner and AOL in 2001 was an early sign, as was the swallowing of YouTube by Google, and the merger of Comcast with NBCUniversal. AT&T is poised to take over Time-Warner, and the Walt Disney Company is acquiring 21st Century Fox. Google has reached a plateau of close to 70 percent of the search engine market. It and rivals like Microsoft's Bing have a clear business model. In the words of internet pioneer Jaron Lanier, ideas are now "minced into anatomized search engine keywords," then "copied millions of times by some algorithm somewhere designed to send an advertisement." The point is less about enlightenment than the production of "bait laid by the lords of the clouds to lure hypothetical advertisers."[32]

True, anyone can now publish on the internet. But getting noticed on the crucial first page of a search result is still difficult. The exact algorithms of search engine placement are notoriously secret. As anyone with a lone blog page has probably noticed, the trick to finding an audience is to devise ways to have a blog positioned as a clickable link from a bigger site.[33]

The few remaining media conglomerates with vast holdings—Disney, Time-Warner, the News Corporation, National Amusements (which controls Viacom and CBS), and Comcast—own a large percentage of the most popular television and print outlets in the United States.[34] Although their holdings are diverse, the effect of their control is often to narrow the range of voices to which most of the American public have easy access. For example, a person who spends her leisure time consuming HBO, Cinemax, Turner Classic Movies, Warner Brothers Films, CNN, and *People* magazine will not have ventured outside the boundaries of the Time-Warner empire. Similarly, watch a lot of ABC's *Good Morning America* or ESPN, or many stations nationwide, and the prevalence of stories about Disneyland should not be a surprise. All are owned by the same Disney parent company.[35] New voices in film, magazines, music, and television will find that gaining a media foothold can be difficult unless they adjust to the demands of the few existing corporations that control many sources.

How Open Is American Society?

This brief history raises the question of how open and free life is. The power of office combined with the persuasive skills of advocates can constrain resistance. To be sure, the right to free speech—the right to persuade—is mostly alive and well in the United States. However, it is not an absolute right, nor is it assured by a perfect marketplace for ideas. In this section we briefly review examples from the fields of government and industry that suggest how far we sometimes stray from the ideal of protected rights of expression.

Governmental Controls

The First Amendment to the Constitution states that "Congress shall make no law . . . abridging the freedom of speech or of the press." But advocates have sometimes been punished for the crime of speaking out. Since World War I, thousands of US citizens have been jailed for distributing pamphlets against war, advocating the overthrow of the government, protesting against the military draft, marching against racial segregation, and joining unpopular political causes.[36] Constitutional protections are often not enough to curb local authorities from using (and misusing) sometimes vague statutes against *libel* (uttering false and defamatory accusations), trespassing, spying, disturbing the peace, and marching without a permit. In addition, many agencies within federal and state governments make extended claims for the right to keep supposedly sensitive information secret. Here are some representative cases.

- Immediately after the 2016 presidential election individuals working with the Trump transition team asked the Environmental Protection Agency to list the names of employees who had worked on President Obama's climate initiatives. Since Trump had been outspoken in his belief climate change was a hoax, some staffers concluded that the request was a witch hunt. "It is a remarkably aggressive and antagonistic tone to take with an agency that you're about to try to manage," a current agency employee said.[37]

- Soon after the terrorist attacks on the World Trade Center and Pentagon, the State Department sought to prohibit Voice of America (VOA) from broadcasting an interview with Afghanistan's Taliban leader, Mullah Mohammed Omar. VOA is a government-supported worldwide radio service providing objective and comprehensive news, as well as explaining US government policy. State Department spokesperson Richard Boucher said, "We didn't think that the American taxpayer . . . should be broadcasting the voice of the Taliban," which has harbored terrorist groups.[38] Norman Pattiz, a member of

The Johnson Treatment

Presidents can extend and magnify their persuasive powers; President Lyndon Johnson excelled in this area. His address to a joint session of Congress arguing for voter rights legislation in March of 1965 is one of the towering achievements of his presidency. He virtually shamed his southern colleagues into relinquishing their stranglehold on voter access. Johnson's rhetoric could be lumbering and labored. And he could be insensitive. But in that speech the angels sang, and the nation finally got a Voting Rights Act that would enfranchise millions.

The former Senate Minority Leader was an incredibly persuasive man in one-on-one meetings. He subjected colleagues to a nonstop barrage of arguments, pleadings, commands, threats, and intimidation until the target could take no more. The experience was known as the Johnson Treatment. Some of what Johnson did was genuine persuasion. Some was simply hammer-lock coercion building off his power in the Senate, and later, as the accidental president.

On January 8, 1964, Johnson announced his "War on Poverty." Sergeant Shriver was living his dream job as head of the Peace Corps. Shriver loved the agency and its mission of humanitarian work performed by young and idealistic Americans. On February 1, Johnson called Shriver to say he was going to announce him as head of the program. Although the idea was inspiring, Shriver knew it would be a hornet's nest of overlapping and competing federal programs. It promised all the organizational headaches that were mostly avoided in the much smaller Peace Corps program. Johnson and his treatment succeeded; three days later Shriver was working to put the program in place. [The Treatment can be heard after a brief pause at http://www.sargentshriver.org/speech-article/president-johnson-and-sargent-shriver-discuss-the-war-on-poverty]

VOA's Board of Governors, disagreed. "I happen to believe that any legitimate news organization in the world would do that interview. And if the United States is going to be a proponent of a free press, it has to walk the walk."[39] The interview was eventually broadcast despite State Department protests.

- Every fall the American Library Association (ALA) sponsors "Banned Books Week" to draw national attention to censorship in some schools and local facilities. The goal of the week is to celebrate the value of free and open access to information.[40] The ALA's Office for Intellectual Freedom also compiles an annual list of books commonly challenged by school libraries, city libraries, or parent groups. The 2015–16 edition included Sherman Alexie's National Book Award winning *The Absolutely True Diary of a Part-Time Indian* (with references to masturbation); Stephen Chbosky's *The Perks of Being a Wallflower* (references to homosexuality, date rape, and glorification of drugs); and Khaled Hosseini's best-selling novel about friendship and betrayal between two Afghan boys, *The Kite Runner* (mentioning rape and violence).[41]

- Between 2008 and 2014 the Department of Environmental Protection in Florida circulated a memo ordering its employees not to use the words climate change, sustainability, and global warming in their communication with the public. The idea of a warming planet was not on the political agenda of Governor Rick Scott. And so the gag order was issued.[42] All of this was happening while coastal roads in the Miami area were regularly inundated by sea water during higher than normal tides.

Issues that involve challenges to freedom of expression frequently require choices between competing values. In many instances, courts and legislatures have weighed the ideal of free expression and freedom of the press against the desire for a peaceful and orderly society. Because advocates for causes have often created inconveniences such as traffic jams or angry crowds, careful vigilance is necessary to be sure that such problems do not become a pretext for curtailing the right to persuade. Similarly, we expect that public institutions such as universities will entertain a broad spectrum of viewpoints. While most college campuses remain open to a wide range of speakers, some in recent years have struggled to provide forums to writers and journalists on the political right. In recent years cancelled or disrupted speakers have included former White House adviser Steve Bannon, think tank scholar Charles Murray, former Breitbart News editor Milo Yiannopoulos, and DailyWire editor Ben Shapiro. Students opposing a speaker can create enough of a disturbance to sometimes trigger the cancellation of an event for safety reasons. But as the University of Chicago's Jerry Coyne has wisely noted, "By all means, let us demonstrate peacefully, write letters and deliver our own counterspeech. But under no circumstances should we try to silence our opponents. That accomplishes nothing. The words 'I favor free speech' should never be followed by 'but.'"[43]

Corporate Controls

Compared to our counterparts in the late 1700s and early 1800s, our knowledge of the world owes less to our neighbors and daily contacts than to the wealth of sources that come via the commercial media. The privately held mass media in the United States have increasingly replaced the back fence, the church, and the town meeting as forums in which issues of the day are discussed. As pioneering media analyst George Gerbner noted, corporations can almost act as "private governments," with the power to buy access to the mass media as the virtual equivalent of the right to operate a private "ministry of culture."[44]

Without question, our lives are enriched by ready access to the products of the nation's varied media platforms and outlets. As we noted above, major corporations—rather than governments or individuals—supply and sometimes impede the flow of information. The much-discussed power of the media involves advertisers, service providers, broadcasters, and individual media corporations, sometimes with a near monopoly in some communities. The danger, of course, is that individual corporate agendas are not necessarily the same as the public's. Consider some of the following cases.

- In 2016 a Georgia medical center cancelled all its advertising and subscriptions to the *Valdosta Daily Times* after the paper reported that board meetings were not public, as specified in the law. Rather than comply, the South Georgia Medical Center decided to punish the paper, even refusing to stock it in the hospital gift shop. As the *Columbia Journalism Review*'s Susannah Nesmith noted, "As the healthcare industry has become a bigger and bigger part of the US economy—and a more prominent advertiser, too—hospitals have become major economic players in many communities. And obviously, local newspapers are weaker than they once were."[45]

- Apple and Google have complied with the requests of the Russian and Chinese governments to purge content of sites viewed as threatening their government's control. The Russian government asked both Apple and Google to pull the app for LinkedIn, the professional social network, based on the fear that data on citizens would be stored on a server outside the country. Chinese regulators asked app stores functioning in their country to register with the government, a not so veiled way to get information about user activities.[46]

- Anyone who wishes to participate in Alaska's annual Iditarod Trail Sled Dog Race is required to sign a waiver that "prohibits them from making remarks deemed harmful to the race or its sponsors from the time they sign up until 45 days after crossing the finish line in Nome."[47] This modern-day gag rule is not unusual. Many organizations require employees to sign pledges not to discuss their salaries or internal decisions with others, even after they have left a company. Regarding the Iditarod prohibition, a Fairbanks newspaper remarked: "the gag order undercuts fundamental principles that have made Alaska and the U.S. what they are."[48]

- Before mid-2010 Microsoft provided the Russian police data about people using pirated copies of Windows software. The huge American corporation allowed itself to be a tool of political repression by aiding police who were anxious to find any reason to raid the offices of dissident writers, journalists, and bloggers. After coverage of this activity in the press, the software giant admitted that the policy was wrongheaded and took steps to end the practice.[49]

- People can be fired for expressing their political beliefs at work. Lynne Gobbell's employer, a vocal Bush supporter, fired her from her insulation-packing job because of the John Kerry bumper sticker on her car. Michael Italie lost his job as a machine operator because he appeared on a local radio program in which he discussed his socialist views. Tim Torkildson, an instructor at an English-language school, was fired because his boss mistakenly concluded that a blog post explaining homophones (words that sound alike but are spelled differently) would associate the school with "the gay agenda."[50]

- Natalie Maines of the Dixie Chicks, during a concert, voiced her frustration about the policies of President George W. Bush. The criticism landed the group on the blacklists of country radio stations and many of their advertisers.[51]

- A fear of offending consumers puts pressure on media outlets to steer clear of significant issues or national problems. Fox Sports asked 84 Lumber to rework their 2017 Superbowl ad to remove the image of a Mexican mother and daughter passing through a portal at the American border.[52] President Trump's displeasure with Mexican immigration had made that image too controversial for the network broadcasting the NFL event.

- One quarter of the editors and reporters who responded to a questionnaire said they avoided legitimate stories if concerned that advertisers or their bosses would disapprove of the subject matter.[53] Self-censorship happens when normally curious and skeptical journalists decide not to pursue a story because of the tensions or risks it will pose for their organizations. Would a critic at *Entertainment Weekly* (owned by Time-Warner) write a scathing review of a movie released by Warner Brothers (also owned by Time-Warner)? Would a favorable article about Tesla automobiles in a struggling city newspaper offend auto dealers, a significant source of display advertising? Would an NBC report on cable subscriber complaints be pulled because NBC is owned by Comcast?

To be sure, the best of the mass media can be commendably independent of the pressures and views of advertisers, but the constant need for high ratings and large circulation numbers is always a factor in the ways ideas are distributed. The founding fathers could not anticipate that public information would be so heavily tied to information industries dominated by major publishing and media corporations. Their idea of popular government was to disperse rather than to centralize influence. They could not have envisioned meaningful discussion as something that would take place through advertiser-based media that frequently has an interest in safe, nonpolitical content.

SUMMARY

The role of the advocate in American society is basic. Few American values are as cherished as the idea of a free and open society. Open and vigorous persuasion rests on the vital corollaries of open access to information and the willingness of public and private institutions to tolerate dissenting views. Advocacy withers under the heavy hand of governmental or organizational oppression.

Throughout history people who have built nations or studied existing societies have disagreed about whether—when left to ordinary people—the power of persuasion can result in decisions that show intelligence and civility. The choices we make as citizens of a nation may never fully satisfy critics of public opinion who distrust its wisdom. But of this we are certain: the greater the diversity of choices within a nation, the more it needs and benefits from vigorous public discussion. We share with Aristotle and the Sophists a faith in communities and societies to find their own ways to enact the values and beliefs of their members.

QUESTIONS AND PROJECTS FOR FURTHER STUDY

1. One of the current battlegrounds over freedom of expression in the United States centers on the internet. In 1998 the Supreme Court struck down legislation that would have put significant curbs on internet content. Develop a position on the question of whether public libraries should employ blocking software that would limit reader access to sensitive sites (i.e., sites that deal with sexual, political, or religious content).

2. We discussed the firing of employees for expressing their political beliefs. Should employers have such powers over their employees? Consider the cases listed in the section on corporate controls. In any of the cases, was the employer justified? Explain your answer.

3. The right to freedom of expression is easiest to defend when we consider the cause to be a good one, but free speech issues often develop from more unpopular roots. In 1977, for example, the American Nazi Party decided to hold a parade and make speeches in Skokie, Illinois. The northern suburb of Chicago has a large Jewish population, many of whom were survivors of Hitler's World War II death camps. If you were the judge presented with Skokie's request to issue an injunction against the march, what would you decide? Try to defend your decision to another member of the class. Look at Nat Hentoff's book, *The First Freedom*, to find out what actually happened.

4. In *The Republic*, Book VIII, beginning at section 554, Plato describes the problems in democratic governments. Read the pages of this section, consider his arguments, and prepare a short summary of his complaints against democracy. Use his analysis as the basis of a paper or a short oral summary presented to other members of your course.

5. The 2001 attacks on the Pentagon and New York's World Trade Center continue to pose serious questions for an open society. How much freedom should we exchange for security? Should we curtail visas for visitors and students? Should we give up some of our privacy for the protection of ourselves and others? How tolerant should we be of airport searches, clandestine government wiretaps, and seizures of property? Choose one of these questions and write an essay for accepting or denying the curtailment of freedom.

6. The text asks if a journalist can afford to pan a movie released by Warner Brothers when both the magazine and the movie company are part of the Time-Warner empire. Survey movie reviews in *Entertainment Weekly*. Is there evidence that

the magazine has a free hand to be critical of films released by another branch of the company?

7. One nonpartisan group that fights media mergers is Free Press (http://www.freepress.net/). Take a look at their website and do one of the following: (a) Identify an issue they cover that you think is significant in preserving the freedoms of advocates in an age increasingly dominated by large media companies. (b) Identify an issue they discuss where you believe they have overstated the risks to our freedom of speech or press. State the reasons for your beliefs.

ADDITIONAL READING

Aristotle, *Rhetoric*, trans. W. Rhys Roberts (Mineola, New York: Dover Thrift Editions, 2004).

Bernard Bailyn, *The Ideological Origins of the American Revolution, Enlarged Edition* (Cambridge MA: Harvard University Press, 1992).

W.C.K. Guthrie, *The Sophists* (Cambridge, United Kingdom: Cambridge University Press, 1971).

Nat Hentoff, Living the Bill of Rights (Berkeley: University of California Press, 1999).

Jaron Lanier, *You Are Not a Gadget: A Manifesto* (New York: Knopf, 2010).

Don Pember and Clay Calvert, *Mass Media Law,* 18th ed. (New York: McGraw-Hill, 2013).

Plato, *The Republic*, Books VII–VIII. Trans. W. H. D. Rouse in *Great Dialogues of Plato,* ed. Eric Warmington and Philip Rouse (New York: Mentor, 1956).

NOTES

1 Lyndon Johnson quoted in Robert Trager, Joseph Russomanno, and Susan Dente Ross, *The Law of Journalism and Mass Communication* (New York: McGraw Hill, 2007), p. 40.

2 This "right"—difficult to interpret in the age of social media—is more implied than explicit in the U.S. Constitution. For a useful primer on the evolution of privacy protections, see Doug Linder, "Exploring Constitutional Law: The Right of Privacy." http://www.law.umkc.edu/faculty/projects/ftrials/conlaw/rightofprivacy.html

3 China Report, Freedom House, 2016, https://freedomhouse.org/report/freedom-press/2016/china

4 Farhad Manjoo, "Apple Silence in China Sets a Dangerous Precedent," *The New York Times*, August 1, 2017, p. B1, B5.

5 Edward Wong and Austin Ramzy, "China Keeps a Tight Lid on Coverage of Sinking," *The New York Times*, June 4, 2015, p, A11.

6 For a useful review of curtailed personal and press freedoms in China see U.S. Department of State, "Country Reports on Human Rights Abuses: China, 2015," https://www.state.gov/j/drl/rls/hrrpt/humanrightsreport/#wrapper

7 "Jailed China Earthquake Activist's Appeal Declined," *Amnesty International Report*, June 9, 2010. http://www.amnesty.org/en/news-and-updates/jailed-china-earthquake-activists-appeal-declined-2010-06-09

8 Mollie Lortie, "In Tibet, environmental group barred from photocopying," *Tibet Post International*, May 16, 2015, http://thetibetpost.com/en/news/tibet/4555-in-tibet-environmental-group-barred-from-photocopying

9 Sharon LaFraniere, "China Aims to Stifle Tibet's Photocopiers," *The New York Times*, May 12, 2010, p. A8.

10 "Report: State of the World, 2015-2016," *Amnesty International*, February 23, 2016, http://www.amnestyusa.org/research/reports/amnesty-international-state-of-the-world-2015-2016?page=3

11 Salman Rushdie, "In Good Faith: The Pen against the Sword," *Newsweek*, February 12, 1990, p. 53.

12 Plato, *The Republic*, Bks 7–10. See also, Karl R. Popper, *The Open Society and Its Enemies Vol. 1*, 5th ed. (Princeton, NJ: Princeton University Press, 1966), p. 42.

13 The dialogue is called *The Gorgias*. For an interesting analysis of Plato's attacks on Gorgias and the teaching of persuasion, see Robert M. Pirsig's best-selling biographical novel, *Zen and the Art of Motorcycle Maintenance* (New York: Morrow, 1974), especially Part IV.

[14] See, for example, William G. Kelley Jr., "Rhetoric as Seduction," *Philosophy and Rhetoric*, 6(2), Spring, 1973, pp. 69–80.

[15] W. C. K. Guthrie, *The Sophists* (Cambridge, England: Cambridge University Press, 1977).

[16] Ibid., p. 270.

[17] Ibid., p. 272.

[18] For a more nuanced assessment of the real Gorgias, see Scott Consigny, *Gorgias: Sophist and Artist* (Columbia: University of South Carolina Press, 2001), pp. 107–118.

[19] Guthrie, p. 183.

[20] Ibid., p. 184.

[21] Aristotle, *Rhetoric*, trans. W. Rhys Roberts (Mineola, New York: Dover Thrift Editions), p. 5.

[22] For a broad overview of ideas feeding the American Revolution see Bernard Bailyn, *The Ideological Origins of the American Revolution, Enlarged Edition* (Cambridge, MA: Harvard University Press, 1992), pp. 1–93.

[23] David McCullough, *John Adams* (New York: Simon and Schuster, 2001), pp. 447–448.

[24] Alan Durning, "Undemocracy and the U.S. Senate," *Sightline Daily*, March 16, 2010, http://daily.sightline.org/daily_score/archive/2010/03/16/un-democracy-and-the-us-senate

[25] Alexander Hamilton, James Madison, and John Jay, *The Federalist Papers*, Ed. Clinton Rossiter (New York: Mentor, 1961), p. 79.

[26] For an overview of the institution's current problems see Thomas Mann and Norman Ornstein, *The Broken Branch: How Congress Is Failing America and How to Get It Back on Track* (New York: Oxford University Press, 2008).

[27] Jefferson quoted in Page Smith, *Jefferson: A Revealing Biography* (New York: American Heritage, 1976), p. 157.

[28] McCullough, pp. 504–505.

[29] Holmes quoted in Jerome Barron, *Freedom of the Press for Whom?* (Bloomington: Indiana University Press, 1973), p. 320.

[30] See, for example, Jackson Diehl, "East Europe on Cultural Fast Forward," in Shirley Biagi (Ed.), *Media Reader* (Belmont, CA.: Wadsworth, 1989), pp. 340–342, and Shadi Hamid, The Future of Democracy in the Middle East: Islamist and Illiberal, *The Atlantic*, May 6, 2014, https://www.theatlantic.com/international/archive/2014/05/democracys-future-in-the-middle-east-islamist-and-illiberal/361791/

[31] See, for example, Frank Rich, "Wallflowers at the Revolution," *The New York Times*, February 6, 2011, Week in Review, p. 8.

[32] Jaron Lanier quoted in Michael Agger, "The Geek Freaks," *Slate*, January 3, 2010. http://www.slate.com/id/2239466/

[33] A Google official quoted in David Segal, "A Bully Finds a Pulpit on the Web," *The New York Times*, November 28, 2010, Sunday Business, p. 6.

[34] FreePress, "Who Owns the Media?" N.D. http://www.freepress.net/ownership/chart, accessed August 1, 2017.

[35] Ibid.

[36] Howard Zinn, *Disobedience and Democracy: Nine Fallacies on Law and Order* (New York: Vintage, 1968), pp. 67–87.

[37] Darius Dixon, "Trump Team's Demands Fuel Fear of Energy Department 'Witch Hunt,'" *Politico*, December 9, 2016, http://www.politico.com/blogs/donald-trump-administration/2016/12/trump-transition-wants-names-of-energy-department-staff-who-worked-on-climate-232424

[38] Felicity Barringer, "State Department Protests Move by U.S. Radio," *The New York Times*, September 26, 2001, p. B3.

[39] Ibid.

[40] American Library Association, "Banned Books Week: Celebrating the Freedom to Read." n.d. http://www.ala.org/advocacy/bbooks/banned

[41] Robert Doyle, "2015–2016 Books Challenged or Banned,", *American Library Association*, http://www.ila.org/content/documents/2016banned.pdf

[42] Tristram Korten, "In Florida, Officials Ban Term 'Climate Change,' *Miami Herald*, March 8, 2015, http://www.miamiherald.com/news/state/florida/article12983720.html

[43] Jerry Coyne, "'Hate speech' Is No Reason to Ban Bannon," *Chicago Tribune*, Feb. 2, 2018, p. 15.

[44] George Gerbner, "Minister of Culture, the USA, and the 'Free Market of Ideas'" in Biagi, pp. 335–339.

[45] Susannah Nesmith, "After a Hospital Reportedly Pulls Ads, Georgia Paper Says It Won't Back Down," *Columbia Journalism Review*, March, 2016, http://www.cjr.org/united_states_project/georgia_hospital_newspaper_feud_open_meetings.php

[46] Farhad Manjoo, "Censors Delight in the World's Reliance on App Stores," *New York Times*, January 19, 2017, p. B1.

[47] Editorial, "Iditarod Gag Rule Shameful" *Fairbanks daily News-Miner*, March 2, 2016, http://www.newsminer.com/opinion/editorials/iditarod-gag-rule-shameful-race-s-ban-on-disparaging-comments/article_95dc4a4e-e032-11e5-90d2-fb5ff64598d7.html

[48] Ibid.

[49] Clifford Levy, "Microsoft Moves to Help Nonprofits Avoid Piracy-Linked Crackdowns," *The New York Times*, October 17, 2010, p. A6.

[50] Jeannette Cox," A Chill around the Water Cooler: First Amendment in the Workplace," *Insights on Law and Society*, Winter, 2015, http://www.americanbar.org/publications/insights_on_law_andsociety/15/winter-2015/chill-around-the-water-cooler.html

[51] Kelefa Sanneh, "Strong, Independent and Taking Their Own Advice," *The New York Times*, August 3, 2006. http://query.nytimes.com/gst/fullpage.html?res=9D00EFDA103FF930A3575BC0A9609C8B63

[52] Sapna Maheshwari, "A Challenge for Super Bowl Commercials: Not Taking Sides, Politically," *The New York Times*, February 3, 2017, p. B2.

[53] Trudy Lieberman, "You Can't Report What You Don't Pursue," *Columbia Journalism Review*, May/June 2000, pp. 44–49.

3

The Language of Advocacy

> Our greatest body of observable social "facts" is not derived
> from what people do, but what they *say* about what they do.[1]
>
> —Hugh Dalziel Duncan

Human language is a marvelous and powerful tool. Most of our early education emphasizes the meaning of words, their placement in sentences, and how sentences form paragraphs. Language, however, is far more than a collection of words and rules for proper usage. While it is the primary instrument for human action and expression, it is also an important part of our consciousness. We *think* in language. The conventional but mistaken view is that language is a residue of a thought rather than its generative source. We also measure the worth of others—their beliefs and attitudes—in their verbal constructions. Words are the primary touchstones for drawing conclusions about others and, ultimately, ourselves as well. As the famed editor Harold Evans reminds us, "Words have consequences."[2] Not only does language describe direct experience as well as past and future events but it also reveals character. It is capable of transmitting both true and false messages with equal flair—although it usually betrays us if we try to conceal our essential nature. This brief chapter about verbal communication highlights the large stake we have in the names and labels we use.

THE NATURE OF LANGUAGE

Most languages are made up of words that are arbitrary; they are created by humans and have significance only when two or more people agree to some general interpretation of the symbol. Everyone assumes the meaning of *chair* is clear, yet one person may visualize a Queen Anne chair while another thinks of a big comfortable recliner. Because words, even ordinary ones, have multiple meanings, we are constantly at risk of misinterpreting the significance felt by others. The fact that the English word *set* has 464 meanings in the Oxford English Dictionary signals the likelihood of confusion.[3]

Linguistic confusion has consequences. A particular phrase may strike its user as harmless, but some listeners may detect prejudice. One person's attempt at humor may offend another person. In 2001 President Bush apologized to the Arab world for using the word *crusade* to describe American antiterrorism efforts. The word "still evokes unpleasant historical memories among Muslim nations."[4] Similarly, *jihad* has a distinctly peaceful connotation for Muslims that is at odds with non-Muslim perceptions. Concepts such as justice, equality, or natural human rights evoke certain feelings in some people and very different feelings in others.

Another key feature in the use of language is that it allows us the capacity to see what *is*, *what might be*, and *what is not*. Kenneth Burke referred to humans as "inventors of the negative," reminding us that there are no negatives in nature, nor probably in most animal perception. Animals live in the moment. In contrast, humans may focus on future possibilities. The negative is a creation of the uniquely human tool of language—often without referents in the material world.[5] Negatives exist as possibilities born of our imaginations. We may not live in a perfect world, but we can verbalize what that might look like. Arthur Asa Berger asks:

> Have you ever wondered why it is that often when you think of a word, the opposite of the word pops into your head? . . . It is because meaning is relational. Nothing means anything in itself, and everything means something because of some kind of relationship in which it is embedded.[6]

We make choices about categories to which a new stimulus belongs—we decide it is *not* one thing but has similarities to another. As Ernst Cassirer explained, humans live in a different reality than the physical world of sensation.[7] Humans live in a symbolic universe. Language, myth, rituals, art, music, and religion are some of the threads that weave the tapestry of our experience. We often see only symbolic reality; physical reality can be overwritten by symbolic experiences. We don't deal with an actual object—we deal with our perception of it, which has been influenced by a myriad of previous symbolic experiences. In Kenneth Burke's words, humans are separated from their "natural condition by instruments of their own making," the verbal equipment that sustains us everyday[8]

We can subdivide meaning into two categories. *Denotative* meanings refer to formal, dictionary meanings for words. The relationship between the word and its meaning is generally clear and not open to much debate. The definition describes essential properties of the referent, but usually without an overtone of judgment. Thus, the word *chair* denotes an object upon which one sits. For most of us that's about all there is. But *connotative* meanings of words provide positive or negative overtones. The relationships between the word and the object are more complex: personal, subject to interpretation, and possibly associated with a certain feeling. If we say that an individual "sits in the chair of power," we mean more than the object upon which the person sits. For some people, the eagle means more than a bird, the flag more than a piece of cloth, and a cross more than a piece of wood. As a result, words can have positive and negative associations simultaneously. For some, abortion is murder. For others, it is a constitutional right. As Lawrence Hosman points out, verbal understandings are always personal, creating judgments about an advocate, message comprehension or recall, and attitudes of acceptance or rejection.[9]

Language is thus based on absorbing the larger culture and the norms of communities we inhabit. At one extreme, we may argue that each word is simply a name of a category of experience, because most languages share thousands of common referents. For example, *horse* in English is *cheval* in French. Other attributes of a culture's language, however, are untranslatable. The reasons may be grammatical, semantic, or experiential. Each language is its own environment, providing special ways to communicate about experience. For example, English is full of binaries like good/bad, true/false. In contrast, Japanese usage emphasizes gradations. "No" in English may become a softer "It's not possible" in Japanese. Even so, the sea of language that is always around us is as all encompassing as the waters that support aquatic life.

THE CREATION OF REALITY THROUGH VERBAL INTERACTION

Formal education is a process of opening windows of language from which to understand reality. Sociology, psychology, communication, history, science, music, politics, and many other fields present specific vocabularies that individuals use to interpret their subjects. Each discipline has its own lexicon that provides a uniquely angled view of the world. If a person becomes a sociologist, they will view events in terms of the structure of communities and the place of individuals within that structure. A clinical psychologist will notice behaviors and will use language that names attributes of an individual's personality.

We can describe any field of study as *words about* a particular aspect of human culture. Knowing the concepts that define bipolar personality or the racially stratified society allows us to see those dimensions of a situation and to grasp their significance. We treat many verbal categories as naturally occurring elements in the universe—rather than a specific conceptual framework. Most of us would have a hard time making sense of the world without using the symbols we have been taught. Language has the primary of function of making the world knowable to ourselves and others. But advocates must remember that the meanings in their messages were constructed and will not necessarily resonate with others. Audiences accept our labeling only if they recognize and share it. Language is a product of exchange and negotiation.

SELF AS A PRODUCT OF HOW OTHERS SEE AND LABEL US

Language and labels have an outsized effect on shaping who we will become. It would be a mistake to underestimate the verbal roots of our own identities. Within the first year of life, individuals are well on their way to creating a sense of self, initially from the attention of parents. But as a child begins to acquire language, they also acquire the capacity to understand that they are presenting a self to others. As George Herbert Mead has noted, we use the feedback we receive from family and peers—their behaviors and words—as mirrors to help us understand who we are. Interaction with others helps us secure a sense of place within communities.[10] We send out verbal signals that confirm, deny, or modify an emerging sense of self. We gradually discern our status, our strengths, and our weaknesses. In the act of communicating with others, we become a whole and self-correcting agent, able to understand the impressions we give, adapting them as needed. *Our perceptions include estimating another's perceptions of who we are.* A continual feedback loop operates as we refine our emerging social intelligence. Thus a post on Facebook or Instagram is always a kind of theater—a personal artifact that will build on what we understand to be our recognizable and natural selves. We learn, internalize, and adjust: fundamental processes that often exist as core attributes of persuaders. The internalization of feedback usually makes us better at mastering settings where others may disagree. In terms of language, the key is frequently the strategic use of terms that reassure rather than alarm. Advocates must build sensitivities toward naming and labeling that surpass what others may deem adequate. An advocate cannot afford to be indifferent to the triggers of their words.

What Advocates Need to Know about Language Use

Naming is consequential and self-defining. It can give us power, or it can handicap our efforts to build trust and seek common ground with others. The chapter concludes with core attributes of symbol using that influence the effectiveness of persuaders.

Meaning Is Fluid

Meanings are in people, not in words. Words evoke different meanings in different individuals. They are relative and are based on shared experiences and common culture. As Dan Rothwell asserts, "When we treat words as things, it is tantamount to eating the menu rather than the food."[11] As society and culture change, so do common meanings of words and their acceptable usages. The words *colored, Negro, black, African American,* and *persons of color* have all referred to the same ethnic group over multiple decades, and each word has varied in its degree of acceptability. Persuader s must work to develop a clear sense of what the audience perceives when a particular word is used.

Most of us operate using a *correspondence view of reality*—that is, we process and understand the material world in similar ways. If you've been surprised by what some people mean by a summer cottage, old car, or inexpensive jeans, you have experienced the limits of the correspondence view. Communication analysis needs something better than the simplistic idea that there are reliable meanings that everyone shares. This improved approach can be called a *phenomenological* view of reality, one that recognizes the variability of meaning.

The phenomenologist accepts that we learn from others and that our self is derived from feedback. But this acceptance is tempered by the expectation that experience is also going to be shaped by individual needs and impulses: that the

Meaning Is Less Transferable than We Think

In theory, communication looks straightforward. When we address others we pass on what we assume are clear ideas with unambiguous meanings. But it's not so easy. It turns out that we aren't very good at transferring even simple information or judgments to others.

All communication is *translation*. Even when the language is the same, words pass through the filter of our experiences. This doesn't mean that we are always in a solipsistic fog. Some statements are relatively obvious and can produce a quick consensus. "Turn right" is not a vague command, but it can be ambiguous if the sender and receiver are facing each other. Even naming simple objects can be problematic—my idea of a camera could be one that uses film and yours could be the digital device in your phone.

These simple challenges with individual words are heightened when we scale up to the meanings of cultural products like speeches, songs, or movies. The hope for uniformity of meaning at this level pretty much goes out the window. For example, ask someone what songs are on their music player. The selections will be personal rather than communal, to the point that one of the parties might find the other's choices unmusical and unlistenable.

The villain here is not just the tricky business of producing concurrent meaning. The use of the term *misunderstanding* sheds some light on the difficulty. The word suggests that the initial communicator is the arbiter in deciding the authentic translation of an idea or thought. The judgment embedded in the term converts what is often a simple difference into an error, which can leave both sides frustrated.

material worlds we share are likely to produce unique understandings. Our personal biographies are likely to feed into interpretations of events that are specific, distinct, and often exclusive to us. Meaning is thus not just a matter of consensus among strangers; it is a mixture of socially mediated *and* personal influences. For example, one of the authors thinks the best time of the year is fall; his friends believe summer is the best. This process of understanding the same phrase (*best time of the year*) or experience in different ways is called *polysemy.* Words can have different meanings and shading. Acknowledging that this exists helps the persuader avoid the simple frustration of discovering that others see different things in the words you have said or written.

Consider an interesting case of polysemy in the negotiations that led to the Camp David Accords. In 1978 President Jimmy Carter worked with Israel's Menachem Begin and Egypt's Anwar Sadat to find a way out of the Arab/Israeli impasse.[12] When the talks seemed to be breaking down, Carter proposed a quick side trip to Gettysburg, not far from Camp David. He reasoned that perhaps a look at a historic Civil War battlefield would help reset the talks. Over three days in 1863 the Confederate and Union armies saw 8,000 of their members slain and 50,000 badly wounded, carnage similar to the 1967 Arab-Israeli Six Day War. Begin and Sadat took all of this in, with detailed narratives provided by Carter and the local National Park staff—but the adversaries saw very different Gettysburgs. Like most visitors, Sadat seemed fascinated by the strategies of the generals leading the two warring armies. He noted the carnage but reveled in stories about military strategy. Begin was sobered by the magnitude of the carnage, and especially the words of President Lincoln, which the Israeli leader interpreted as a call for political leadership to rise above the brutal factionalism of civil war. For Begin, Gettysburg was less a preserved chessboard of moves and countermoves than a reminder of the horrible price of strife between neighbors. Even the same physical space of an old battlefield was open to very different understandings about its significance.

Terms Are Expressive or Instrumental

The distinction between *instrumental language* and *expressive language* is important in persuasion message design. Understanding these contrasting categories contributes to coherent messages that help the advocate communicate effectively.

Much of our everyday language can be considered instrumental. This is the language of simple nouns, articles, and other terms that name the obvious and communicate simple thoughts. Instrumental terms are words that have settled meanings. Mathematics uses instrumental language; we rarely quarrel over the meanings of mathematic signs. "Your car is parked in the back lot" is a sentence of instrumental terms; it stipulates but does not judge. To be sure, this function is obvious and not very interesting.

Expressive language does not simply name an object or obvious thought; *it also judges it.* Advocates need to focus on expressive terms, which can enhance or ruin a persuader's chances. Expressive terms communicate attitudes. They have what rhetoricians call *tendency.* To use them is to explicitly praise or blame. For example, calling someone a fool or a saint is expressive terminology that seeks acceptance of the attitude embedded in it. In a conversation about some of our family members we might easily find ourselves saying that Aunt Jane is ambitious; her husband is lazy, and their kids are fantastic math wizards. Notice that in every case the word that is doing most of the heavy lifting is a term of judgment linked to a specific referent.

Expressive terms that praise are called *god terms*; those that disparage are *devil terms*. Nouns, verbs, and adjectives make up the bulk of this language. These contrasting terms can be easily paired as contrasting judgments, for example:

patriot versus zealot
honest versus corrupt
eloquent versus windbag
confident versus brash
thoughtful versus insensitive

The perspective of the person doing the labeling determines whether the god term or the devil term is applied.

Linguist George Lakoff provides a similar list summarizing the polar opposites that divide American progressives and conservatives.

God Terms for Political Progressives	God Terms for Political Conservatives
Stronger America	Strong Defense
Broad Prosperity	Free Markets
Better Future	Lower Taxes
Effective Government	Smaller Government
Mutual Responsibility	Family Values[13]

An enhanced sensitivity to labeling options can help the designer of a message make use of every opportunity to make their case. God and devil terms are essentially one-word arguments offering an attitude. Imagine that you are writing advertising copy for a client's brand of ice cream. Will you call it smooth and creamy or rough and lumpy? The best choices are obvious. In this context the first terms are god terms, the second two offer good reasons to try another brand. The important principle underlying this example is that it is always the persuader's choice to find the labels that are most apt to create the intended impression.

With masterful advocates, expressive language adds potency to a thought. Verbal effectiveness is cumulative: at once giving precision to ideas while affirming the credibility and good sense of the source. Consider the fluency of Robert Hughes, the former art critic of *Time* magazine and an accomplished essayist. Hughes was a born advocate. His target in this case: American television:

> The power of television goes beyond anything the fine arts have ever wanted or achieved. Nothing like this Niagara of visual gabble had even been imagined a hundred years ago. American network television drains the world of meaning; it makes reality seem dull, slow, and avoidable. It is our "floating world." It tends to abort the imagination by leaving kids nothing to imagine: every hero and demon is there, raucously explicitly, precut—a world of stereotypes, too authoritative for imagination to develop or change. No wonder it has predisposed American artists toward similar stereotypes. It is stupidly compelling, in a way that painting and sculpture, even in their worst moments of propaganda or sentimentality, are not.[14]

This effective use of language and imagery—"Niagara of visual gabble," "abort the imagination," "stupidly compelling"—is a significant part of the persuader's art: to find the right terms of judgment that reflect the exact feelings or attitudes that they want their target audience to understand. Of course these terms also serve a sometimes darker function of undermining a worthy idea by using devil terms to sabotage its acceptance.[15] As in all communication, the language of incisive comment can also be the language of the bully.

The Power to Name Is the Power to See

Nothing is so disorienting and exhilarating than introducing an idea that has the effect of turning the world as we think we know it upside down. And so it is with the *Sapir-Whorf hypothesis,* a theory of language use and acquisition that proposes a very different relationship to experience than what we usually assume.

Edward Sapir and Benjamin Lee Whorf argued that language is the basic port of entry for nearly all forms of higher experience.[16] In any society, the linguistic system shapes ideas and guides mental activity; "the structure of a culture's language determines the habits of thought and behavior in that culture."[17] To be sure, we don't need the word hot to understand that we will burn our finger if holding it too close to a fire. Our sensory organs enable us to directly experience the heat. But most of modern life involves *characterizations* of other's actions and motives—ways of looking at the outside world that are guided by acquired vocabularies. Perception guided by language creates worlds from which it is difficult to escape. Racism in children, for example, is verbally created. If children live in a family environment that thinks of differences from themselves as less desirable, they are guided to see ethnic differences. They acquire the impulse for racist actions often from the language of peers or parents, not their daily interactions with others.

It is interesting to note how our evolving vocabulary creates new sensitivities and sometimes lets old ones die. Fifty years ago Americans did not talk about attention deficit disorder, sexual harassment, posttraumatic stress syndrome, or perimenopause. These physical conditions have not evolved recently, but we now have names for them that give us new ways to see. Vocabularies function as environments. Like all environments, they determine our perceptions of the known world.

We don't consciously focus on what we do not name. A great deal of higher order cognition depends upon language. Hence, we get to the startling and counterintuitive conclusion that *language guides thought*. This is the core hypothesis of Sapir and Whorf. Language is the great engine of consciousness. For example, Asian words and grammars more easily accommodate the idea that something can be and not be at the same time. That's a different sensibility that affects the ways we think about our place in a culture. The writer Yiyan Li noted that when she moved to the United States she wrote more and more in English. She felt like being "orphaned" from her native language was "a kind of suicide."[18]

At certain levels this kind of linguistic relativity is obvious. We organize our educational system mostly around the idea of literacy. Reading and writing are justifiably considered the gateways to a rich cognitive life. There's good reason to worry if Johnny doesn't want to read or isn't acquiring the kind of extended vocabulary we expect through each stage of the graded school system. Even at advanced levels, educational processes emphasize vocabulary expansion. Working as a lawyer is functionally the process of making use of the generative power of legal terminology. Similarly, it's not unreasonable to assume that a doctor is more likely to see medical conditions she has names for. Even the hard sciences that are ostensibly about the physical and material worlds owe a great deal to discoveries that come through windows created in metaphors, analogies, and paradigms.[19] For example, computer pioneer Steve Jobs more or less fell into the idea of a seeing a monitor as a desktop, not a television. That idea obviously became the generative source for how certain features such as typewriter-like keyboards and visual buttons would come to define the home computer.[20]

Consider another example: most of us at a party see a room full of people. But a student who has just finished a course in Abnormal Psychology is probably going to notice more: perhaps the bipolar behavior of the guy in the corner, the clinical depression evident in the young woman who went on at length about her family, and the obvious paranoia of the couple engaged in survivalist activities. *We tend to notice what we can name.* Depression, paranoia, bipolar: this partial lexicon of mental health diagnosis reveals maladies we might otherwise miss. Even so, taking the theory as a core operating principle in communication is a hard sell to many who see language as a residue rather than a driver of experience. We routinely underestimate the verbal roots of most of our perceptions: constructions that only come to life because we have the right verbal equipment.

The Sapir-Whorf hypothesis is controversial, and linguists continue to argue over the relationship of language and thought. For some, the claim that semantic structures of different languages produce distinctive worldviews is too much of a closed system.[21] Yet anyone unfamiliar with a process who hears it described in concrete language will suddenly see connections that would previously not have been noticed. This applies as much to the rhetoric of science as to the rhetoric of intentions. In the first case, we know the laws of physics by their names, but we need names for their features in order to recognize the effects. In the second case, the author can still remember the thrill of new insight after encountering Kenneth Burke's statement that language allows us to think in negatives.

Every Society Has Its Own Ultimate Terms

Another feature of language that persuaders need to consider is what rhetorical scholars call *ultimate terms*. These words and phrases represent ideas and values that are so widely accepted that their presence in a message is likely to produce a nod of agreement. Ultimate terms represent the central beliefs of a society; in the United States, words like justice, fairness, equality, freedom and honesty are ultimate terms. Advocates using this language rightly expect that they will not be challenged. It would be unexpected for someone to defend the opposite, such as injustice or inequality.[22]

Persuaders should rename their reasons and arguments in ultimate terms. Think of this language as giving the user a free pass. The centrality of these words within the culture makes it nearly impossible to alienate a persuadee. So if John is having a difficult time persuading Mary that a single-payer health plan would be good for the United States (i.e., essentially making Medicare available to all), he might try to frame his advocacy in the kinds of ultimate terms that are not easily doubted or denied. "A single-payer system like Britain's," he could argue, "makes it more likely that everyone has *equal access*, that basic medical care is a *human right* that should be guaranteed to all in a *democratic system*." In short, he's reframed his point of view in the debate as an affirmation of some core US beliefs. Any persuader needs to ask if they are giving their ideas the best launch by renaming them in ways that reflect common cultural values.

Most Groups Have Their Own Lexicons

Language is always a changing river. A printed dictionary is a useful repository of meanings, but it is always going lag behind shifts in usage often generated by the young. Consider the *lexicon* that was in vogue for young women in the 1920s. This was the age of the *flappers*—women with a newfound sense that they controlled their own destinies and were less dependent on outdated role models. A 1922 edition of the *New York Times* included a brief dictionary to help readers puzzling over terms used by newly empowered women.

> *Oil Burner: girl who chews gum*
> *Princess Mary: girl about to be married*
> *Young Otis: chap from the country*
> *Egg Harbor: free-admission dance*
> *Ankling along: taking a walk*
> *Red Mike: boy who never goes out with a girl*
> *Darb: can be relied on to pay the checks*
> *Flat-wheeler: chap whose idea of entertainment is a walk*
> *Jammed: intoxicated*
> *Smudger: one who does all the new dances*
> *Wrinkle: a chaperone*[23]

As we have already noted, language has an important passkey function. The words we use formally or in casual conversation mark us as members of ethnic, religious, ideological and professional communities. Language leaves markers that say more about us than what the words designate. Name a special skill or occupation and, like anthropologists, we can begin to construct the features of a modern tribe. For any group, we can build a lexicon of significant terms that function as indicators of membership. This applies to 14-year-olds as much as it applies to lawyers, doctors or high school wrestlers. Indeed, from a linguistic point of view, learning the terms relevant to a group or subject is one of the functions of learning a new activity. We may not be fluent in the language of contract law, for example, but we can easily recognize from their rhetoric someone who probably is.

As we have seen, adolescents can be counted on to develop their own age-specific lexicon, often not accepting its use by parents or other would-be interlopers. Functioning as a true peer—with the language to support it—can be a significant advantage in boosting an advocate's credibility. But think also of a school principal trying to talk to a ninth-grade class in *their* manner of speaking. It probably will not work since it is faking an unearned status. Students would probably respect the principal more if he used language appropriate to the authority figure he is.

The persuader is interested in lexicons because they represent potential gains and losses in connecting with another group. But there are potential pitfalls. If you've learned part of a group's lexicon, should you use it? How authentic will they judge you to be if they find you are *misusing* one of their passkeys? The persuader must be sure he or she is knowledgeable enough to use the special language of the group. Otherwise, advocates should avoid using inside language, or they risk losing credibility.

Language Can Be a Tool of Mystification

There aren't many forms of address where *not* understanding what has been said has per-

> ### The Grammar of Hubris
>
> Rhetoricians like to say that language has its way with us. The phrase implies that everyday language steers us to conclusions that usually promise more than we can deliver. Our choice of words can convert the unlikely into the likely, the improbable into the possible. When we tie a wish to an action verb, we create expectations for things that may never materialize.
>
> The Vietnam era, and more recently Afghanistan and Iraq, confirmed this tendency. Substantive reasons for caution were obscured behind the neon glow of action verbs.
>
> It's natural that we place ourselves in the driver's seat. We assume we can be in charge because our language so easily lets us imagine it. If we round up individual culprits and put them in a lineup, they all look more or less innocent: verbs like *affects, makes, destroys, results in, causes, starts, produces, alters, stops, triggers,* and so on.
>
> In the right circumstances, these can be useful terms. In the rhetoric of a leader determined to make his or her mark on the public stage, they can turn lethal. Fantasies of power and control impose more order on human affairs than usually exists. Blame our overly deterministic language, along with the hubris that comes with being the world's preeminent military power.

suasive advantages. But mystifications provide one such case. *Mystification* denotes the use of specialized terms as signs of an individual's authority. Mystifications usually come from specific professional lexicons and implicitly signal expertise; they are unearned attempts to quell another's skepticism. This is often the effect of *bureaucratese*, a kind of "formal, stilted language that is unfamiliar to people who lack special training."[24] We may put our faith in the expert, just as we do when an auto mechanic tells us the throttle shutter, diaphragm, and inlet needle are not working in our old car's carburetor. The field of communication is similarly littered with dozens of names for particular rhetorical maneuvers—*anthypophora, aposiopesis, congery, hypocatastasis*—and many more. Left in their original Latin or Greek, they can make even a struggling pedant sound like a king of the academic anthill.

We can't recommend mystification as a rhetorical strategy. Deceiving people by communicating in the signs of expertise rather than comprehensible explanation is dishonest, a form of language-based coercion. Language has lasting significance only when—through experience or agreement—we use it in ways that are beneficial to others.

SUMMARY

Psychologist Stephen Pinker reminds us that "language is so tightly woven into human experience that it is scarcely possible to imagine life without it."[25] Through language we construct an image of ourselves. Through interaction with others, we come to know who we are, how we fit in, and what we are supposed to do.

Consciousness itself is a product of our access to language. We think in words. The acts of naming things and feelings allow us to acquire preferences, attitudes, and judgments that affect how we perceive the world. Indeed, the Sapir-Whorf hypothesis proposes that the elemental process of experience is triggered by naming. Not having a word for an experience means we may well not have the experience itself.

Effective advocates consider the possible effects of their word choice on others. Naming is a strategic tool. God terms, for example, seek a positive attitude from a receiver, just as devil terms attempt the opposite. Conscious word choice is elemental in controlling a message and producing intended effects in receivers. Succeeding in this process means that several tactical questions need to be considered. Is my language right for this audience? Does the group have a special lexicon that I should adopt? What are the ultimate terms that mean the most to this audience? And how can they and the expressive god and devil terms I select add to the effectiveness of my case? This type of analysis helps the persuader harness language to influence the audience in accepting key attitudes or new and specific behaviors.

QUESTIONS AND PROJECTS FOR FURTHER STUDY

1. Describe a course of study that used language that guided you to see something interesting that you had been missing. What were the key terms?

2. Google a political speech such as a campaign address or the president's annual State of the Union Address. Circle expressive terms that argue the speaker's

point of view. How would opponents hearing those terms alter them for their own counter-persuasive message?

3. In the same address you examined above look for ultimate terms. How useful do you think they might be in tamping down potential opposition to the ideas they are used to describe?

4. Describe some of the terms in the lexicon of a group you belong to (i.e., a theater performance group). Could you detect an imposter or new member by their inability to understand the terms? How important is the language to feeling fully a part of the group?

5. Cite a film or television show (i.e., *Ghostbusters*) where one of the characters uses verbal mystifications to foreclose debate or doubts about his or her credibility.

6. If you have lived in a culture with a different language, what perspectives or ways of thinking were encouraged by the use of particular words or grammatical forms?

ADDITIONAL READING

Kenneth Burke, *Language as Symbolic Action* (Berkeley: University of California Press, 1966).

Sonja K. Foss, Karen A. Foss, and Robert Trapp, *Contemporary Perspectives on Rhetoric, 30th Anniversary Edition* (Long Grove, IL: Waveland Press, 2014).

Harold Evans, *Do I Make Myself Clear?* (New York: Little, Brown, 2017).

Geoffrey Nunberg, *Going Nucular: Language, Politics, and Culture in Confrontational Times* (New York: Public Affair Press, 2004).

Steven Pinker, *The Language Instinct: The New Science of Language and Mind* (New York: Penguin, 2009).

Richard Weaver, *The Ethics of Rhetoric* (Davis, CA: Hermagoras Press, 1985).

NOTES

[1] Hugh Dalziel Duncan, *Communication and Social Order* (New York: Oxford University Press, 1962), p. 144.

[2] Harold Evans, *Do I Make Myself Clear?* (New York: Little Brown, 2017), p. 3.

[3] "Most definitions," Quora.com, March, 20 2015, https://www.quora.com/What-word-in-the-English-language-has-the-most-meanings

[4] Geoffrey Nunberg, *Going Nucular* (New York: Public Affair Press, 2004) p. 42.

[5] Sonja K. Foss, Karen A. Foss, and Robert Trapp, *Contemporary Perspectives on Rhetoric, 30th Anniversary Edition* (Long Grove, IL: Waveland Press, 2014), p. 203.

[6] Arthur Asa Berger, *Signs in Contemporary Culture: An Introduction to Semiotics* (Salem, WI: Sheffield, 1989), p. 173.

[7] Ann Gill, *Rhetoric and Human Understanding* (Long Grove, IL: Waveland Press, 1994), pp. 9–10.

[8] Kenneth Burke, *Language as Symbolic Action* (Berkeley: University of California Press, 1966), p. 16.

[9] Lawrence Hosman, "Language and Persuasion," in James Dillard and Michael Pfau (Eds.), *The Persuasion Handbook* (Thousand Oaks, CA: Sage, 2002), 372.

[10] George Herbert Mead, *Mind, Self and Society*, Ed. Charles Morris (Chicago: University of Chicago Press, 1970), p. 142.

[11] Dan Rothwell, *Telling It like It Isn't* (Englewood Cliffs, NJ: A Spectrum Book, 1982), p. 48.

[12] Lawrence Wright, *Thirteen Days in September* (New York: Knopf, 2014).

[13] George Lakoff, *Don't Think of an Elephant: Know Your Values and Frame the Debate* (White River Junction, Vermont: Chelsea Green, 2004), p. 94.

14 Robert Hughes, *The Spectacle of Skill* (New York: Knopf, 2015), pp. 88–89.

15 For a more extensive overview of how god and devil terms are used see Richard Weaver, *The Ethics of Rhetoric* (Davis, CA: Hermagoras Press, 1985), pp. 211–230.

16 See John Carroll and Joseph Casagrande, "The Function of Language Classifications in Behavior," in Alfred Smith (Ed.), *Communication and Culture* (New York: Holt, Rinehart & Winston, 1966), p. 491.

17 Stephen W. Littlejohn, Karen A. Foss, and John G. Oetzel, *Theories of Human Communication*, 11th ed. (Long Grove, IL: Waveland Press, 2017), p. 114.

18 Quoted in Jiayang Fan, "A Kind of Suicide," review of *Dear Friend, From My Life I Write to You in Your Life*, *The New York Times Book Review*, February 19, 2017, p. 9.

19 Thomas Kuhn, *The Structure of Scientific Revolutions, 50th Anniversary Edition* (Chicago: University of Chicago Press, 2012), pp. 92–94.

20 Walter Isaacson, *Steve Jobs* (New York: Simon and Shuster, 2011), pp. 127–128.

21 See, for example, John Gumperz and Stephen Levinson, "Linguistic Relativity Re-examined" in John Gumperz and Stephen Levinson (Eds.), *Rethinking Linguistic Relativity* (Cambridge, UK: Cambridge University Press, 1996), pp. 1–20.

22 Ultimate terms serve many different ideologies and cultural perspectives. For a full discussion see Kenneth Burke, *On Symbols and Society*, Ed. Joseph Gusfield (Chicago: University of Chicago Press, 1989), pp.192–199.

23 Ben Schott, "A Ponzi Scheme for Flappers," *The New York Times*, December 2, 2012, p. E1.

24 Diane Halpern, *Thought and Knowledge: An Introduction to Critical Thinking*, 5th ed. (New York: Psychology Press, 2014), pp. 141.

25 Steven Pinker, *The Language Instinct: The New Science of Language and Mind* (New York: Penguin, 2009), p. 17.

PART II

Perspectives on the Nature of Persuasion

4

Persuasion
and Reasoning

> Fix reason firmly in her seat, and call to her tribunal every fact, every opinion.[1]
>
> —Thomas Jefferson

Persuasion is sometimes considered a field apart from the processes associated with reasoning and argumentation. That was not the approach of the ancients like Aristotle or Cicero, who mixed observations about the psychology of audiences with insights on the nature of public debate and practical argumentation. The current tendency to partition the subject owes a great deal to the hyperspecialization of the modern university curriculum, which has moved persuasion away from its roots in philosophy. But the fact that reasoning is about linkages and how we perceive them argues for consideration of the best ways to put claims and evidence together. We naturally organize and communicate ideas with the intention of establishing connections that others recognize as making sense. We hope compelling reasons might be sufficient to overcome resistance. In formal debates—and even in everyday interactions—we count on the reasonableness of words and arguments to persuade.

There is also some urgency to reconsider reasoning practices, since we have entered a period in US public life when some political advocates show little interest in defending their claims with evidence or good reasons. The writer and editor Harold Evans describes a "retreat from reason to assertion," citing a sample instance of candidate Donald Trump talking to supporters in 2016.

> We have to stop illegal immigration. We have to do it. (Cheers and applause) We have to. Do it. Have to do it (Audience: USA! USA! USA!).[2]

Notice that the second and subsequent statements in the sequence simply repeat the claim. The tradition in oral argument is to use those positions to amplify or prove the first statement.

This post-fact era has triggered heated debates between many groups, particularly President Trump and the nation's largest news organizations. For the first time in their modern history, many mainstream journalists have reassessed the journalistic norm of not calling out a source for lying.[3] Historically, the usual process was to fact-check the suspect claims; if an error was discovered, journalists would then contact the source to see if they wanted to correct the misstatement.

Reasoning is generally perceived as a serious process, but comedy owes a great deal to the rudiments of logic. Humor in most forms is premised on *intentional* violations of the rational. It is an important cultural vehicle for celebrating the threshold where sense becomes nonsense. Our laughs serve as signs that we hold membership in the society of the sane. In the whimsical Wallace and Gromit animation epics, for example, the faithful dog Gromit must face all forms of mayhem in service to his owner's love of both untested contraptions and a good English cheese.[4] Only the wary canine seems to understand the logic coming from Wallace's tunnel-like brain.

We get the same wonderful effects of deliberate disconnectedness watching some of the earlier films of Melissa McCarthy, Amy Poehler, or Jim Carey, all performing characters whose verbal and physical actions are slightly askew.

In an ideal world, all persuasion would be grounded in good reasons and clear rationality. But individuals are not always willing to commit the necessary mental energy to the task of determining whether conclusions have significant rational justifications.[5] And we need to acknowledge that *our* reasons for accepting ideas are sometimes more personal than uniform. Individuals may sometimes disagree about what constitutes good reasoning, but persuaders should test the strength of their evidence before drawing conclusions. In a chilling example of the importance of reasoning, authorities before the 9/11 attacks detained a flight school student who was very interested in learning how to fly an airliner but completely disinterested in learning to land it.[6]

UNDERSTANDING PRACTICAL ARGUMENTS

> ### Debased Debates
>
> Election season brings out a cycle of televised debates ostensibly to allow the public the chance to compare candidates. True argumentation can reveal both a person's views and their character. As usually formatted, the broadcast debates don't achieve the lofty goals they allege.
>
> A public debate done correctly should deliver a purposeful clash of views where claims and evidence are tested against a series of counterarguments. Among others, Aristotle was certain that acts of public advocacy had a cleansing effect on the body politic. He believed we are wiser for subjecting our ideas to the scrutiny of others. Most of us do a form of this when we talk through a pending and important decision. We often want friends to help us see potential problems with our proposed course of action.
>
> In open societies such as ours we expect to hear the contrasting opinions. It's a wonderful process when properly formatted. As devised by most political operatives and journalists—a political debate is usually little more than a joint press conference. There is generally a moderator, and each side is given only a minute or two to respond to the statements of opposing candidates. These compressed political debates owe more to theater than to evidence-oriented argumentation.

Stephen Toulmin, Richard Rieke, and Allan Janik note that reasoning "is a collective and continuing human transaction, in which we present ideas or claims . . . and offer the appropriate kinds of 'reasons' in their support."[7] *Claims* linked to *premises* and *evidence* are what we mean when we use the term *argument*. In the context of controversy, claims are assertions, vulnerable to challenge, that we hope we can convince others to accept. Some claims are never stated in public because we feel we do not have the rational means to defend them. We may privately believe assertions that the "French are lazy" or "New Yorkers are pushy." But when we *publicly* express our conclusions, we enter the realm of reasoning, because we assume that our assertions will be able to withstand the critical scrutiny of others. Phrases such as "I know . . . ," "It's true that . . . ," and "It would be difficult to doubt . . . ," all carry a tone of certainty that implies we can provide evidence to back up our views.

Statements of common knowledge that go on to support such claims are called *premises*. Premises can be axiomatic and obvious, as with those we could trot out to support the claim it's a nice day: for example, "a sunny day with a temperature of 65 degrees constitutes 'nice weather' for Indianapolis in November." We usually don't need to verbalize premises for the obvious. But we could, if someone wanted to challenge a point. Regarding the claim about pushy New Yorkers, the key premises would be less universal, but some people would accept them as true. More aggressive behavior can be the result of living in a densely populated metropolitan area. *Evidence* is different. We cite evidence when we have specific data—examples, statistics, testimony—to support our claims. Evidence establishes a benchmark against which a receiver can measure claims. If someone developed a scale to measure citizen affability in major cities, the data could offer evidence for the claim about New Yorkers.

Aristotle was among the first to put practical reasoning at the center of persuasion theory. He criticized other teachers of persuasion in ancient Greece for neglecting the important role that practical reasoning plays in winning converts. "Persuasion is clearly a sort of demonstration, since we are most fully persuaded when we consider a thing to have been demonstrated."[8] A statement is persuasive and credible either because it is directly self-evident or because it appears to be proved by other believable statements. Aristotle called everyday forms of these arguments containing facts or judgments *enthymemes*, noting that they "are the most effective of the modes of persuasion."[9] We will have more to say about the special nature of enthymemes after a brief review of the baseline for reasoning: the formal argument.

Analytic Arguments

Formal logic starts with the ideal of the *analytic argument* where claims necessarily follow from a series of widely accepted premises or assertions of evidence. An argument is *analytic* when its conclusion is contained in (absolutely follows from) its premises.[10] In this reasoning sequence, the claim is necessary rather than probable because acceptance of the premises dictates acceptance of the conclusion.

Although the messy variability of real life rarely allows us to construct valid and true analytic arguments, this ideal provides a tantalizing model for persuaders. Who would not like to have ironclad arguments that cannot be refuted? Mathematics provides an example of **analytic arguments**. Mathematical symbols—unlike ordinary language—are completely unambiguous and value free. For example, $2 + 5 = 7$ is analytic because its conclusion (the sum of 7) necessarily follows from its premises (universally accepted definitions of what 2, 5, and + mean). Similarly, the equation $(3 \times 6^2 \div 4) - 25 + 8 = 10$ uses a rigid logic that leads to an unchallengeable result. Anywhere in the world, a mathematically competent person—whether a socialist, capitalist, Muslim or Christian—could be expected to reach the same conclusion by correctly applying universally accepted rules and premises. We can also use letters rather than numbers to represent analytic arguments. For example:

1. If A then B.
2. A.
Therefore,
B.

In this argument—sometimes also called *deductive* or *syllogistic*—the relationship defined in the first premise ("If A is present then B is also present") sets up a reasoning sequence that leads irreversibly to the claim. We can substitute ordinary language in place of letters or numbers to give the same argumentative form a concrete setting.

Premise: If Harry decides to go to Europe this summer, Jane says she will go with him.
Premise: Harry is going to Europe in the summer.
(Therefore)
Claim: Jane will also be in Europe this summer.

The most interesting characteristic of valid analytic arguments is that there is no way to deny the *force*—persuasiveness or potency—of their claims if you accept the soundness of their premises. In fact, the conclusion is contained *in* the premises.

Developing a series of statements that embody a built-in certainty has attracted scholars and scientists for hundreds of years. The idea of asserting a string of statements of fact that cannot be refuted is extremely alluring. Philosophers from Descartes to Bentham hoped that humankind would benefit from a logic that used known premises to reach certain and unchallengeable conclusions. They were intrigued by the possibility that people could move beyond the fictions, falsehoods, and exceptions common to ordinary discussion. As "a system of necessary propositions which will impose itself on every rational being," notes Chaïm Perelman, the idea of the valid empirical argument promises timelessness and dispute-free truth.[11]

But life is messy. It is difficult to construct valid analytic arguments about ordinary events, especially when—as is frequently the case with persuasion—issues under discussion involve values and judgments. As a result, many persuasive statements use the general *form* of analytic arguments, but their actual *force* is less than their form implies.

Consider Article 18 of the "Baptist Faith and Message" notes that a woman should "submit herself graciously" to her husband's leadership. The statement notes that "A wife is to submit herself graciously to the servant leadership of her husband even as the church willingly submits to the headship of Christ. She . . . has the God-given responsibility to respect her husband and to serve as his helper." Many premises and pieces of evidence were offered for these claims, for example:

Premise: Ephesians 5:22–23 notes that a husband's relationship with his wife should be like Christ's "rule" over the church.
Premise: The Bible is the word of God.
(Therefore)
Claim: Wives should submit to the leadership of their husbands.

Although the Southern Baptist statement raised eyebrows when it was announced, the argument on its own terms is analytic. *If* the Bible "is the word of God," and if its content must be followed by believers, *then* claims derived from the testimony of the Bible seem to be binding. Those who accept both premises would find it hard to reject the conclusion.

The farther we move away from purely denotative languages such as mathematics, the less likely we are to locate valid analytic arguments that can fully deal with the complexities of the real world. Ordinary language is less precise than numbers. It frequently communicates attitudes and judgments as well as simple descriptions. The symbols 2 or %, for example, have single stipulated meanings. It would be extremely odd to hear that a friend liked the number 7 better than the number 2, or grew anxious at the sight of a percent sign. By contrast words such as *is, allows,* or *cannot* may seem to define precise relationships, but fall short.

As we noted in the last chapter, language carries our values and feelings. In certain contexts we may feel good or bad, angry or pleased about subjects represented with *connotative words*—symbols with widely varying associations. For example, thousands of years of human history have failed to produce agreement about what constitutes a democracy or even truth itself.[12] In fact, most persuasive claims *cannot* be constructed to apply to all cases, categories, or people. The claim "all As are Bs" is easy to state and manipulate as an abstract expression, but it is much more difficult to make comparable categorical assertions that would help settle real human differences. People, groups, and cultures are rarely all of anything. In the realm of human affairs, the only statements that can be made without citing useful exceptions are either obvious ("water is necessary to sustain life") or trivial ("all children have parents").

Practical Enthymemes

Of what use is formal logic if it is so conditional and limited? Drawing conclusions about real events comes down to *probabilities*. Aristotle shrewdly noted that this kind of everyday argument was somewhat analytic, because ordinary persuasion finds its premises in the probable existing opinions of audiences rather than in categorical truths (the "alls" and "if-thens") of analytic arguments.[13] The conclusions of what he called *enthymemes* are *contingent* on audience acceptance; they are not certain. Because enthymemes spell out logical relationships based on generally accepted opinions,[14] they must be at least partially judged by how well the persuader has used audience beliefs as premises for persuasion. Use them well, and you succeed. Miss the norms and beliefs that an audience holds dear, and you will fail. In everyday life, the audience is the arbiter of the force of the argument.

Here, for example, is an enthymeme that Aristotle cites to show how to argue from accepted beliefs to persuasive claims. He's talking about his culture's long list of humanlike Gods such as Zeus or Apollo:

> Thus it may be argued that if even the gods are not omniscient, certainly human beings are not. The principle here is that, if a quality does not in fact exist where it is *more* likely to exist, it clearly does not exist where it is *less* likely.[15]

Or, in a simpler diagrammatic form:

Premise: Even gods are not omniscient.
Premise: (Since the gods are better than people . . .)
Claim: Certainly human beings are not omniscient.

Note that the premise "the gods are not omniscient" is a statement of *social belief,* not (at least for most of us) a truth for which there could be universal agreement. The reasoning sequence makes sense only if the premises are accepted. What we lose in certainty we gain in our awareness that conclusions and truths are often *intersubjective*, meaning they are *socially constructed* within a culture and validated by a degree of consensus.[16]

Demonstration and Argumentation

We can approach the distinction between formal arguments and practical enthymemes from another useful perspective. Aristotle observed what many analysts of reasoning continually rediscover: that the reasoning of analytic arguments takes the form of a *demonstration*, and that everyday persuasion requires far less certain *argumentation*. The terms are helpful because the differences between the two are enormous. A mathematics problem is usually a demonstration because its final sum is self-evidently true. The transformation of the various operations into a conclusion is, in practical terms, beyond discussion. No one spends much time deliberating over claims that are self-evident by definition or direct observation. In contrast, everyday argumentation is not so much concerned with *Truth* as with the possible agreement of readers or listeners. We may argue a point to a resistant audience using a wide variety of reasoning skills, but we know that we cannot sweep away all of their doubts in the same way that we can correct a mistaken sum in a math problem.

Aristotle noted that practical reasoning works from generally accepted opinions. Demonstrations work from basic premises where it would be "improper to ask any further for the why and wherefore of them."[17] A math teacher demonstrates how to solve a given problem; she would be puzzled (understandably) if she were asked to argue her case. But there probably are no universally accepted procedures for *demonstrating* conclusions such as "the United States is the most democratic society on earth." In broad swaths of human action there are fewer ways to make claims that are immune from potential disagreement. Real world persuasion is thus subject to the acceptance of a particular audience. In locating persuasive ideas to build arguments, we meet our audiences on the ground of their own convictions.[18]

Factual and Judgmental Claims

Implicit in our discussion so far is the important but often misunderstood distinction between arguments that contain **claims of fact** and those that argue **claims of judgment.** Facts hold out the possibility of being proven true or false. Judgments, in contrast, express priorities, preferences, or values that may differ from individual to individual. Generally speaking, the force of an argument focused on a claim of judgment will not be as great as a well-constructed reasoning sequence in support of a claim of fact.

Persuaders frequently mistake claims of judgment for claims of fact, thereby overestimating how powerful proof can be in silencing disagreement. After all, a claim of fact should be provable beyond doubt. The culprit that leads us to mistakenly assume we are simply demonstrating a fact is the simple word *is*. Is and other indicative verb forms (i.e., was and were) have an aura of finality that makes judgmental claims sometimes *seem* factual. For instance, the statement "Barack Obama was a better president than George W. Bush" is not a statement of fact. We can utter this claim with all the finality and certainty that we can muster. But neither it nor its opposite will ever be universally true. There is simply no single standard for judging an individual's presidency as there would be for, say, determining the acidity of tap water. As applied to an individual's performance on the job, better can legitimately be defined in different ways. One person may rank a president's foreign policy decisions higher than their domestic policies; someone else may reverse the importance of those issues. By contrast, *factual* claims are statements that hold the promise of being demonstrated true or false for all people.[19] Some examples of factual claims are listed below.

- American teens text an average of 60 times *a day*, spending 6 hours on social media sites in a 24-hour period.[20]
- North Korea can launch missiles with nuclear weapons.
- There are more acres of forest in the Northeast now than there were in 1912.
- Google is the most common search engine used in the United States.
- Smoking increases a person's chances of contracting lung cancer.
- Drivers talking on cell phones increase their chances of being in an accident.
- There was never a massacre by Islamic terrorists in Bowling Green, Kentucky.[21]

These statements share the *possibility* of being conclusively shown to be right or wrong. We say possibility because the available evidence is sometimes insufficient to discover the truth about actual events. For example, we know (it is an unchallenged fact) that the baby of aviation hero Charles Lindbergh mysteriously disappeared from his family's Hopewell, New Jersey, home. We also know that a carpenter, Bruno Richard Hauptmann, was convicted of the crime of kidnapping in a gaudy 1935 trial and was later executed. But there are still doubts that Hauptmann committed the crime.[22]

The most common claims in the realm of persuasion are judgmental. These cannot be proved or settled by citing supporting facts, nor can they be known in the same way that we know the truth of a statement such as "Texas was once a part of Mexico." A judgmental claim involves the assignment of personal preferences to persons, objects, or ideas. The words we use in these claims indicate how we feel about what we are describing. The object of our attention is good, bad, worthwhile, dangerous, or desirable, reflecting our preferences about what is right or wrong, decent or indecent, moral or immoral, important or insignificant. Listed below are examples of judgmental claims.

- Professional athletes are grossly overpaid.
- Albuquerque, New Mexico, has the best Tex-Mex cuisine in the country.
- Insurance companies unfairly discriminate against young car drivers.
- Legalized gambling is a legitimate way for governments to raise revenue.
- Pixar is the best studio for animated features.
- The sound quality of MP3 technology is poor.

Note that in every statement, there is a word that gives a judgmental spin to the claim. Words like *grossly, best, unfairly, legitimate,* and *poor* express *feelings* about the qualities of ideas or objects. We can prove to the satisfaction of most reasoning people that "smoking increases a person's chances of contracting lung cancer"—a valid cause-and-effect factual claim with ample proof to support it. But we cannot prove with the same certainty that "Unitarian Universalism is the most socially inclusive American religion."

This is not to say that the old axiom warning us not to argue about religion or politics is correct. It isn't. We *must* debate our preferences with others, and with all the logic we can muster. After all, preferences and values are the basis of most of the laws and codes we live by. The only caution is that it is unreasonable to expect that persuasion will put all contrary positions to rest in the same way that a piece of evidence may prove that a defendant is guilty beyond any reasonable doubt.

Implied and Stated Components of Arguments

When we make passing comments about noncontroversial subjects, as we have noted, the logical relationships that lead to assertions hardly need to be explored at all. For example, the claim that "it is too hot today" is usually accompanied by obvious evidence (high temperature and humidity, bright sun, etc.) that makes it unnecessary to provide supporting reasons. If pressed, however, we *could* make the reasoning behind almost any assertion explicit by writing down all relevant claims and premises. A complete argument about the weather might include a factual premise ("the thermometer reads ninety-two degrees") and a judgmental premise that interprets the significance of the facts (ninety-two degrees is, by our criteria, too hot). This argument diagrammed as an enthymeme could be represented in simple form:

Factual Premise: The thermometer reads ninety-two degrees.
Judgmental Premise: (implied but not stated) A temperature of over ninety-two is too hot.
(Therefore . . .)
Claim: It is too hot today.

Talk about stating the obvious. But that's the point. It is often unnecessary to make all of the premises (and sometimes even the claims) of our arguments explicit. Aristotle reminds us that we can count on our listeners to supply parts of the reasoning sequence. He was perhaps the first to offer the savvy persuasion advice that a successful persuader often uses the audience's beliefs coactively rather than asks for entirely new beliefs. The pioneering advertising guru Tony Schwartz said the same thing. The skillful persuader uses the audience as a workforce. When you focus on persuading them using *beliefs they already hold*, they are essentially participants in their own persuasion.[23] Key words or images are enough to activate premises that the audience already accepts.

There are other times when we need to locate hidden premises to expose the unstated relationships on which assertions are based. In effect, we need to reconstruct arguments to discover unstated assumptions that are perhaps hindering agreement. What we are frequently looking for are called **warrants** for arguments. Though often unstated, warrants authorize the inferential leap from evidence to claims.[24] For example, consider the claim that "Islam promotes violence and religious intolerance." This view has been expressed many times since the attacks on the Pentagon and World Trade Center on September 11, 2001. The argument is somewhat varied from source to source,[25] but in diagrammatic terms it takes this form.

Claim: Islam promotes violence against the West.
Premise: ISIS and their counterparts in Pakistan and elsewhere foment a holy war against the United States.
(Unstated warrant: ISIS is a representative segment of Islamic thought.)

Aside from the claim itself, *the most debatable assertion is implied rather than explicitly argued.* Many thoughtful analysts believe that ISIS is no more representative of Islamic thought than Jim Jones or David Koresh were of Christian thought. Militant Islam is rejected by most who practice the faith.[26] Cases like this are a reminder that sometimes the premises most in need of closer analysis are easily overlooked.

Reasoning to Discover and to Defend

Reasoning is used both to discover ideas and to rationalize them; this is an important distinction. We can employ the processes of logic to investigate topics. For example, we might research rates of HIV infection in the United States to determine their prevalence. The reasoning of persuasion, however, more typically *defends* what we believe we already know. As a persuader on a given topic, your view is probably more or less fixed; what you hope to alter is the attitude of your listeners. Logic in persuasion is thus a kind of rationalization: a process of finding defensible reasons in support of cherished positions. And persuasion is often suspect because of this. We tend to be wary of advocates who have adopted arguments that seem more convenient than fully tested.

Ideally, the best persuasion flows from arguments that were *formed in the process* of discovery. Aristotle's teacher, Plato, made the telling point that elaborate efforts at persuasion without equally intense efforts to discover the best or true may result in the exploitation rather than enlightenment of an audience.[27] When we wonder if celebrities use the services they endorse in advertisements, we are using this principle. An endorsement ideally carries at least the superficial implication that the famous spokesperson has made a discovery that they are comfortable promoting. We can be forgiven the more cynical view that most endorsements are little more than cash-for-comments transactions.

Finding Good Reasons for Claims

Having considered some of the primary issues related to logical persuasion, we are now in a better position to offer some practical guidelines. Communication scholar Karl Wallace assessed practical messages in terms of *a theory of good reasons.* According to Wallace, "Good reasons are a number of statements, consistent with each other," in support of statements that ask others to make choices.[28] They provide explanations for the judgments that the persuader hopes the audience will find acceptable. Good reasons frequently summarize what members of a society already accept as valuable. As Wallace advises, "One can scarcely declare that something is desirable without showing its relevance to values." Persuasion, then, is "the art of finding and effectively presenting good reasons."[29] Consider this example with a judgmental claim and its good-reason premises.

Claim: Companies that direct advertising to very young children are engaged in unethical conduct.

Reason #1: Young children lack sufficient experience and sophistication to discount for the puffery in advertising.

Reason #2: Ethical persuaders will not exploit gullible audiences who lack the ability to weigh the motives of communicators.

Note that Wallace's point is especially affirmed in the second reason. As a statement of support it communicates a widely endorsed value that condemns exploitation. You may agree, disagree, or find fault with one or both of the reasons. Sometimes one person's common sense is another's irrationality, especially when cultural traditions and differences have affected one's experiences. But within the same culture we can usually sense when we have located reasons that will hold up under public scrutiny.

Some reasons function as factual evidence, as in the first premise above. Many can be tested scientifically. Yet practical reasoning frequently boils down to what might be called the ethical pivots of common sense. When we isolate the premises that we intend to use in support of a claim, our sense of what works is often based on *judgments about the appropriateness of conduct* that we hold in common with others in the culture. Learning and rationality is a lifelong process of acquiring norms about "what goes with what," and what contexts are friendly or hostile to certain ideas.

Alleged Logic–Emotion Distinction

In the *Rhetoric*, Aristotle identified three forms of proof available to the persuader: ethical, logical, and emotional.[30] Ethical proof (*ethos*) focuses on the advocate's character. Logic (*logos*) is the search for good reasons. And emotional content (*pathos*) points to how deeply we feel about a claim or its evidence. Although he did not specifically note that the presence of one meant the absence of another, popular usage over hundreds of years has had that effect. Ask the average person to analyze an advertising pitch or a pamphlet from a group seeking social change. Many will come up with a variation of Aristotle's distinction. Some parts of the message will be identified as containing logical reasons and other parts as containing emotional appeals. The presence of one suggests the absence of another.

We think the assumption that the presence of emotional content means the lack of logical content is a significant error of analysis. We call this the *false dualism of logic and emotion*. Wallace hoped that the acceptance of good reasons as the substance of discourse would mean the disappearance of distinctions between logical proof and emotional proof, which he called "weasel concepts."[31] Yet too many experts who study messages closely continue to separate logic and emotion. Thus, a law school professor regrets that "emotion can activate any behavior which has not been inhibited by reason."[32] An expert on political communication notes that the statements of most politicians are "nothing more than emotional appeals."[33]

There are two problems with the urge to make this false distinction. One is that we have increasing evidence to rethink reason and emotion as *complementary processes*.[34] One fuels the other. In actual practice, a sense of reasoned justification usually *increases* our emotional attachment to ideas. When we feel that we have a strong case for a point of view, our sense of urgency in communicating that commitment is usually enhanced.[35] Think about your experiences with the emotion of anger. Most of us have been warned to calm down and not let our emotions get the better of us. Presumably—as conventional thinking goes—too much emotion will shortchange our capacities for reasoning. In fact, your anger probably develops in proportion to the good reasons—the logic—you have for it. Reasoning motivates our emotions and serves as a register of conviction.

Aside from the fact that the term *emotional* is nearly useless as a critical judgment, a second problem is that this distinction is sometimes a way to dismiss an argument we don't like or can't understand. The label *emotional appeals* sometimes serves the intellectually dishonest function of dismissing an idea. Emotion is sometimes viewed as a back door to persuasion: the last refuge for those who don't have reasoned arguments to offer. There is perhaps no easier way to dismiss an opponent's views than to claim that "they have resorted to the rants of emotional appeals." In his groundbreaking analysis of Adolf Hitler's rhetoric, critic Kenneth Burke noted that it was not enough to simply characterize Hitler's words as the ravings of a fool. To do so, he noted, "contributed more to our gratification than our enlightenment."[36] Instead, Burke's analysis assumed that Hitler had a logic for his actions and that his claims had found a receptive audience.

COMMON FORMS OF DEFECTIVE REASONING

Textbooks that address reasoning almost uniformly attempt to provide readers with the logician's equivalent of the Rock of Gibraltar—some sturdy reference points that will simplify the problem of navigating toward sound reasoning. If we know what good reasoning is, then it follows that there must be systematic ways to classify forms of bad reasoning. "A *fallacy*," notes philosopher Max Black, "is an argument which seems to be sound without being so."[37] Fallacies take the form of strong statements that have force, while none actually exists. No list is inclusive. And none of us can engage in advocacy very long without committing some of these fallacies. We include only the most common mistakes or subversions of logic.

Ad Hominem

Before Donald Trump was elected, he got into a public fight with comedian Rosie O'Donnell. Ms. O'Donnell criticized Trump for his treatment of a contestant in his Miss USA pageant. Trump responded with ad hominems, noting that Rosie was "not smart," "crude," "disgusting," "a slob," and "an animal."[38] *Ad hominem* occurs when statements worded as arguments are actually directed against *persons* rather than their *ideas*. The language is personal and negative, often in an attempt to deflect attention away from the merits of an argument to alleged and largely irrelevant defects of an individual or a group. Taped private conversations of Richard Nixon in the White House revealed crude epithets about Supreme Court members, publishers, and people he considered enemies.[39] Trump has taken the process further, publicly calling out critics and members of the press with abusive language most Americans thought they would never hear from a president.[40]

We are now awash in mean-spirited commentary from the web to newspapers to prime-time cable talk shows. These screeds describe politicians as "pinheads," "too old," "a loser," or a "jerk"; a reporter may be a "windbag," "stupid," or a "fanatic." In many ways these insults are as old as politics, but there is now a crucial difference. Web comments are frequently posted by unidentified persons. Respondents to articles and other content can now say anything without having to identify themselves and risk being associated with their intemperate attacks. Ad hominem has thus been given an unfortunate new life—a refuge for individuals unable or unwilling to expend the effort to argue the merits of ideas. A reliance on personal invective is an indication of a person's resistance to finding the higher ground of better public discourse, where choices should be defended based on good reasons.

False Cause

Are tornados attracted to mobile home parks? Do the world's roosters keep the sun on schedule? Is composing a Ninth Symphony tempting death? A persuader who has fallen victim to the fallacy of *false cause* mistakenly assumes that because two events have occurred together, one has caused the other. Ordinary discourse is full of false-cause reasoning.

Hiding in the Bushes

Many of us grew up pulling what we thought was the great stunt of sneaking up on a neighbor's house, ringing the doorbell, and then hiding in the nearby bushes. Serious crime it wasn't. But there is clearly something wrong with this prank. It's never good when we can abuse the trust of others without paying a price.

Today, an equivalent behavior is scanning internet sites and posting anonymous comments. Many popular sites allow anonymous comments; others do not. We invite trouble when a person is free to weigh in on almost any topic without fulfilling the basic social responsibility of signing the opinion. Hashtags representing various avatars allow us to escape the moral consequences of owning our comments, depriving the human recipients of our criticism the right to know who we are. Many reactions to online stories are ill-considered, mean-spirited, offensive, and hostile. Some swirl in virtual cesspools of rhetorical maliciousness.

Character assassination by proxy is never pretty and makes us a coarser culture. From a communications point of view, concealing one's identity is considered a fundamental breach of faith. Before the existence of the internet, there were whisper campaigns, witch hunts, and unattributed pamphlets—including those alleging communist treason that pointed fingers at many artists in the 1940s and 50s whose careers were ruined when they were investigated by the House Un-American Activities Committee and blacklisted. Engaging in criticism comes with the duty to identify oneself. Doing so anonymously is a moral cop out.

Arguments from false cause proliferate primarily from *mistaking correlation for causation*. For example, the Physicians Committee for Responsible Medicine reports that mortality rates are more than twice as high in neighborhoods that are close to fast-food restaurants.[41] There is a tendency to assume that the coexistence of two elements means that one causes the other. Poorer Americans, who tend to have more health problems, often live in urban neighborhoods where many commercial businesses are located, including fast-food restaurants. Obesity has been correlated with a number of social concerns. While it is rightly linked to significant health problems, there is little evidence for false-cause allegations that obese drivers cause the United States to use more gasoline and create more carbon dioxide, or that obese passengers cause plane crashes.[42] As the author of one study notes, identifying obesity as a primary cause for multiple woes amounts to little more than making fat people scapegoats for problems with deeper causes.[43]

In an age when much of our survey research looks for causes within correlations, even seasoned scientists with the best intentions can fall victim to this fallacy. For example, many studies over the years have suggested the moderate levels of alcohol can have beneficial effects on men and women who want to avoid heart problems or diabetes. Some of these correlational studies find lower rates of these diseases in people who drink moderately (typically one or two glasses of wine or their equivalents). But as another researcher has pointed out, those who drink in moderation may just be better at managing their lives and health. They "tend to do everything right—they exercise, they don't smoke, they eat right and they drink moderately."[44] Many of these other factors could play a role in helping to reduce rates of disease. An advocate should exercise caution if the force of a claim rests on correlational data.

Non Sequitur

A *non sequitur* occurs when a conclusion does not follow from the reasons that have been cited. This can happen visually with the juxtaposition of two disparate elements. For example, the magazine *Coastal Living* ran a headline, "Bring on the watermelon margaritas!"—and placed a photo of two young children directly under it.[45] More generally, this problem arises when elements that seem to be related are—in actual fact—at odds with each other. Non sequiturs may leave us perplexed that a person could say or do two things and not recognize that they are contradictory behaviors. For example, imagine following a car with the declaration "Conquer Cancer" on its license plate—and then noticing the driver smoking a cigarette.

Non sequiturs seem to be more common in our lives, partly because our distractions with other tasks sometimes let obvious inconsistencies slip by us. University professors advocating the glories of the marketplace may miss the irony of extolling the advantages of a system while being shielded by tenure from suffering any of its economic challenges. Even well-trained professionals can sometimes miss the big picture. A friend of one of the authors was present when a doctor broke the news to his 92-year-old cancer patient that the radiation therapy she was on had not worked. Her tumors had grown, and she had perhaps a month left to live. As he exited her room, he reminded her that her last radiation treatment would be in two days.

Circular Argument

Sometimes the reasons cited for a claim are little more than a rewording of the claim. Supporting premises in *circular arguments* are just restatements that have the structure of claims that imply good reasons, but start and end with the same idea. Parents regularly use this form of argument: "Do it because I said so." The phrase that follows *because* is essentially a duplicate of the original statement.

Circular arguments can cut short public debate on pressing issues by narrowly focusing on only unchallengeable claims. By August of 1968, for example, the United States had committed 541,000 troops to the Vietnam War. Many leaders in

Congress and in the Johnson and Nixon Administrations argued that because we were so deeply committed to the defense of South Vietnam, we should stay to see the war through. The fact of being at war became its own justification for delaying our departure from Vietnam until over 58,000 American lives had been lost.[46] Many have argued that we have repeated this fallacy again with the United States' ongoing military involvement in Afghanistan.[47] "We can't win, but we can't afford to lose" is the common refrain, and another way of saying that "we need to stay because we're already there."

Fallacy of Oversimplification

Categorical claims appear to have more force because they are unqualified and emphatic. The *fallacy of oversimplification* is perhaps the most common disease of our distracted age. We want to make simple conclusions that exclude troublesome exceptions. We often think like journalists who are given 45 seconds of airtime to tell a complex story. Imagine a television news reporter trying to detail in very limited time that the government of Cuba is sometimes politically repressive *and* educationally progressive, or that the most urban state in the nation (New Jersey) is also a leader in farmland preservation, or that most residents of Manhattan are usually from somewhere else.

Human action is usually far more complex than our efforts to describe it. Our desire to capture essential points relevant to a persuasive case is often at odds with real-world complexities that cannot be represented in Twitter-length epigrams. *Prevention* magazine, for example, has rated San Francisco one of the most walkable cities in the United States. But it also has one of the highest rates of pedestrian deaths in accidents involving cars.[48] Can we acknowledge that both statements are true? Can we make our minds bend to two different but complex truths?

Simple declarative statements are sometimes inadequate to characterize multifaceted realities; simplification is often the same as distortion. Even so, it is possible to use language to signal complexity that should not be oversimplified, as in the examples below.

> His strengths are also his weaknesses.
> While this is true in certain circumstances, there are important exceptions.
> We take comfort in this belief, but discovering its truth may be a challenge.
> The effects of this problem are more evident than its root causes.

Because the statements are tentative, they might seem to weaken a person's persuasive case. On the other hand, thoughtful listeners may assign more credibility to a source that seems open to natural complications and ironies than to one who is categorical and simplistic.

HOW PERSUASION AND LOGICAL ARGUMENTATION DIFFER

Thus far, we have shown how a claim supported by reasonable premises can lead to persuasion. We labeled this single logical unit an argument and noted that Aristotle discovered everyday forms of argumentation (enthymemes) that routinely appear in most types of persuasion. Does it follow that we can use the words persuasion and argumentation interchangeably? Is persuasion always subject to the rules of practical reasoning? The answer to both questions is "no," because factors other than reasoning influence what people believe. We close this chapter with an explanation of why we think persuasion is more than the construction of reasoned arguments, vital though they are.

Denial Often Defeats Reasoning

Under repeated and hostile questioning from members of the opposition party, former British Prime Minister James Callahan used to respond to statements of disbelief with the same expression of frustration: "I can *tell* you the truth, but I *can't make you see it.*" How right he was. *Denial* is a potent antidote to even the best sequence of persuasive logic. Callahan expressed perfectly the persuader's lament. We have all had the experience of communicating to the human equivalent of a brick wall.

Self-interest often trumps what looks like a winning hand. Tell teens that the volume levels are too loud on their MP3 players, and the result can be that they listen at even *higher* levels.[49] Even by the end of his second term many Republicans still doubted that Barack Obama was born in the United States.[50] Persuasion is not easy. And persistence of inaccurate or incorrect belief is common. When we are asked to give up cherished beliefs, views of the world that have become part of the comfortable furniture of our lives make change difficult. Our psychology immunizes us against the infection of others' ideas, just as our biology marshals its defenses against toxic bacteria. The instinct for ideological self-preservation works as an immune system rejecting unwanted or unacceptable conclusions. Workers at Apple Computer even had a name for it. The brilliant and innovative Steve Jobs who headed the company often rejected what his engineers said was possible. He had a "reality distortion field," they noted, denying vital truths that made Jobs the volcanic manager he was.[51]

Denial routinely functions as an effective shield that can be used to ignore reasoning that takes one to an unpleasant conclusion. Smoking and the industry that supports it is an interesting case. All of us have habits that threatening our health. But tobacco use is a special case; publicity about its dangers have crept into every corner of American public life. Appeals to quit smoking are pervasive and constructed in arguments that have a lot of force. Cessation will increase the chances of a longer life and fewer debilitating illnesses. But it is easy to find smokers who will explain that (1) they understand it is a behavior that carries some risks, and (2) they still do *not* intend to quit. A common end-run around smoking-effects evidence is to challenge some of its credibility, or simply not to deal with it.[52] The likelihood of getting smokers to quit increases if you immerse them in prolonged exposure to antismoking arguments through extended group contact. The most widely accepted way to effect behavioral change of almost any kind is to provide a supportive environment while simultaneously making it impossible to escape to a state of denial.[53]

It is rare to find someone involved in what appears to have been a bad decision who is willing to pay the psychological price of a full *mea culpa*. A former Lehman employee who sold the kind of mortgage securities that would eventually bring down his firm (and very nearly the entire economy) is a notable exception in confessing "I have blood on my hands."[54] More typically, others at the firm were reluctant to accept blame for creating financial products that were unsustainable. They, and counterparts at other banks, point to failures of the regulators rather than admit responsibility.[55] Part of what is going on in the denial of the obvious is *motivated reasoning* (see chapter 6).

Persuasion's Self-Interest and Argumentation's Public Interest

Our earlier point about the mistake of assuming that logical and emotional appeals are discrete is relevant to a related distinction between persuasion and argumentation. As we have noted, someone else's logic may not necessarily be your logic. Hence, we may sometimes miss or ignore another person's good reasons. To put it another way, reasoning may be *personal and specific*, appealing to an individual's needs rather than to a collective sense of the good or the True. The conventional view of logic is that it should be able to withstand scrutiny by many different people. But it is useful to momentarily contrast the difference between persuasion's self-interest and logical argument's public interest.

All persuasion must provide a series of reasons for winning the approval of audiences, but not all legitimate persuasion involves good reasons. As we have noted, the good reasons of arguments are intended to convey the reasonableness of the claim to a wide diversity of people. Make a claim about, say, climate change or the advantages of using debit rather than credit cards, and the reasons should make sense to people with different interests and backgrounds. By contrast, while persuaders frequently employ rational argumentation, they also rely on their abilities to use appeals to satisfy what are sometimes more clearly *personal* claims.

All of us have personal needs for affection, for approval from others, for high self-esteem, and so on. We can be motivated by appeals that promise to satisfy these needs. For example, jurors in a courtroom are sometimes cautioned by the judge to ignore attempts at flattery by lawyers eager to win their cases. Appeals to the need for approval are—for the judge, at least—out of place in the legal system's attempt to reconstruct the historical record of what the defendant did or did not do.[56] Yet, persuasion frequently depends on just such identification—on efforts to recognize and appeal to individual needs and motivations.

One reason television or internet advertising can be effective is that it reaches the viewer as a private rather than a public person. We accept advertising appeals made to us in our homes that we might reject as a member of a live audience. We might view a commercial passively, but if we view the same ad in a theater, we may hear groans of disbelief from the audience.

Consider the classic case of an advertisement for skin cream to remove "ugly age spots" that used to run on network television. Like most cosmetic ads, it promised a way to *purchase* greater satisfaction about the way we appear to others. The commercial for Porcelana Cream opened with a picture of four middle-aged women playing cards. One of the women is obviously ill at ease as she looks down at her hands holding the cards. We hear her think to herself, "These ugly age spots; what's a woman to do!" Her embarrassment is painfully clear. The solution is obvious—purchase the product to remove the spots and the problem.

From an argumentative point of view, the commercial is hopelessly flawed. Would personal friendships really be at stake because of a few skin blemishes? Of course not. Based on just a few seconds of the commercial, we *can* believe that there are individuals anxious enough about their acceptance to believe that even minor blemishes could put them at risk. It appeals to the kinds of very private fears that most of us experience from time to time. To dismiss the ad as irrational misses the point. The appeal to fear of rejection is *not* intended to stand up under the scrutiny that we give arguments.

SUMMARY

In this chapter we have looked at the role that reasoning plays in persuasion. We defined reasoning as the process of supporting controversial claims with premises and evidence that function as good reasons. Reasons are good when they build on value-based premises that are as sensible for others as they are for ourselves. They have force when their linkages are so strong that they seem to demand our acceptance. Some of the claims and premises of arguments may involve judgments that can never fully be argued away; others may be factual and produce nearly universal acceptance.

We also noted that there is a great deal of misunderstanding about reasoning and about what it can and cannot do. For example, the most direct route to attitude change is sometimes by appealing to private but powerful motivations, such as a person's need to feel wanted by others. These individualized appeals are not necessarily irrational emotions nor unreasonable grounds for forming attitudes, but neither are they the kinds of statements that can stand up as reasons that would help shape a consensus of support in a public gathering. Advertising is full of motivating appeals, which frequently have the effect of allowing people to reward themselves or to sanction a certain feeling. Topics of greater consequence, such as efforts to reconstruct the guilt or innocence of a defendant in a trial, demand more rigorous defenses.

Using Aristotle's writings as a guide, we looked at the unique features of practical arguments called enthymemes. Enthymemes have two special features that make them different from the formal analytic arguments used by scientists, mathematicians, and logicians. First, the claims in enthymemes are probable or preferable, since they deal with practical subjects where preferences often mingle with facts. Second, usually one or more of their parts (claims or premises) may be implied rather than stated; enthymemes replicate effective persuasion by building from what an audience already knows or accepts.

Like all forms of reasoning, enthymemes and other forms of argument can be made from premises of dubious quality. In fallacies like ad hominem, false cause, non sequitur, and circular argument, the premises of some arguments may present only the illusion rather than the reality of logical support. The task of the effective persuader is to avoid these superficial linkages in favor of arguments with genuine good reasons.

QUESTIONS AND PROJECTS FOR FURTHER STUDY

1. Locate a persuasive essay written by an opinion writer or blogger. After studying the column, summarize the claims and premises the author has used. Be careful to look for implied as well as stated premises. Make a judgment about the quality and adequacy of the author's arguments.

2. Search-engine algorithms attempt to read our interests so that ads specific to us can be placed on some of the web pages we see. Search for material on the stage and film actor Christopher Plummer, for example, and you may find that subsequent pages include ads pushing the availability of local plumbers. Cite a recent example of the non sequiturs algorithmic logic has produced in your own web use.

3. This chapter describes practical reasoning by comparing several categories of opposites. Briefly explain the differences between each of the following contrasting terms, indicating which term identifies a characteristic of practical reasoning: demonstration vs. argumentation; analytic arguments vs. enthymemes

4. Explain the statement in this chapter that analytic arguments offer "a tantalizing model for persuaders." Construct a simple argument with two premises and a conclusion that takes the form of an analytic argument.

5. We note that one of the most common mistakes people make with regard to reasoning is the assumption that they can prove a claim of preference or judgment. Cite your own example of a claim of preference that might be mistaken for a claim of fact. Why is the claim not provable with the same certainty as a claim of fact?

6. Some individuals and media assert more than they argue. Illustrate the difference with reference to online news sources such as The Daily Beast, Twitter, or Instagram.

ADDITIONAL READING

Aristotle, *Rhetoric*, trans. W. Rhys Roberts (Mineola, New York: Dover Thrift Editions, 2004).

Isabelle Blanchette, "The Effect of Emotion on Interpretation and Logic in a Conditional Reasoning Task," *Memory and Cognition*, July, 2006, pp. 1112–1125.

Al Gore, *The Assault on Reason* (New York: Penguin, 2007).

Chaïm Perelman and L. Olbrechts-Tyteca, *The New Rhetoric: A Treatise in Argumentation*, trans. John Wilkinson and Purcell Weaver (Notre Dame, IN: University of Notre Dame, 1969).

Stephen Toulmin, Richard Rieke, and Allan Janik, *An Introduction to Reasoning* (New York: Macmillan, 1979).

Karl R. Wallace, "The Substance of Rhetoric: Good Reasons," *Quarterly Journal of Speech*, October, 1963, 139–249.

NOTES

[1] Jefferson quoted in Al Gore, *The Assault on Reason* (New York: Penguin, 2007), p. 45.

[2] Harold Evans, *Do I Make Myself Clear?* (New York: Little Brown, 2017), p. 16.

[3] Dan Barry, "In a Swirl of 'Untruths' and 'Falsehoods,' Calling a Lie a Lie," *The New York Times*, January 26, 2017, p. A21.

[4] See, for example, *The Curse of the Were-Rabbit* (2005).

[5] For a discussion on audience motivations to seek out logical relationships in persuasion see Daniel J. O'Keefe, *Persuasion: Theory and Research*, 3rd ed. (Thousand Oaks, CA: Sage, 2015), pp. 98–100.

[6] Jeffrey Toobin, "Crackdown," *The New Yorker*, November 5, 2001, p. 59.

[7] Stephen Toulmin, Richard Rieke, and Allan Janik, *An Introduction to Reasoning* (New York: Macmillan, 1979), p. 9.

[8] Aristotle, *Rhetoric*, trans. W. Rhys Roberts (Mineola, New York: Dover Thrift Editions, 2004), p. 5.

[9] Ibid.

[10] See Toulmin, Rieke, and Janik, pp. 125–35.

[11] Chaïm Perelman and L. Olbrechts-Tyteca, *The New Rhetoric: A Treatise on Argumentation*, trans. John Wilkinson and Purcell Weaver (Notre Dame, IN: University of Notre Dame, 1969), p. 2.

[12] For further discussion of this point see Richard Weaver, *The Ethics of Rhetoric* (Chicago: Henry Regnery, 1953), pp. 7–9.

[13] Lloyd Bitzer, "Aristotle's Enthymeme Revisited," *Quarterly Journal of Speech*, December 1959, pp. 399–408.

[14] Aristotle, *Topics*, Book I, Chapter. 1.

[15] Aristotle, *Rhetoric*, pp. 101–102.

[16] For a more nuanced assessment of how the Sophists dealt with the apparent dichotomy between certain truth and intersubjective truth, see Nathan Crick, "The Sophistical Attitude and the Invention of Rhetoric," *Quarterly Journal of Speech*, 96 (February, 2010), pp. 25–45.

[17] Aristotle, *Topics*, Book I, Chapter 1, http://classics.mit.edu/Aristotle/topics.1.i.html

[18] Ibid. For further discussion of the differences between demonstrations and arguments, see also Perelman and L. Olbrechts-Tyteca, pp. 13–14.

[19] A good case has been made by sociologists of knowledge and others that very little knowledge about human affairs is completely free of our own values. In a practical way, however, certain obvious facts are largely free of subjective interpretations. The reader interested in how social values can shape what we claim to know might start with Peter L. Berger's and Thomas Luckmann's *The Social Construction of Reality* (New York: Doubleday, 1967).

[20] Amanda Lenhart, "Teens, Smartphones and Texting," March 19, 2012, *Pew Internet and American Life Project*, http://www.pewinternet.org/~/media/Files/Reports/2012/PIP_Teens_Smartphones_and_Texting.pdf

[21] The claim was asserted and then withdrawn by a White House spokesperson in 2017. Jim Rutenberg, "'The Massacre That Wasn't:' a Fake News Turning Point," *New York Times*, February 6, 2017, pp. B1, B3.

[22] For a convincing case arguing Hauptmann's innocence, see Ludovic Kennedy, *The Airman and the Carpenter* (New York: Viking, 1985).

[23] Tony Schwartz, *The Responsive Chord* (New York: Anchor Books, 1974), p. 73.

[24] Thomas Hollihan and Kevin Baaske, *Arguments and Arguing*, 3rd ed. (Long Grove, IL: Waveland, 2016), p. 109. See also Toulmin, Rieke, and Janik, p. 110.

[25] See, for example, Andrew Sullivan, "This is a Religious War," *The New York Times Magazine*, October 7, 2001, p. 44, and Salman Rushdie, "Yes, This Is About Islam," *New York Times*, November 2, 2001, p. A25.

[26] See, for example, Fareed Zakaria, "The Jihad against the Jihadis," *Newsweek*, February 12, 2010, http://www.newsweek.com/2010/02/11/the-jihad-against-the-jihadis.html

[27] Richard Weaver, *The Ethics of Rhetoric* (Chicago: Henry Regnery, 1968), pp. 11–12, and Plato's *Phaedrus*, trans. R. Hackforth (Indianapolis, IN: Bobbs Merrill, Library of the Liberal Arts, 1952), pp. 119–22.

[28] Karl Wallace, "The Substance of Rhetoric: Good Reasons," *Quarterly Journal of Speech*, October 1963, p. 247.

[29] Ibid., p. 248.

[30] Aristotle, *Rhetoric*, Book I, Chapter 2.

[31] Wallace, p. 249.

[32] Gray L. Dorsey, "Symbols: Vehicles of Reason or of Emotion?" in Lyman Bryson, Louis Finkelstein, R. M. McIver, and Richard McKeon (Eds.), *Symbols and Values: An Initial Study* (New York: Cooper Square, 1964), p. 445.

[33] Murray Edelman, *The Symbolic Uses of Politics* (Chicago: University of Illinois Press, 1967), p. 137.

[34] Isabelle Blanchette, "The Effect of Emotion on Interpretation and Logic in a Conditional Reasoning Task," *Memory and Cognition*, July, 2006, pp. 1112–1125.

[35] For classic statements of this view, see Gary Cronkhite, "Logic, Emotion, and the Paradigm of Persuasion," *Quarterly Journal of Speech*, February, 1964, pp. 13–18; and Samuel Becker, "Research on Emotional and Logical Proofs," *Southern Speech Journal*, Spring, 1963, pp. 198–207.

[36] Kenneth Burke, *The Philosophy of Literary Form*, 3rd ed. (Berkeley: University of California Press, 1973), p. 191–192.

[37] Max Black, "Fallacies," in Jerry M. Anderson and Paul J. Dovre (Eds.), *Readings in Argumentation* (Boston: Allyn & Bacon, 1968), p. 301.

[38] Jacques Steinberg, "Back to 'Talking Smack' with Rosie, Donald and Barbara," *The New York Times*, January 11, 2007, http://www.nytimes.com/2007/01/11/arts/television/11feud.html?n=Top%2fReference%2fTimes%20Topics%2fPeople%2fO%2fO%27Donnell%2c%20Rosie&_r=0

[39] Leonard Garment, "Richard Nixon, Unedited," *The New York Times*, October 19, 2001, p. A23.

[40] See Jasmine C. Lee and Kevin Quealy "The 305 People, Places and Things Donald Trump Has Insulted on Twitter: A Complete List," *The New York Times*, January 20, 2017, p. E1.

[41] "Just the Facts," *Good Medicine*, Summer, 2005, p. 23.

[42] Gina Kolata, "For a World of Woes, We Blame Cookie Monsters," *The New York Times*, October 29, Sec. 4, 2006, p. 14.

[43] Ibid.

[44] Roni Caryn Rabin, "There Goes Your Excuse for Drinking," *Globe and Mail* (Canada), June 19, 2009, p. L4.

[45] Stuart Elliott, "Two Marilyns, Six Scotches and 20 Hamburger Toppings," *The New York Times*, November 29, 2013, p. B2.

[46] This is admittedly a simplification of a very complex issue. There were obviously many reasons for the U.S. commitment to support the South Vietnamese. One reporter who has written extensively on both the early and later phases of our involvement is David Halberstam. His first book, *The Making of a Quagmire* (New York: Random House, 1965), points to the dilemmas brought on by heavy military involvement in a land war. His second book, *The Best and Brightest* (New York: Random House, 1972), partially reconstructs the circular reasoning behind what became the no-win situation for the United States.

[47] See for example, John Barry, "Obama's Vietnam," *Newsweek*, January 31, 2009, http://www.newsweek.com/2009/01/30/obama-s-vietnam.html

[48] Dashka Slater, "On the One Hand," *Sierra Magazine*, May/June 2011, p. 28.

[49] "New iPod Listening Study Shows Surprising Behavior of Teens," *Science Daily*, February 28, 2009, http://www.sciencedaily.com/releases/2009/02/090218135054.htm

[50] Josh Clinton and Carrie Roush, "Poll: Persistent Partisan Divide Over 'Birther' Question," *NBC News*, August 10, 2016, http://www.nbcnews.com/politics/2016-election/poll-persistent-partisan-divide-over-birther-question-n627446

[51] Walter Isaacson, *Steve Jobs* (New York: Simon and Schuster, 2011), pp. 117–124.

[52] For a humorous look at how twisted the logic of smoking can become, see the film, *Thank You for Smoking* (2005).

[53] Most twelve-step programs ranging from alcohol abuse to spousal abuse work this way. For one example, see Claudia Pinto, "Helping Kids Quit," *Modern Healthcare*, April 20, 1998, p. 62.

[54] Louis Story and Landon Thomas Jr., "Tales from Lehman's Crypt," *The New York Times*, September 13, 2009, Sunday Business, p. 1.

[55] Ibid., p. 7.

[56] A similar distinction is sometimes made between persuasion that moves us intellectually and conviction that moves us personally. See Perelman and Olbrechts-Tyteca, pp. 26–31.

5

Theories and Models of Source Credibility

> Many people assume that because young people are fluent in social media
> they are equally perceptive about what they find there.
> Our work shows the opposite to be true.[1]
>
> —Sam Wineburg

In 2017 the National Hockey League filed court papers demanding that data relating to head trauma research conducted at Boston University be turned over to the League's medical advisors. Some sixty studies in peer reviewed journals documented permanent brain damage (Chronic Traumatic Encephalopathy or CTE) in players. Part of the collected data came from players who had who agreed to donate brain tissue after they were deceased. The reason for the NHL's request was to see if there were grounds for challenging the findings of widespread CTE. The League was apparently searching for flaws in the research that would confirm the NHL Commissioner's declaration that "the relationship between concussions and the asserted clinical symptoms of CTE remains unknown."[2] Several years earlier the National Football League had made the same claim before finding ways to be more proactive in preventing head injuries. Years earlier, tobacco companies also attempted to raise doubts about the quality of the research linking their products to cancer and other health problems.

We are in a period when even well-designed medical studies administered and conducted by the best clinicians are subject to suspicion. Cancer researcher Stephen Hecht notes, "the only people who think science is wrong are the people who are going to be hurt by it."[3] In this case as in so many others, the decision about *whom* to believe should come down to the quality of the research design and, more to our point, sources who are expert and unbiased enough to make a claim of fact. Persuasion may appear to be primarily messages and ideas, but the qualifications of sources should be deciding factors in whether messages and their evidence are accepted.

Although we are not always conscious of the process of assessing **source credibility**, we usually run a quick calculation for every request we receive. What do we know about the source? Has unsettling new information about a familiar topic come from a group or individual we can trust? What does the source gain or lose in associating themselves with messages that ask us to yield? Questions like these are vital. Consider some examples.

- A digital ad campaign for the Twentieth Century Fox film, *A Cure for Wellness* (2017), created fake news sites. One was named The Salt Lake City Guardian, and the fabricated online newspaper posted an article using the logo of the Centers for Disease Control and the headline "Trump Orders CDC to Remove All Vaccination Related Information from Website."[4]Many who viewed the site did not realize it was a publicity stunt for the movie; instead, they accepted it as confirmation of their suspicions about vaccine safety and reposted the misinformation on social media outlets. How do consumers defend themselves against "fake news?" And how aggressive should social media outlets be in verifying the authenticity of an item posted on its site?

- A respected medical journal published an article that reviewed the research behind public health guidelines to reduce sugar intake, concluding that the warnings were based on low quality evidence. The review was funded by the Life Sciences Institute, which receives money from companies like Coca-Cola and Hershey's.[5] Should the review's assessment be trusted?

- In 2012, offensive lineman Jacob Bell announced he was retiring from the Cincinnati Bengals over concerns about potential diminished mental capacity from head injuries.[6] Given recent news about the effects of accumulated concussions in contact sports, what would you say if you were the parent of a child who asks to try out for the high school football team?

- Bernard Madoff perhaps best illustrates misplaced faith in a source. The financier for decades issued bogus reports of steady returns (10 to 12 percent) to thousands of individual investors. Madoff eventually confessed to operating a $50 billion Ponzi scheme, in which he used money from new investors to pay dividends to other clients. Investors were acquainted with Madoff through country clubs and social networks. His offices were in impressive buildings in New York and London, and—as one aide noted, "he appeared to believe in family, loyalty and honesty."[7] What signs could investors have noticed that should have made them more cautious?

- Every ten years the United States government conducts a census with the goal of identifying basic demographic information. The results have significant effects, from the apportionment of federal funds to the number of representatives for a state. It's an enormous task, completed primarily by sending questionnaires to homeowners. The 2010 effort urging Americans to comply with requests for information represented the largest public media campaign ever attempted.[8] The specific goal was to get individual families to return completed questionnaires; the compliance rate was 74 percent. Analysts segmented Americans into groups based on tendencies to comply or not. The most difficult group was what they called the "cynical fifth," roughly a fifth of the population characterized as harboring deep suspicions about government and any large institutions.[9] Reaching these people takes enormous effort. What kinds of appeals might have helped secure their compliance?

Source credibility always figures into calculations about how people will respond to requests for action or change. But as this chapter demonstrates, the processes that accompany granting authority to a source are anything but simple. Persuasion theorists have found contradictory reactions of audiences to *high- and low-credibility sources*. In significant numbers, individuals can surprise us by believing sources they should dismiss and resisting others worthy of trust.

THE THREE MEANINGS OF CREDIBILITY

Credibility is a pivotal term in the study of persuasion that has evolved over time. Generally, estimates of credibility involve assessing how the reputation of a persuader will affect the way a given audience will respond. For some, credibility means good character, sincerity, or integrity. For others, it is a synonym for proven expertise, or a reputation for fair-minded objectivity. These are prescriptive definitions; they remind us of what we should do. But social science adds a descriptive one as well, defining credibility as what is *believable* to others, even when the qualifications or objectivity of the source should raise doubts. These perspectives sometimes blend together. At other times, each one presents an opportunity to explore the different paths sources have for achieving their goals.

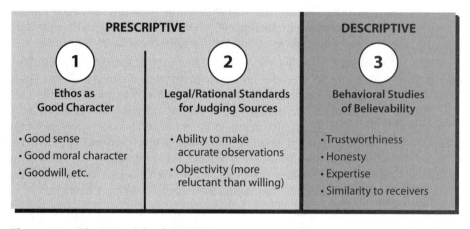

Figure 5.1   Three models of credibility

Ethos as Good Character

One of the oldest terms associated with the qualities of an advocate is the Greek word, **ethos**. For Aristotle, ethos was one of the three major forms of influence. He wrote in *The Rhetoric* that the ideal persuader should put the audience in the right emotional frame of mind (*pathos*), state the best arguments (*logos*), and have the right kind of character (*ethos*). The persuader "must not only try to make the argument of his speech demonstrative and worthy of belief; he must also make his own character look right."[10]

Aristotle labeled the components of good character as good sense, good moral character, and goodwill. "It follows," he noted, "that anyone who is thought to have all three of these good qualities will inspire trust in his audience."[11] If the audience members perceive that a persuader has good sense, good moral character, and good intentions, they are more likely to believe that a persuader's judgments are reasonable and justified. Add in the element of goodwill—the important idea that the persuader seems to have honorable intentions toward the audience—and we have a sense of what kinds of advocates are likely to be successful.

Ethos is the personal or professional reputation the persuader brings to the persuasive setting or constructs in the process of communicating. We usually have little difficulty recognizing the general traits of credibility. We identify high ethos sources as fair, trustworthy, sincere, reliable, and honest. Their knowledge about a subject may be seen as professional, experienced, and authoritative; their manner of presentation may be perceived as energetic, active, open-minded, objective, bold, or decisive.[12]

In his classic memoir *Zen and the Art of Motorcycle Maintenance*, writer Robert Pirsig explored how character is revealed in ordinary life. On his cross-country trip, his old motorcycle developed engine problems. Below is his description of two mechanics who were asked to diagnose the problem.

> The shop was a different scene from the ones I remembered. The mechanics, who had once all seemed like ancient veterans, now looked like children. A radio was going full blast and they were clowning around and talking and seemed not to notice me. When one of them finally came over he barely listened to the piston slap before saying, "Oh yeah. Tappets."[13]

Pirsig eventually paid a $140 repair bill for services that failed to remedy the engine problem. He later discovered that the noisy piston was caused by a damaged twenty-five cent pin accidentally sheared off by another careless mechanic. "Why," he wondered, "did they butcher it so?" What evidence did they provide that indicated they were less than fully competent mechanics?

> The radio was the clue. You can't really think hard about what you're doing and listen to the radio at the same time. Maybe they didn't see their job as having anything to do with hard thought, just wrench twiddling. If you can twiddle wrenches while listening to the radio that's more enjoyable.
>
> Their speed was another clue. They were really slopping things around in a hurry and not looking where they slopped them. More money that way. . . .
>
> But the biggest clue seemed to be their expressions. They were hard to explain. Good-natured, friendly, easygoing—and uninvolved. They were like spectators. You had the feeling they had just wandered in there themselves and somebody had handed them a wrench. There is no identification with the job. No saying, "I am a mechanic." At 5 PM or whenever their eight hours were in, you knew they would cut it off and not have another thought about their work. They were already trying not to have any thoughts about their work on the job.[14]

Pirsig argued that a good mechanic is a person of high ethos who can match the precise tolerances of machinery with a rigorous and analytic mind.

The Rational/Legal Ideal of Credibility

The second means of determining credibility is through the use of formal guidelines for judging expertise and reliability. From the *rational/legal perspective*, statements or views deserve to be believed if their sources meet certain general standards for accuracy and objectivity. The courts use these guidelines, as do the sciences, journalists and individuals who have basic critical thinking skills. The jumble of texts and sources on the internet has not made the task easier, especially for younger Americans[15] Even so, it is essential that persuaders and their audiences understand these guidelines.

Robert and Dale Newman describe a source as believable if she or he tells the truth "with no concern as to whether any specific audience or reader will in fact believe it."[16] Their assessment provides a bridge between ethos and rational credibility—and summarizes the most meaningful ways to test a source's credibility.

The difference between a persuader's ethos and his rational credibility rests on objective criteria that exist apart from the beliefs of people in specific settings. Only an audience can decide if they believe a persuader has good character, but the rational/legal rules for judging sources are constructed to apply to all audiences. Members of a jury, for example, may initially have strong suspicions that a defendant of a different social background is guilty of the charges brought against him or her. But under courtroom guidelines for assessing sources, they must disregard their personal preconceptions and decide a case based on the rules of evidence. The witness who is instantly likable because she or he is outwardly like the jurors (in dress, and education level, for example) may only be capable of giving hearsay (overheard or secondhand) evidence. Under rational/legal rules governing sources, hearsay testimony will usually not be permitted by a judge. Witnesses must be experts or have personal knowledge about the events that took place.

Ability.   How do we determine if someone can tell the truth or make intelligent observations about a specific subject? The first crucial test is measuring the extent to which an authority has been able to observe and make considered judgments. Were they eyewitnesses to events, or did they get information secondhand from another source? Do they have the training, experience, access to information, and knowledge to know what to look for? Can their testimony be corroborated by others?

A person with a rare medical condition, for example, will want to be sure that the health professional had the expertise to reach an accurate diagnosis. If the condition is rare and a nonspecialist family doctor did the analysis, it would be appropriate to seek a second opinion from a specialist before making any major decisions. Expertise, experience, and corroboration by other experts are all commonsense criteria for judging a source's ability.

Objectivity.   *Objectivity* is the ability to set aside personal needs or prejudices as frames of reference for understanding an event. Journalists aspire to it; scientists claim it; and most academics assert that it is a core value in their research. Complete objectivity, however, may be impossible; arguably, human creativity and imagination sometimes benefit from passions that are

Questioning Questionable Sources

The idea of rigorous assessment of the potential veracity of a source is critical, not just in legal proceedings where the stakes are obviously high, but in all walks of life. To be sure, we do look for sources we can trust. But in our overcommunicated society, qualifying a source of information as reliable sometimes is based on little more than recognizing the name of the source.

Many Americans seem to lack the basic skills to detect motives that reveal glaringly obvious biases. Individuals are frequently too generous in accepting conclusions from questionable advocates: for example, relying on British Petroleum as a source for information about the Deepwater Horizon explosion and oil spill in 2010; agreeing with a National Hockey League doctor that stories of head trauma among players are overblown; or assuming Walmart is a reliable source of information on the treatment of their employees. Companies will always put the best face on a significant problem, but accepting their narratives without subjecting them to critical analysis is a mistake.

created by having a point of view. Even so, we prize sources who can render events and observations with high degrees of accuracy and fairness. Weather forecasting, forensic science, space science, and structural engineering are just a few fields where accuracy is needed. And we hope that journalists can make reasonably accurate accounts of civil or political upheavals unfolding in distant parts of the world. But objectivity is usually more a matter of degrees than absolutes. The origins of human motivation can be obscure, and the desire to explain the unknown can lead to decisions based on prior beliefs and values rather than objective truths.

Indeed, we often *expect* personal investments will shape the comments and responses of groups and individuals. In such cases, credibility is said to be *willing*, which makes it somewhat suspect. **Willing sources** make claims that confirm judgments or state facts that are flattering or self-serving.[17] We mentioned the natural tendency to fill in unknowns with assumptions and beliefs, and there is an even stronger impulse to put the best face on the actions of groups or institutions to which we feel a certain allegiance. Thus press releases from university public relations offices can be counted on to report institutional successes rather than failures. ABC television finds significant news value in motion pictures released by their owner, the Disney Company.[18] After the economic meltdown of 2008 many former executives at banks and financial business defended the reasonableness of business practices that caused the crash but made them wealthy.[19]

Willing sources confirm our natural inclination to rationalize events in terms of what we want to see or believe about ourselves. Doctors who are paid handsome fees by pharmaceutical companies to educate others about the benefits of a particular drug are willing sources. If a competitor's drug would treat a patient's condition more effectively, can you count on the doctor to do the right thing and forgo the brand they have endorsed?[20]

In contrast, **reluctant sources** take positions that *go against* their own interests. The idea of reluctant testimony is based on a sturdy principle: "It is assumed that sane individuals will not say things against their own interests unless such testimony is true beyond doubt." If a witness gains little from his or her own testimony, it is probably very credible.[21] After leaving her position, a former assistant secretary of education said she was wrong to believe that constant testing was essential for measuring progress and improving American schools.[22] Similarly, a police commissioner admitted his department was guilty of neglect by not properly handling evidence on a series of drunk-driving convictions.[23] Neither person gained by admitting their mistakes while holding positions of responsibility, lending credibility to their testimony. Similarly, **negative evidence**—the absence of data where you would expect to find it—can be its own form of reluctant testimony. For example, despite President Trump's assertions of widespread voter fraud in presidential elections, there was little evidence of illegal voting.[24]

The continuum between the willing and the reluctant source is heavily weighted at the willing end of the scale. Like gold nuggets in a stream, reluctant testimony is rare and valuable. The task left to persuaders and audiences searching for strong evidence is to find high-ability sources who are at least not obviously willing—that is, not so tied to their own self-interest that they are incapable of seeing merit and truth in opposing viewpoints.

Source Credibility as Believability

A third perspective on credibility comes from experimental studies after World War II on the formation of attitudes about sources. Psychologist Carl Hovland was instrumental in redefining *credibility as believability,* spawning hundreds of studies of source traits that usually indicated audience preferences for messages from sources exhibiting *expertise, trustworthiness,* and *attractiveness.*[25] His study with Walter Weiss of audience responses to high- and low-credibility sources is considered a classic.[26] The researchers asked students at Yale University to complete opinion questionnaires that measured the students' attitudes on four different topics. After completing the questionnaires, the subjects read pamphlets arguing pro and con positions on the same four areas. All participants read identical texts on the four issues. One of the issues addressed whether it was currently (1950) possible to build an atomic-powered submarine One group was told that the pamphlet they were reading came from the Russian daily, *Pravda.* A second but demographically similar group was told that the source was the widely respected physicist, J. Robert Oppenheimer. Another topic was whether the popularity of television would decrease the number of movie theaters in operation. The opinion on this subject was attributed either to *Fortune Magazine* or to a gossip columnist. The study was designed to hold every variable constant except for the sources to which the pamphlets were attributed.

Did the attributions make a difference? Was there a greater attitude change in the groups who believed in the integrity of their sources? Not surprisingly, many of the respondents agreed with opinions when they were attributed to high-credibility sources. Oppenheimer and *Fortune,* for example, were ranked as more believable than *Pravda* and the gossip columnist. Did high credibility translate into greater agreement with the source? The answer was a qualified yes. The experimenters measured shifts in attitudes by responses to the initial questionnaires with changes in attitude measured in a second questionnaire. The net change in attitudes was not large, but it was always greater for those who believed they had read a pamphlet prepared by trustworthy sources.[27] Analysts who have studied and replicated this research have noted that in order to see even a *slight* advantage for a credible source, the researchers had to create *extreme* differences in communicator credibility. Overall, studies confirm that a high credibility source usually has some advantages over a low credibility source.[28]

The problems involved in designing precise experimental studies are complex.[29] As the pioneer researcher Arthur Cohen noted years ago, a "persistent theoretical problem is that of disentangling the main components of credibility. Is it expertness or trustworthiness, perception of fairness or bias, disinterest or propagandistic intent, or any combination of factors which is responsible for the effects of credibility on attitude change?"[30] A source can be studied by focusing on one specific dimension (dress, gender, age, perceived intelligence, the decision to include both sides of an argument), on a broader identity (a writer for the *New York Times,* a representative of the United States Government, a member of the Chamber of Commerce, or a felon), or the content of a particular ad.

There is also evidence to suggest that the *medium* through which a message is sent affects the credibility of the source. Because they provide more data about a source's demeanor, and appearance, for example, radio and television naturally allow a more personal focus.[31] Print, in contrast, reveals fewer personal details. Many of us feel we know something about the character and personality of CNN's Anderson Cooper or Sirius XM's Howard Stern. In contrast, few Americans know anything about the *New York Times*'s Dean Baquet, even though the executive editor of that paper arguably has a larger role in setting the nation's news agenda.

As we have noted, even the simplest communication setting contains a multitude of source variables that are difficult to isolate and study. Efforts to control for these factors have raised as many questions as answers. Despite these limitations, research into how sources are judged by audiences has produced useful observations, some of which are summarized below.

1. *For many people high credibility means trustworthiness.* The concept of trust lies on or near the surface of most individual assessments of sources. Receivers are more willing to accept what a persuader says if they believe that his or her intentions are honorable. Trustworthy sources are seen as people who will not abuse their access to an audience. Audiences who believe that they are being used, deceived, or carelessly misled will pay little attention to an advocate's ideas.[32]

2. *Individual characteristics are likely to affect a receiver's assessment of the importance of a reliable source.* These factors include the amount of knowledge the receiver possesses on the topic, initial attitudes, involvement with an issue, memory for possible counterarguments, and many other factors.[33]

3. *High-credibility sources increase confidence in a message, especially if receivers have taken enough time to fully consider arguments or evidence.*[34] Sources matter most with audiences that are centrally (rather than peripherally) processing a message. See the section on elaboration likelihood theory in the next chapter for a detailed discussion of this distinction.

4. *With some exceptions, sources matter least with internet content.* Since websites often aggregate materials from other media, users tend to focus less on questions of authorship and reliability.[35] As the opening quotation of this chapter notes, that can be a problem for younger and ostensibly savvy users of digital media.

5. *Similarities between communicators and audiences do not necessarily pave the way for influence.* Researchers have sometimes found that listeners judge similar sources "as more attractive than dissimilar sources."[36] However, the fact that there is prior agreement between people on a range of topics does not guarantee that they will more easily influence each other.[37]

6. *Physical attractiveness increases a persuader's chances with audiences.* While intense audience involvement with a subject is usually more important, several researchers who have studied audience reactions to persuaders have concluded that attractive sources (and celebrities) have an advantage, especially against nonexpert sources.[38]

7. *The advantages of high quality sources tend to disappear over time.* Demonstrating what is sometimes called the *sleeper effect*, some studies have shown

that people tend to forget their initial impressions of an advocate while retaining at least a general sense of the point of view expressed. "The increased persuasion produced by a high-credibility source disappears. Similarly, the decreased persuasion produced by a low-credibility source vanishes."[39] This is good news for advertisers, political campaigners running negative ads, and other sources who may create initial negative impressions. It also accounts for the common observation:, "I don't know where I heard this, but . . ." *If* the person remembered the source, he or she might be less inclined to recite what they heard.

8. *Prescriptive standards (see previous discussion of models of credibility) often have little effect on overall persuadability.* If a source is introduced purely with reference to their high credentials, the additive value of their expertise is less than one would hope.[40] Even persuaders who carefully document the origins of their information often do not fare much better than less candid advocates.[41] There is also some evidence to suggest that homegrown internet bloggers can seem as credible to many receivers as those with special training and expertise.[42] This result should be disturbing since there is a world of difference between the news gathering potential of, say, the British Broadcasting Corporation and the much more modest efforts of a TMZ.com. The web user can be influenced more by factors such as presentation than by the knowledge of a source.

9. *Audiences seem to learn information regardless of a source's reliability.* A political campaign commercial on television may teach the viewer more about the political views of a candidate than an objective news report with ostensibly higher credibility.[43] And there is some evidence to suggest that the internet has found audiences that are receptive to conspiracy theories, bogus medical remedies, and dubious historical facts.[44] Research suggests that users are not very curious about the credibility of internet sources, assuming that there is little difference between the web materials and more professionally edited media such as television or magazines.[45] We seem to absorb—if not fully accept—views regardless of our assessments of the quality of the source.

10. *The needs of receivers often override extensive consideration of a persuader's credibility.* The acceptability of a source is sometimes based on factors far removed from rational source credibility criteria. Gary Cronkhite and Jo Liska ask, "Do listeners always attend to public and television speakers because they consider the sources to be believable? Sometimes that is the reason, of course, but persuasion in such formats also proceeds as a matter of mutual need satisfaction." At times, "likability, novelty, and entertainment are valued more highly" than traditional standards of competence and trustworthiness.[46]

11. *Warning receivers that they are about to hear from a low-credibility source significantly weakens reception of the source's message.* This form of *inoculation* is one of the most reliable credibility effects.[47] We will revisit this important finding in the next chapter.

12. *A credibility-enhancing description of the source has the most beneficial effect if it comes at the beginning or middle of a message, rather than at the end.*[48]

As we have seen, the qualities that make a given source attractive to an audience have been the subject of much speculation. In ancient Greece, credibility was inherent in the quality of a person's character—a good persuader should be a virtuous person. For critical thinkers and the courts, credibility resides in sources that have high expertise and reasonable objectivity. For social scientists who are concerned with how attitudes are formed, source credibility means believability, with criteria set by what a given audience will accept.[49]

CREDIBILITY AS AUTHORITY

Although a message often stands or falls on the weight of its ideas and arguments, this is not the case with the five source-based strategies discussed below. Each represents a dimension of persuasion that depends as much on an advocate's attributes—on their implied authority—as on the ideas presented.

Legitimation

Within every culture and community, there are individuals who have the power to give at least superficial legitimacy to almost any idea or cause they endorse. *Legitimation* adds a sense of success or importance to a gathering, such as when a president chooses a local forum for an appearance. The presence of politicians, business leaders, entertainers, artists, clergy, or important civic leaders lends legitimacy to a gathering.

Sources that have the power of legitimation are usually celebrities or charismatic leaders. Celebrities can have influence through notoriety, even when their actual achievements may be modest.[50] American advertising pages are filled with celebrity endorsements for everything from drinking milk to wearing the right wristwatch. Many more accept roles as spokespersons for social and political action groups. Charlize Theron and Alec Baldwin, for example, have been spokespersons for People for the Ethical Treatment of Animals. Hollywood legends Clint Eastwood and Bruce Willis have appeared at Republican Party events. Interestingly, in these cases the legitimization can be reciprocal. Actors may gain from their association with serious causes; and the causes can trade on the notoriety of some of their supporters.

It is standard procedure in advertising to present a celebrity as a contented user of a product. As early as the 1880s, tobacco companies sought to identify their products with athletes and actors.[51] Endorsements by celebrities reached their peak on network television in the late 1950s when many stars, program hosts, and even some news reporters were expected to sell their sponsor's products. This strategy is still evident today, although tempered by the lightning speed of social media through which reports of unacceptable celebrity behavior can reach an audience immediately, sabotaging a campaign that has linked a product to a celebrity.[52] A suddenly toxic public figure can be a tricky public relations knot to untangle.

Charisma is another form of legitimization. Sociologist Edward Shils describes charismatic leaders as "persistent, effectively expressive personalities who impose

The Mistake of Assumed Agency

We think of people as the *authors* of their actions and ascribe responsibility for the choices made. As ordinary as this pattern of thinking is, it can be overextended. We often assign intentionality to individuals or groups for whom the term is, at best, a stretch. The pronoun *they* is sometimes the culprit. If we do not understand the actions of those who appear different, we may resort to stereotypes and assigning purpose and intention that does not exist.

A friend who is a geriatric psychotherapist is dismayed that staffs in nursing facilities so often assume that patients are "acting out" if they are unruly. The problem with ascribing intention is that most of the residents have dementia, which robs them of agency. Their behavior is not representative of what they would do if the neural pathways available to them for most of their lives were still intact. Assuming volition leads to punishing the patient rather than acknowledging that their behavior is tied to deteriorating mental abilities.

We make other mistakes in ascribing agency. For example, we assume that the office of the president can resolve multiple national challenges. The economy is one example. Most economists believe the chief executive cannot significantly change the course of the economy. A more accurate view is that it's an engine without a single engineer. Indeed, most presidents would welcome the chance to be as powerful as is widely believed.

themselves on their environment by their exceptional courage . . . self-confidence, fluency, [and] insight."[53] Charismatic figures are forces of history; we often define eras by their presence. They can be as diverse as Mohandas Gandhi in India, Nelson Mandela in South Africa, and Martin Luther King in the United States. All were powerful in challenging actions that limited civil liberties. As Shils notes, "it is also possible to apply the general characteristic of charisma to all individuals who can establish ascendancy over human beings by their commanding forcefulness or by an exemplary inner state which is expressed in a being of serenity."[54] John Kennedy garnered an enormous following in places like Berlin. Bill Clinton produced similar results in Ireland, as did Barack Obama in his first presidential visit to Europe.[55] Other leaders who owed part of their effectiveness to the force of their public images and personalities included: Adolf Hitler, Theodore Roosevelt, Franklin Roosevelt, Louisiana's Huey Long, France's Charles de Gaulle, and Cuba's Fidel Castro. To be sure, charisma does not buy instant success with an audience. But the presence of this elusive quality primes most audiences to levels of receptivity that ordinary sources usually cannot match.

Anonymity and Identity Concealment

Arguably, the migration of news and opinion to the internet has made it possible for anyone with a computer to react to blogs, news stories, reviews, and other forms of public discussion. Read online sources like Slate or the Huffington Post, and reader responses—some thoughtful, others obscene or ill considered—are appended to most stories. If you submit a letter to a traditional magazine or newspaper, you will be asked to sign your name and sometimes give your home address and phone number. But some internet-based media will post any and all responders, even those who provide a web name that conceals their identity to users of the site. For example, the posted comments on an article about former vice presidential candidate Sarah Palin on Slate included responses, ad hominem attacks, and counterarguments from people identified as "opus 512," "Beckingorder 25," "pdavidcATL," "DBloom75," and others.[56]

Some observers have noted that the internet opens up discourse. Anonymity can make individuals more honest in relaying their views.[57] But we think *identity concealment* carries more negatives than positives. The more scurrilous the comments are, the more cowardly the advocate seems. When there is no way to determine the source of a comment or opinion, we lose the transparency that is vital to open societies.

There are two problems with cloaking one's own advocacy behind a scrim of anonymity. One is ethical, and the other is practical. The ethical issue speaks to whether someone commenting on other persons or their ideas should be able to do the equivalent of wearing camouflage: that is, to be a participant in an exchange without the usual obligations for civility that is implicit in making oneself known to others. There's good reason why a civil society reserves its wrath for hit-and-run drivers, secret police, cyberbullies, and the like. We have a moral obligation to be accountable for our actions. Advocates who seek to change the views of others through assertions and especially accusations have an obligation to identify themselves.

Taking responsibility for our views is its own good reason for identifying ourselves. But there is a second practical reason to shun anonymity. There is some evidence that a person is likely to be taken *less* seriously if their remarks are anonymous.[58] As Stephen Rains notes, "Although anonymity may make one more comfortable participating in a group's discussion, it may also undermine perceptions of one's contributions."[59] Hiding behind anonymity weakens credibility.

Two-Step Flow

Early research on voting influences conducted in the 1940s and 1950s by Paul Lazarsfeld and Elihu Katz showed that the conclusion that mass media sources have direct and immediate influence on the audience was too simplistic. They observed that even in persuasion scenarios where the mass media *appear* to be the dominant sources of influence, there are usually at least two layers of influence at work. The concept of *two-step flow* is simple but important. Key media outlets often have their greatest effects on leaders who are especially attentive to their content—the first step. Opinion leaders then relay versions of those messages to people in their circle of influence—the second step.[60] (See figure 5.2.) The interesting fact about two-step flow is that motivated leaders act as *multipliers* of an original message. They add to the credibility of a message because they are personally known to their followers. The idea that peers are likely to influence each other is a durable principle of persuasion.

The two-step flow from media to opinion leaders to ordinary recipients is evident in many settings. The nation's most powerful print news sources (the *New York Times*, the *Washington Post*, the *Associated Press*, *The Wall Street Journal*, and a few others) frequently influence the topics covered by national television journalists. This pattern is repeated in the flow of ideas on contemporary social problems, new trends, and political positions. Ministers, priests, and rabbis pass on what they have learned from the media to their congregations. Bloggers interpret media stories for their readers. In individual families, one member might be a political news

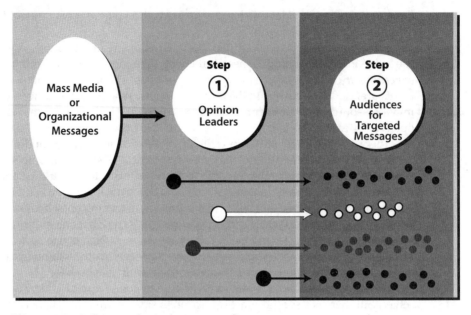

Figure 5.2   Influence through two-step flow

junkie, another a sports addict, or a film enthusiast—all of whom relay media-initi-
ated messages to other members of a household or to friends.

In applying two-step flow to persuasion campaigns, strategists frequently calculate how to work through opinion leaders so that they can be turned into local
agents of advocacy. A savvy health campaign directed to athletes, for example, may
target team leaders or coaches to be the sources of warnings about the risks of drug
use or excessive weight loss.[61] The same approach is behind the idea of *buzz marketing*. In this kind of selling, individuals working with the persuader are instructed to
praise a product's qualities to friends and acquaintances, usually on social media
and without the recipient's knowledge that they are really talking to a *shill* (a paid
audience member).[62] In these instances there is one constant: the idea of using personal influence *not* in place of the mass media but as the last stop in the persuasion
chain that starts with media sources.

Source/Placebo Suggestion

One of the most fascinating forms of authority-induced influence is the effect
of placebos on our sense of well-being. A placebo is a harmless and chemically neutral agent presented to a patient as treatment for an illness. Its most familiar form is
a sugar pill, but it may also include impressive machines, bundles of herbs, or virtually any object or symbol system that implies therapeutic power. The potency of
placebos lies partly in their powers of mystification. The *inability* to understand
medical terminology, complicated equipment, and medicines enhances the possibilities for success. Ironically, a more thorough understanding of the limitations of
treatments might take away the mystery that is the basis of the cure.

The remarkable fact about placebos is that they often work. When administered by medical authorities or other credible agents, placebos can have very real therapeutic benefits: an outcome known as the *placebo effect*. Frequently, the mere *suggestion* that a person is receiving a therapeutic treatment is sufficient for actual healing to begin.

The power of suggestion can have significant physical and mental effects. Jerome Frank notes that "expectations have been shown to affect physiological responses so powerfully that they can reverse the pharmacological action of a drug."[63] Some studies indicate that success in treatment with placebos ranges from 30 to 60 percent. And for the treatment of conditions with a subjective dimension—such as depression and allergies—effectiveness may even by higher.[64] Much to the chagrin of the pharmaceutical industry, improvement rates for patients receiving placebos *for pain* can easily rise to 50 percent, sometimes rivaling the results of new and expensive drugs.

Although recent studies have challenged some of the claims made for placebos in clinical trials,[65] there is little doubt that treatments involving subjective outcomes are greatly affected by medical symbols and the high expectations associated with them.[66] The chemistry of drug therapy is sometimes superseded by the potency of expectant attitudes about a high credibility source. Such *expectancy* may be enough to produce a link between mind and body that triggers the release of endorphins that block symptoms and create an enhanced sense of well-being. Whether we take a placebo in a medical study or decide that a doctor's language qualifies him or her as an expert, our expectations may lead to compliance and (in certain kinds of treatment) substantive improvement.

We can assume a parallel set of outcomes in settings that go beyond conventional therapies. Any authority—shaman, faith healer, acupuncturist, psychotherapist or motivational speaker—who enjoys the unqualified faith of a persuadee may set some of the same wheels in motion. Results from placebo studies often demonstrate that we cannot afford to be too eager to dismiss faith-based or alternative treatments.

Authoritarianism and Acquiescence

History is filled with examples of strong leaders who have used official authority and persuasion to reshape the attitudes and actions of compliant people. Hitler, Mussolini, and Japan's Tojo were widely portrayed in the United States as having hypnotic control over their followers during World War II. In his classic study of the true believer, Eric Hoffer noted that especially for people who see themselves as society's victims rather than beneficiaries, strong insurgent leaders can be especially seductive.

> People whose lives are barren and insecure seem to show a greater willingness to obey than people who are self-sufficient and self-confident. To the frustrated, freedom from responsibility is more attractive than freedom from restraint. . . . They willingly abdicate the directing of their lives to those who want to plan, command and shoulder all responsibility.[67]

This is the central ideal of *authoritarianism:* a natural tendency among some to defer too readily to unambiguous authority.

T. W. Adorno was the lead researcher of the first major English language analysis of social conditions and personality traits that give rise to excessive obedience to authority.[68] Influential academics, some of whom had escaped from Austria at the start of World War II, traced the origins of a multitude of central European personality traits, including anti-Semitism, "susceptibility to antidemocratic propaganda," ethnocentrism (judging others by one's own cultural values), and predispositions toward fascism. Their efforts to determine how patterns of upbringing instilled such traits are less important here than the fascinating questions their study brought into focus. Are certain kinds of listeners especially susceptible to appeals based on authority, especially official sources? Are some types of audiences attracted to the rigid ideological certainties of a demagogue (i.e., Hitler's stereotypes of Jewish failings)? And what psychological needs are satisfied when total allegiance is promised to a leader?

The *F (Antidemocratic) Scale inventory* probed for signs of authoritarian submission in a paper and pencil test. This inventory of attitudes consisted of claims, such as the ones listed below, to which the respondent could agree or disagree. (In this sample, agreement with the statements raises the F score, indicating authoritarian attitudes.)

- Obedience and respect for authority are the most important virtues children should learn.

- Every person should have complete faith in some supernatural power whose decisions will be obeyed without question.

- What this country needs most, more than laws and political programs, are a few courageous, tireless, devoted leaders in whom the people can put their faith.[69]

The researchers found that anti-Semitism, rigidity, ethnocentrism, undue respect for power, and other traits tended to cluster within many of the same people. They theorized that the clustering was tied to styles of family life. They also learned that authoritarianism can be identified in segments of almost any population. Some people may be psychologically hardwired to seek a place in the social order and to follow official authority eagerly.

The dilemma this research raises, of course, is that while every society has an important stake in the rule of law, the failure of ordinary people to challenge unjust or inhuman leadership can coarsen the same society. There have been times (in colonial America, for example, or in the decisions of the former Soviet republics to declare autonomy) when disorder arguably served justice. Only with the advantage of hindsight can we fully gauge when the price of obedience has been too costly. For instance, it is now easy to criticize German submission to Hitler and his lieutenants during World War II. Nearly every discussion of that conflict questions how so many people in the democratic and relatively well-educated nation could have accepted the blatant xenophobia and racism of the Third Reich.[70] Others have also questioned why many Americans accepted the decision to incarcerate 117,000 Japanese Americans in roughly the same period[71] and the hundreds of enemy combatants currently held without trial or legal representation in U.S. military prisons.[72] Slick Hollywood war films played their parts in demonizing the enemy in World War II, as have many post-9/11 warnings about threats posed by our enemies. But a more complete answer must also consider the psychology that induces some individuals to exchange their freedoms for a sense of collective security.

A clue to these dynamics came in perhaps the most infamous of all clinical experiments in psychology. In the study Stanley Milgram offered an up close view of decent people obeying oppressive authority. His famous shock -box studies in the 1960s measured the degree to which ordinary people would follow problematic orders from a responsible official. The research design was ingenious, even though university research boards today would not allow the stress placed on the subjects.

Milgram advertised for volunteer teachers to help conduct what was characterized as a learning experiment. Those whom he selected were asked to assist him in teaching the learner—in reality, a confederate with Milgram. Each time the learner answered a question incorrectly, the teacher who was the actual subject of the experiment was instructed by Milgram to administer an electrical shock. This scheme of reward and punishment was ostensibly designed to help improve the skills of the learner.

In *Obedience to Authority*, Milgram explained how the subject teachers were introduced to the setting.

> After watching the learner being strapped into place, he is taken into the main experimental room and seated before an impressive shock generator. Its main feature is a horizontal line of thirty switches, ranging from 15 volts to 450 volts, in 15-volt increments. There are also verbal designations which range from slight shock to danger-severe shock. The teacher is told that he is to administer the learning test to the man in the other room.

The learner actually received no shock at all. The point of the experiment was to see how long a person ordered to inflict pain on a protesting victim would continue to comply in a concrete and measurable situation.[73] The dilemma faced by the subject teachers was one of obedience. At what point should they refuse to obey the commands of the experimenter? The suffering of the learner pressured the subject teachers to reject the instructions. Yet, the experimenter, a legitimate authority to whom the subject felt some commitment, gave orders to continue.[74] Many did continue, even when the learner cried out in pain. Had the learners actually been wired to the shock box as the subjects were led to believe, they would have suffered physical and emotional injuries.

To witnesses of this research, the subjects who continued to obey Milgram appeared to be sadistic. But Milgram concluded otherwise, citing the very human tendency to shift responsibility to a higher and seemingly legitimate authority. He notes that "relatively few people have the resources needed to resist authority. A variety of inhibitions against disobeying authority come into play and successfully keep the person in his place."[75]

Admittedly, there are differences between a setting in which a subject agrees to carry out the orders of a researcher and a persuasive situation in which a popular advocate elicits support from an autonomous collection of individuals.[76] The subject's desire to be helpful in an experiment exceeds the average listener's motivations to accept the views of advocates. French social psychologist Gustave Le Bon authored a book on the psychology of crowds in 1895, a time of industrialization and urbanization that upended rural traditions. We doubt that most people in open societies today are the "servile flock ... incapable of ever doing without a master" that he described.[77] Even so, any observer of contemporary American politics and scores of other hierarchical settings will readily see how references to authority function as effective appeals.

SUMMARY

In human communication, the content of a message is almost always understood in terms of the quality and acceptability of a source. As we noted at the beginning of this chapter, there are many questions about the nature of credibility that still need answers, and there are many ways to describe how credibility enables persuaders to succeed. We outlined three forms of credibility. First, audiences expect that those seeking their support will demonstrate positive traits of character, common sense, and goodwill. Second, in settings such as the courtroom and the laboratory where audiences are prepared to weigh evidence to determine truth, sources are best measured by their abilities to observe events accurately and objectively—the rational/legal model of credibility. Third, we described a believability standard that has less to do with the search for truth or good character than with existing audience dispositions. Specific personal attributes of persuaders are judged to be more or less attractive, shaping audience acceptance.

High credibility can also be understood as a kind of authority. We briefly examined five strategic forms of source-centered persuasion: legitimation and charisma; anonymity/identity concealment; the two-step flow of relaying mass media messages to audiences through opinion leaders; inducements to acceptance using verbal and placebo mystifications; and authoritarianism and acquiescence. Some receivers are especially susceptible to official sources. They combine the disposition to act on the words of others with what can be a dangerous desire to relinquish responsibility to others.

An audience's awareness of an advocate's character is often the first important benchmark in the communication process. It follows that the sheer force of a dominating advocate remains one of the compelling benchmarks in persuasion.

 QUESTIONS AND PROJECTS FOR FURTHER STUDY

1. Using any search engine such as Google, pick a controversial topic (i.e., abortion or illegal aliens) and generate a random list of websites discussing it. Answer some of the following questions: Do any of the websites make statements about their own credibility? What cues or signals are included to suggest high credibility? How do you think individuals would respond to the absence or presence of credibility claims?

2. Billy Ray's 2003 riveting feature film *Shattered Glass*, recreates the true story of Stephen Glass, a respected staff writer for *The New Republic*, *Rolling Stone*, and other publications. We now know that Glass fabricated many of his stories, nearly destroying *The New Republic* in the process. View the film and assess the credibility issues Glass raised for his increasingly doubtful coworkers. How serious a problem was the reporter's fabrication of stories? In what other fields is one's personal credibility of equal or greater importance? Does an information source make an implicit contract with a reader or consumer?

3. Observe some of the experts and spokespersons making guest appearances on network news programs (i.e., CNN's *Anderson Cooper 360*, PBS's *Newshour*, *CBS Evening News*, etc.). Note if the introductions of the guests establish their ethos

for the audience. Assess the credibility of one or two experts using both the rational/legal model and the experts' own claims.

4. Locate several magazine advertisements that use prestige and legitimation as a persuasive strategy. Describe the verbal and visual symbols that help sell the product.

5. Observe a legal proceeding in your area. Study the way the prosecution and defense attorneys or journalists attempt to establish or discredit the credibility of specific witnesses. (As an alternative, watch a film where the plot pivots on source credibility: *The Rainmaker* [1997], *The Verdict* [1982], *Erin Brockovich* [2000], *A Civil Action* [1998], and *Spotlight* [2015].)

6. Using films, television programs or national politics, identify a figure who seems to exhibit some of the characteristics of the authoritarian personality. Explain the reasoning behind your choice.

7. From your own experiences with family members or with people at work, describe the two-step flow of influence. What media source(s) did an opinion leader use? In your judgment, was the advocacy of the opinion leader more effective than if the audience had heard from the media source directly?

8. From the list below,[78] identify and defend eight credibility traits that would help (1) a male member of a persuasion course advocating a compulsory year of government service for all 18-year-olds or (2) a senator from your state urging a cross section of citizens to support a 15 percent pay increase for all members of Congress.

fair	good speaker	respectful
good	right	honest
trustworthy	loyal	admirable
just	patient	correct
sincere	straightforward	reliable
valuable	unselfish	nice
virtuous	impartial	calm
moral	frank	friendly
professional	experienced	energetic
authoritative	has foresight	bold
aggressive	active	open-minded
decisive	proud	objective

 ## ADDITIONAL READING

T. W. Adorno, Else Frankel-Brunswik, Daniel J. Levinson, and R. Nevitt Sanford, *The Authoritarian Personality* (New York: Harper and Brothers, 1950).

Gary Cronkhite and Jo R. Liska, "The Judgment of Communicant Acceptability" in Michael Roloff and Gerald Miller (Eds.), *Persuasion: New Directions in Theory and Research* (Beverly Hills, CA: Sage, 1980), pp. 101–39.

Andrew Flanagin and Miriam Metzger, "Perceptions of Internet Information Credibility," *Journalism and Mass Communication Quarterly*, Autumn, 2000, pp. 515–540.

Andrew Flanagan and Miriam Metzger, "Digital Media and Perceptions of Source Credibility in Political Communication," *Oxford Handbooks Online*, September, 2014, oxfordhandbooks.com.

Carl Hovland, Irving L. Janis, and Harold Kelley, *Communication and Persuasion* (New Haven, CT: Yale University Press, 1953).

Stanley Milgram, *Obedience to Authority: An Experimental View* (New York: Harper & Row, 1974).

Robert P. Newman and Dale R. Newman, *Evidence* (Boston, MA: Houghton Mifflin, 1969).

Chanthika Pornpitakpan, "The Persuasiveness of Source Credibility: A Critical Review of Five Decades of Evidence," *Journal of Applied Social Psychology*, Vol 34, 2004, pp. 243–281.

Barbara Warnick, "Online Ethos: Source Credibility in an 'Authorless' Environment," *American Behavioral Scientist*, Vol. 48, October, 2004, pp. 256–265.

NOTES

[1] Wineburg quoted in Brooke Donald, "Stanford Researchers Find Students Have Trouble Judging the Credibility of Information Online," *Stanford Graduate School of Education*, November 22, 2016, https://ed.stanford.edu/news/stanford-researchers-find-students-have-trouble-judging-credibility-information-online

[2] Juliet Macur, "The NHL's Problem with Science, *The New York Times*, February 8, 2017, pp. B8, B12.

[3] Ibid., p. B12.

[4] Sapna Maheshwari, "The News Was Fake. The Regret? That's Real," *The New York Times*, February 17, 2017, pp. B1–B2.

[5] Anahad O'Connor, "Study Tied to Food Industry Tries to Discredit Sugar Guidelines," *The New York Times*, December 20, 2016, pp. B1 and B5.

[6] Lynn Zinser, "Bell Chooses Health over More Football," *The New York Times*, May 10, 2012, http://fifthdown.blogs.nytimes.com/2012/05/10/bell-chooses-health-over-more-football/?_r=0

[7] Julie Creswell and Landon Thomas Jr., "The Talented Mr. Madoff," *The New York Times*, January 25, 2009, pp. B1, B8.

[8] Jerome Williams, Nancy Bates, Michael Lotti, and Monica Wroblewski," Marketing the 2010 Census," in David Stewart (Ed.), *The Handbook of Persuasion and Social Marketing, Volume Three* (Santa Barbara CA: Praeger, 2015), p. 147.

[9] Ibid., p. 132.

[10] Aristotle, *Rhetoric*, trans. W. Rhys Roberts (Mineola, New York: Dover Thrift Editions), p. 59.

[11] Ibid., p. 60.

[12] These are high credibility indicators cited by Jack L. Whitehead, Jr. in "Factors of Source Credibility," *Quarterly Journal of Speech, 54* (1968), p. 61.

[13] Robert M. Pirsig, *Zen and the Art of Motorcycle Maintenance: An Inquiry into Values* (New York: William Morrow, 1974), p. 32.

[14] Ibid., pp. 33–34.

[15] Donald, "Stanford Researchers."

[16] Robert P. Newman and Dale R. Newman, *Evidence* (Boston: Houghton Mifflin, 1969), p. viii. We are indebted to the authors of this book for the general scheme developed in this section.

[17] Ibid., p. 79.

[18] Robert McChesney, *Rich Media, Poor Democracy* (New York: The New Press, 2000), p. 54.

[19] Louise Story and Landon Thomas Jr., "Tales from Lehman's Crypt," *The New York Times*, September 13, 2009, Sunday Business, pp. 1, 7.

[20] Alex Spiegel, "How to Win Doctors and Influence Prescriptions," National Public Radio, October 21, 2010, http://www.npr.org/templates/story/story.php?storyId=130730104

[21] Newman and Newman, p. 79.

[22] Alan Wolfe, "The Education of Diane Ravitch," *The New York Times Book Review*, May 16, 2010, p. 14.

[23] Allison Steele and Joseph Slobodzian, "Philadelphia Breath-test Readings Off for 1,147 Cases," *Philadelphia Inquirer*, March 24, 2011, http://www.philly.com/philly/news/20110324_Phila__breath-test_readings_off_for_1_147_cases.html

[24] "Debunking The Voter Fraud Myth," *Brennan Center for Justice, NYU School of Law*, January 31, 2017, http://www.brennancenter.org/analysis/debunking-voter-fraud-myth

[25] Carl Hovland, Irving L. Janis, and Harold Kelley, *Communication and Persuasion* (New Haven, CT: Yale, 1953).

26 Carl Hovland and Walter Weiss, "The Influence of Source Credibility on Communication Effectiveness," *Public Opinion Quarterly 15* (1951), pp. 635–650.

27 For a review of this study see Philip G. Zimbardo, Ebbe B. Ebbesen, and Christina Maslach, *Influencing Attitudes and Changing Behavior*, 2nd ed. (Reading, MA: Addison-Wesley, 1977), pp. 94–98, 125–27.

28 For an exhaustive review of the literature on source credibility see Chanthika Pornpitakpan, "The Persuasiveness of Source Credibility: a Critical Review of Five Decades of Evidence," *Journal of Applied Social Psychology*, Vol 34, 2004, pp. 243–281.

29 For more detailed analyses of experimental research on source credibility see: Kenneth Andersen and Theodore Clevenger, Jr., "A Summary of Experimental Research in Ethos," in J. Jeffrey Auer (Ed.), *The Rhetoric of Our Times* (New York: Appleton-Century-Crofts, 1969), pp. 127–151; Jesse G. Delia, "A Constructivist Analysis of the Concept of Credibility," *Quarterly Journal of Speech*, December 1976, pp. 361–375; Icek Ajzen and Martin Fishbein, *Understanding Attitudes and Predicting Social Behavior* (Englewood Cliffs, NJ: Prentice-Hall, 1980), pp. 13–27, 218–228; and Dominick A. Infante, Kenneth R. Parker, Christopher H. Clarke, Laverne Wilson, and Indrani A. Nathu, "A Comparison of Factor and Functional Approaches to Source Credibility," *Communication Quarterly*, Winter 1983, pp. 43–48.

30 Arthur R. Cohen, *Attitude Change and Social Influence* (New York: Basic Books, 1964), p. 26.

31 See, for example, Steve Booth-Butterfield and Christine Gutowski, "Message Modality and Source Credibility Can Interact to Affect Argument Processing." *Communication Quarterly*, Winter 1993, pp. 77–89.

32 For more on assessments of motives, see our discussion of attribution theory in chapter 6.

33 Pornpitakpan, pp. 256–264.

34 Zakary Tormala, Pablo Briñol, and Richard Petty, "Multiple Roles for Source Credibility under High Elaboration: It's All in the Timing," *Social Cognition, 25* (August 2007), pp. 536–552.

35 Barbara Warnick, "Online Ethos: Source Credibility in an 'Authorless' Environment," *American Behavioral Scientist*, Vol. 48, October, 2004, pp. 256–265; Andrew Flanagan and Miriam Metzger, "Digital Media and Perceptions of Source Credibility in Political Communication," *Oxford Handbooks Online*, September, 2014, oxfordhandbooks.com

36 Herbert W. Simons, Nancy N. Berkowitz, and John Moyer, "Similarity, Credibility, and Attitude Change: A Review and Theory," *Psychological Bulletin*, January, 1970, pp. 2–4.

37 Michael Sunnafrank, "Attitude Similarity and Interpersonal Attraction in Communication Processes: In Pursuit of an Ephemeral Influence," *Communication Monographs*, December 1983, pp. 273–284.

38 Peter A. Andersen, *Nonverbal Communication: Forms and Functions*, 2nd ed. (Long Grove, IL: Waveland, 2008), pp. 271–273. See also Pornpitakpan, p. 248.

39 Charles Kiesler, Barry E. Collins, and Norman Miller, *Attitude Change: A Critical Analysis of Theoretical Approaches* (New York: John Wiley and Sons, 1969), p. 108.

40 William J. McGuire, "Attitudes and Attitude Change" in Gardner Lindzey and Elliot Aronson (Eds.), *Handbook of Social Psychology, Third Edition, Volume II* (New York: Random House, 1985), p. 263.

41 Wayne N. Thompson, *Quantitative Research in Public Address and Communication* (New York: Random House, 1967), pp. 54–55.

42 Thanomwong Poorisat, Benjamin Detenber, Vani Viswanathan, and Helen Nofrina, "Perceptions of Credibility: A Comparison of User-Generated and Expert Generated Websites," International Communication Association Annual Meeting, 2009.

43 Thomas E. Patterson and Robert D. McClure, *The Unseeing Eye: The Myth of Television Power in Politics* (New York: Putnam, 1976), pp. 22–23.

44 See, for example, Stephen Rains, "The Anonymity Effect: The Influence of Anonymity of Sources and Information on Health Websites," *Journal of Applied Communication Research*, May, 2007, Ebscohost, February 14, 2011.

45 Andrew Flanagin and Miriam Metzger, "Perceptions of Internet Information Credibility," *Journalism and Mass Communication Quarterly*, Autumn, 2000, pp. 515–540.

46 Gary Cronkhite and Jo Liska, "The Judgment of Communicant Acceptability," in Michael Roloff and Gerald Miller (Eds.), *Persuasion: New Directions in Theory and Research* (Beverly Hills, Sage, 1980), p. 104.

47 Pornpitakpan, p. 257.

48 Ibid., p. 249.

49 For a more detailed discussion of different assumptions for assessing credibility see Cal Logue and Eugene Miller, "Rhetorical Status: A Study of Its Origins, Functions, and Consequences," *Quarterly Journal of Speech*, Feb. 1995, pp. 20–28.

[50] Richard Sennett argues that the trivia that flows from the celebrity-making machinery of the mass media increasingly eclipse a person's genuine accomplishments. It may now be easier to be a celebrity—to be well known—than to sustain public attention on an agenda for social action. See Richard Sennett, *The Fall of Public Man* (New York: Vintage, 1978), pp. 282–87.

[51] Daniel Pope, *The Making of Modern Advertising* (New York: Basic Books, 1983), p. 228.

[52] For research on some effects of celebrity endorsements see Clinton Amos, Gary Holme, and David Stutton, "Exploring the Relationship Between Celebrity Endorser Effects and Advertising Effectiveness," *International Journal of Advertising, 7*(2), 2008.

[53] Edward Shils, "Charisma," in David Sills (Ed.), *The Encyclopedia of the Social Sciences*, Vol. 2 (New York: Macmillan, 1968), p. 387.

[54] Ibid.

[55] Andy Barr, "Obama Still a Rock Star in Europe," *Politico*, March 30, 2009, http://www.politico.com/news/stories/0309/20682.html

[56] Jacob Weisberg, "Did Sarah Palin Really Say That?" *Slate*, January 28, 2011, http://www.slate.com/id/2283069/#add-comment

[57] See, for example, Steven Rains and Craig Scott, "To Identify or Not Identify: A Theoretical Model of Receiver Responses to Anonymous Communication," *Communication Research*, February 2007, pp. 61–67.

[58] Stephen Rains, "The Impact of Anonymity on Perceptions of Source Credibility and Influence in Computer-Mediated Group Communication," *Communication Research*, February, 2007, pp. 100–125.

[59] Ibid.

[60] Denis McQuail and Sven Windahl, *Communication Models for the Study of Mass Communication* (New York: Longman, 1993), pp. 62–63.

[61] For summaries of interesting applications of the research by Lazarsfeld and Katz, see "Quick Read Synopsis of Politics, Social Networks, and the History of Mass Communications Research: Rereading *Personal Influence,*" *The Annals of the American Academy of Political and Social Science, 608*, November 2006, pp. 315–342.

[62] "What's the Buzz about Buzz Marketing," *Knowledge@Wharton*, January 12, 2005, http://knowledge.wharton.upenn.edu/article.cfm?articleid=1105&CFID=2739428&CFTOKEN=16196988

[63] Jerome D. Frank, *Persuasion and Healing* (New York: Schocken, 1974), p. 137.

[64] Margaret Talbot, "The Placebo Prescription," *The New York Times Magazine*, January 9, 2000, pp. 34–39, 44, 58–59; F. J. Evans, "Placebo," in Raymond Corsini (Ed.), *The Encyclopedia of Psychology*, 2nd ed. (New York: John Wiley and Sons, 1994), Vol. 3, pp. 91–92.

[65] Gina, Kolata, "Placebo Effect Is More Myth than Science, Study Says," *The New York Times*, May 24, 2001, p. A20.

[66] Fred Guterl, "How Real Is the Placebo Effect?" *Newsweek*, June 18, 2001, p. 49.

[67] Eric Hoffer, *The True Believer: Thoughts on the Nature of Mass Movements* (New York: Harper and Row, 1966), p. 109.

[68] T. W. Adorno, Else Frankel-Brunswik, Daniel J. Levinson, and R. Nevitt Sanford, *The Authoritarian Personality* (New York: Harper and Brothers, 1950). The study is considered a classic, although serious questions have been raised about its complex attitude-research methodology in 1950. See for example, Roger Brown, *Social Psychology* (New York: Free Press, 1965), pp. 509–26.

[69] Adorno et al., p. 248.

[70] See, for example, Daniel Goldhagen, *Hitler's Willing Executioners: Ordinary Germans and the Holocaust* (New York: Knopf, 1996), pp. 3–48.

[71] Charles Goodell, *Political Prisoners in America* (New York: Random House, 1973), p. 87.

[72] See Joseph Margulies, *Guantanamo and the Abuse of Presidential Power* (New York: Simon and Schuster, 2006), pp. 3–61.

[73] Stanley Milgram, *Obedience to Authority: An Experimental View* (New York: Harper and Row, 1974), pp. 3–4.

[74] Ibid., p. 4.

[75] Ibid., p. 6.

[76] For a useful discussion of Milgram's study and the problem of obedience, see Roger Brown, *Social Psychology*, 2nd ed. (New York: Free Press, 1986), pp. 1–41.

[77] Gustave LeBon, *The Crowd* (New York: Viking, 1960), p. 118.

[78] Whitehead, "Factors of Source Credibility," pp. 59–63.

6

The Mind in Persuasion

> There is nothing more practical than a good theory.[1]
>
> —Kurt Lewin

W e can study persuasion from many angles. We can survey audience attitudes or behaviors before and after exposure to messages and sources.
We can deconstruct messages to see how their logic works. We can also
identify common strategies for gaining compliance. But at some point a persuader
must make judgments about what is going on internally with the receiver. Because
persuasion involves changes in attitudes and/or behavior, it requires the discovery
of the *psychology* involved in the process. Researchers have developed theories to
make predictions about outcomes when receivers contemplate a message. Models
help us forecast the potential effects of persuasion inputs (a given source, a set of
appeals, a certain medium).

Theories of attitude change are essential in understanding persuasion. Theories and models make the process much more transparent. They offer systematic
answers to important questions, such as: what is going on internally when someone we like says something we dislike? How do we handle the hundreds of
requests for money, time, or attention that bombard us daily? What are the likely
mental processes that occur when an idea we oppose aligns with one we like? Our
answers may be tentative rather than certain, but theories about human action give
the persuasion analyst a clear predictive advantage.

THE MEASURES OF PERSUASION EFFECTIVENESS

Attitudes

Pick an issue, product, or controversial event, and the chances are good we
have an identifiable attitude about it. Beliefs and values—often the unexamined
inheritances of growing up in specific communities and cultures—provide the
foundations for **attitudes**. A person who values progress might combine it with a
belief in a person's fundamental right to basic medical care to produce a favorable
attitude toward a single-payer health system, as in Canada.

Attitudes are topical and sometimes transitory; they emerge in everyday conversation as judgments we *may* be prepared to act on.[2] In other words, attitudes are
our *predispositions* toward ideas, objects and individuals. In addition to emerging
from our beliefs, attitudes can also be learned from others and then adopted as our
own. The strength of our attitudes are a combination of beliefs and the weight
assigned to them. Persuaders often think of attitudes as strong, weak, or neutral. It
is essential to make estimates of attitude strengths when planning messages.[3]

Attitudes precede and therefore influence behavior. We expect the two to align.
To be sure, there is not always a link between what we think and what we do. A

person may accept the idea that smoking is detrimental to one's health but still smoke. Similarly, persons who express acceptance of the principle of equality may still behave in ways that are discriminatory toward a particular group. Other factors may also keep attitudes and behaviors out of alignment. Pleasing someone may be temporarily more important than acting on an attitude. As we will see in the discussion of cognitive dissonance theory below, individuals are capable of a kind of denial that allows them to ignore how certain actions violate expressed attitudes. Even so, we are always interested in internal attitudes because they can grow into overt action. Sufficient experiences or the accumulation of evidence over time can eventually result in behavior that reflects attitudes.

One feature of an individual's attitudes is certain: they are deeply shaped by our interactions with others. What passes as information in our daily lives frequently carries implicit attitudes that we accept as fact. When someone tells us about their nightmare visit to an emergency room, the story and its details can easily feed into a shared feeling that the U.S. health-care system is still broken. We convert experiences and face-to-face conversations into durable views on which we may act. In addition, we obtain a great deal of information from media sources. Many of our attitudes are shaped by what we see and hear on topics are varied as sex, fashion, or public policy. This is why users of Twitter, Instagram and Facebook are studied by analytics companies who assess the extent to which a personal habit or activity is indicative of an attitude.[4]

Such observational learning is sometimes called *modeling* or vicarious modeling. By listening and watching others, we form positions about what is right and wrong, good and bad. When we emulate those we admire, we accept some of their attitudes and reenact them. As social animals, we naturally bend toward social acceptance and validation.

Behaviors

An attitude is an inner state. *Behavior* involves more observable human action; it can be seen by others. A political poll asking respondents what they think about an issue will usually result in the expression of an attitude. But voting itself is a behavior. When someone says they really like the cars made by a company, it is reasonable to expect that the attitude will convert into the act of purchasing the brand. However, human behavior is not always predictable; it is marked by ambiguity. What we say does not always translate into what we do. We know our friends mostly by their *verbal action*, the attitudes they express in comments that can be heard by others.

Generally speaking, the more information people have about an issue, the greater their *attitude-behavior consistency*.[5] That is, what they say generally fits with the ways they act. Studies indicate that attitude-behavior consistency is also affected by a strong vested interest; the greater the potential impact of an attitude on ourselves or significant others, the greater the behavioral consistency.[6]

This brief overview of attitudes, and behavior sets the stage for the remainder of the chapter. Theories and models that predict specific effects are invaluable when analyzing attempts to change attitudes or behavior.

Essential Theories and Models of Persuasion

Theory applied to the rich variability of human action lacks the precision and predictability of, say, the laws of physics. Persuasion theories do, however, allow us to estimate plausible outcomes from certain kinds of messages. While space prevents an exhaustive list, we include concepts with significant explanatory power for how the mind processes specific appeals.

Theory of Cognitive Dissonance

Theories dealing with consistency and balance are among the most important persuasion concepts. These theories generally assume that individuals will feel uncomfortable if new information presents an inconsistency, motivating them to reduce discrepancies by changing attitudes or behaviors. Although these theories are not ironclad predictors of how attitudes can be altered, they present the possibility of identifying how we might induce others to change. For example, suppose that you found out that a close friend has been charged with theft of a piece of artwork owned by the university. If the information disturbs you, would you change your attitude about your friend? Consistency theory predicts that the contradiction of having a thief as a friend may force a realignment of attitudes. In short, the knowledge of your friend's behavior may reduce your positive attitude toward him. The theory predicts that persuasion happens when apparent contradictions between two *related* attitudes or behaviors force a realignment of them toward a state of mental "consonance."

To envision how imbalance produces change, consider that—for any attitude—there is at least one related attitude that should be consistent. If the related attitude is inconsistent, it may produce what Leon Festinger identified as *cognitive dissonance*, or mental stress.[7] Consider another example. Imagine that you have discovered that a distant ancestor in your family owned slaves before the civil war. How would you feel? Writer Cynthia Carr remembers her shame when she learned that fact about an ancestor. She sought to resolve the resulting dissonance by telling an African American friend.[8] Like the character of Fanny who is adopted by a slave-owning family in the film version of Jane Austen's *Mansfield Park* (1999), Carr had the urge to express her disappointment by publicly disowning any association with the racism and cruelty that the dissonance produced.

In understanding this model it helps to think of all individuals as collections of attitudinal or behavioral preferences, each represented by a continuum. Individuals have attitudes or active behaviors that can be located somewhere along the continuum between agree–disagree or like–dislike. Sometimes we are indifferent or neutral on a topic: for example, the subject of the second president of the United States:

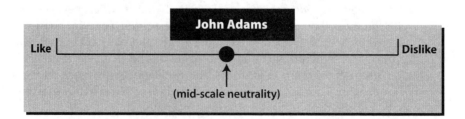

At other times, our position is well defined, as is usually the case with the third president:

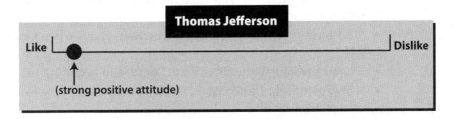

Most Americans revere Thomas Jefferson. Yet he owned slaves, refusing to free them even at the end of his life. How does this information alter our view of Jefferson? Festinger's theory predicts dissonance, hence the need for an attitude realignment that will bring about *consonance*.

The basic assumption of the theory is that dissonance causes tension and that inconsistency will motivate people to do something to reduce the uncomfortable imbalance. The more important or critical the attitude or behavior, the more dissonance one experiences. The pressure to change increases with the perceived relevance of the two out-of-sync elements. In the model below, dissonance reduction means that a positive attitude toward Jefferson will be downgraded. It also predicts that the very low opinion of slavery might be moderated by considering Jefferson in the context of his time.

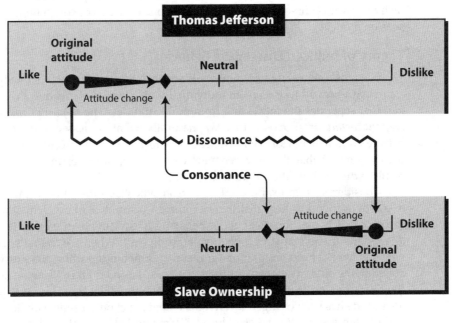

Figure 6.1 Cognitive Dissonance

Many types of arguments gain force by laying out apparent contradictions that imply the need for change. Consider a few examples:

- "I can't understand why you signed a year-long lease if you want to move to Arizona next month."
- "TSA security screening at airports is excessive, but we don't want another 9/11."
- "I know smoking is a health risk, but I can't seem to quit."
- "I always thought Disney World was a bit hokey, but I have to admit that I had a pretty good time."

Each instance poses a consistency dilemma that invites attitude moderation.

We can, of course, rationalize away the dissonance designed into a message. First, you can simply dismiss the source or validity of the conflicting information. For example, one may not accept data about teen smoking from the Tobacco Institute or gun safety from the National Rifle Association. Second, a person may reduce dissonance by finding new supportive or consonant information or sources. For example, one may reason that it is far better to be a little overweight than to keep smoking. Or an individual may disregard messages that drinking alcohol has risks, focusing instead on studies that suggest that drinking wine reduces the likelihood of heart attacks.[9]

Festinger and other dissonance theorists also account for the possibility of complete denial.[10] Our capacity to compartmentalize actions and words can leave many of us blissfully untroubled by our contradictions.[11] Self-awareness requires a level of analytical rigor that is unevenly spread across our species. Even so, the predictive power of dissonance theory remains one of the most compelling of all persuasion models.

Theory of Induced Discrepant Behavior

The most interesting variation on dissonance theory involves a strategy of *first requesting a new behavior* from an individual with the goal of creating a dissonance gap that separates the individual from prior attitudes. The **theory of induced discrepant behavior** proposes that we naturally want to lessen the discrepancy between a new behavior we have been *encouraged* (but not forced) to try out. The theory predicts that the new behavior will open up a dissonance gap that may result in diminishing the old attitude.

Consider several examples. If a person who has little interest in politics is asked by a friend to help distribute campaign pamphlets in a neighborhood, the theory predicts that the sheer act of behaving like a campaign worker is likely to *decrease* the friend's apathy, a genuine attitude shift. When we *willingly* take on a new behavior, it becomes part of our identity, sometimes putting pressure on us to abandon the older discrepant attitude that says "I don't do this." Having helped in the campaign means that the original apathy about politics must be altered. Hence, an attitude has been changed by an inducement to act out of sync with it.

We can see the theory of induced discrepant behavior at work in an award-winning documentary, *The Education of Shelby Knox*.[12] Knox was a high school junior in Lubbock, Texas, who argued that the school board needed to open its facilities to gay and lesbian classmates. The response from the board was "no." The denial of the use of facilities triggered city hall demonstrations in support of the LBGQ community. Counterdemonstrations also took place; an out-of-town group protested with placards suggesting AIDS was "God's Curse" for being homosexual. Shelby decided to join her friends in support of the students' Gay-Straight Alliance. Shelby's mother—who described herself as a conservative Christian Republican—tried to understand her daughter's emerging activism. But she was concerned to have her daughter out on a picket line alone and reluctantly marched with Shelby and others in the Gay-Straight Alliance. Ms. Knox's sign simply said "Judge Not.". The theory predicts that the inducement to support her daughter probably also had the effect of moving Ms. Knox toward the position that the group was advocating.

The authors have seen countless students take on speech or essay topics where they had to argue or defend a point of view. Even though initial interest in the topic may have been low, it was not unusual after the presentation to discover that the single most persuaded person in the room was the writer/speaker. Induced behaviors are powerful motivators for realigning related attitudes.

Marketing professionals use the same process. If you are a regular user of Brand A toothpaste but notice that Brand B is on sale at half price, you might be induced to try the sale item. The act of purchasing Brand B is a new behavior that is a little out of sync with your preference for Brand A. If Brand B works well, you now have a gap between your long-term preference and your recent buying behavior. Would you buy Brand B again? Probably. You have already taken on the behavior of a purchaser of that product. The old preference could yield to the new reality that either brand is acceptable.

It is important to remember that you can't force someone into a new behavior and expect to create dissonance. In fact, the *stronger* the threat of force, the *less* dissonance an individual may experience. Individuals must retain free choice to experience the sense that their behavior and beliefs or attitudes are not consistent.

Stimulus-Response Theory

A simple and well-known learning model also has relevance to persuasion. The most famous example of *stimulus response theory* is Pavlov's dog. Classical conditioning is a learning procedure in which a neutral stimulus is paired with a reflex response. Dogs naturally salivate when presented with food (a normal reflex response), but Pavlov discovered that he could trigger the same response with a neutral stimulus if the dogs learned to associate food with that stimulus. He rang a bell each time he fed the dogs. After repetitions of the procedure, the dogs learned an association between the bell and food. They would then salivate at the sound of the bell alone. The ringing triggered a conditioned (learned) response.

Learning theories center on the relationship between stimuli and responses. Infants enter the world with a clean slate. They *learn* what behavior is acceptable, what is right, and what not to do. Most learning theories assume reinforcement helps to cement a sought-after response.[13] Throughout life we learn to seek favorable rewards and to avoid unfavorable ones. Positive rewards reinforce certain attitudes and behavior. If we are told enough that we are good, beautiful, or smart, we begin to believe it and act accordingly. The stimulus of a teacher's praise reinforces the student's motivation to do good work. To the extent this linkage works, a *conditioned response* is a predictable outcome.

Robert Cialdini argues that we need mental shortcuts—fixed-action patterns—that work well most of the time (this topic is revisited in the section on elaboration likelihood theory). We use these mental shortcuts (*judgmental heuristics*) in making everyday decisions. For example, we are conditioned to equate expensive items with quality or social status. Named brands are preferred to generic brands. Much of the process of getting people to comply with requests and suggestions is based on these preprogrammed, automatic, shortcut responses to external stimuli.[14]

Research demonstrates that we are more likely to be attracted to those who hold similar attitudes. The stimulus is the discovery of shared attitudes; the response is attraction. Similar attitudes have a reward value for us because the interaction confirms our view of the world and related issues. Attitudes that are rewarded will grow stronger. People also make decisions by learning to associate consequences with proposals. The feelings become connected with the object. In the language of learning theory, we are conditioned to expect a particular result. Thereafter, we identify the proposal itself with our feelings about the consequences. Conditioning works by arousing a dislike or like without the necessity of repeating the consequences—just the mention of the object is sufficient.

Advertising uses this concept daily. When someone mentions Progressive or GEICO insurance, what images come to mind? The super-helpful Flo? An Australian gecko with perfect diction? These icons with cheeky humor keep the two brands near the top of the charts in terms of audience recognition—a form of stimulus-response. If you conducted a taste test in which you changed the labels of an expensive wine and a cheap wine, which do you think your friends would choose? Would the stimulus of an expensive label predispose them to favor that bottle? If you were purchased two paintings from a local artist and signed one Smith and the other the name of a hot new artist in Los Angeles, which do you think would receive more money at an auction? The same process is used when advertisers use a famous spokesperson. They hope we will suspend judgment and attach our good feelings about the celebrity (the stimulus) to their product. As a result, we respond to the person and not to the attributes of the product. The key is the power of association between objects and images.

Inoculation Theory

An *inoculation* message is a warning not to be taken in the communication that follows. The strategy of inoculation is entrenched in many forms of persuasion—from political campaigns to court trials to prevention messages in many health campaigns. The theory predicts that a persuader who delivers a warning about a future message from a different source inoculates an audience against that source's persuasive effects.[15] When trial lawyers begin their opening statements by noting that the other side "will try to convince you . . . " they are attempting to inoculate the jury. Likewise, when politicians "get out in front" of a problem by revealing a mistake they made years ago, they are engaged in inoculation. The rule of thumb is to admit the problem early, explain it, then move on in the hope that opponents will not have the advantage of being the first to raise the issue with voters.

Think of inoculation in terms of its metaphoric origins. Just as immunization can prevent disease by introducing a benign form that triggers the body's defenses, persuaders can introduce a problematic topic to lessen the impact of subsequent messages. Inoculation promotes resistance to persuasion. There is strong evidence to suggest, for example, that exposure of preteens to antismoking messages featuring inoculation elements ("Films, friends and the giant tobacco industry will try to convince you that smoking is cool.") work quite well.[16] It is less effective for reaching older teens, who have been barraged with warnings about sexual activity, driving, dating, drugs, and more. This problem introduces a second form of inoculation.

If we have heard too much about any topic, we can be immunized to resist future similar messages. By the time the average American has reached adulthood, there are few opportunities to deliver fresh warnings, especially on entrenched health or social issues such as smoking, binge drinking, gambling, excessive credit card use, and so on. The persuasion and counter-persuasion that bounces around popular culture on these topics may result in a generalized resistance to all social action campaigns.

Attribution Theory

Fritz Heider noted that it is human nature to try to make sense of the world and the behavior of others by assigning responsibility, blame, and motives.[17] *Attribution theory* is a mainstay of research in the social sciences, education, and the analysis of consumer behavior. We receive messages, decode them, and interpret them. By analyzing the broad situation or context of an action, *we attribute a motive, an intention or reason for a persuader's behavior.* Drama and storytelling engage the audience with invitations to consider *why* a character has done something. We are constantly reading each other's words and actions so that we can assign meaning to them. As the influential thinker Kenneth Burke reminded us, human action is purposive. We expect that we will be able to account for other people's actions by uncovering or learning their motivations.[18]

Even though they are often left unspoken, attributions of motives are a part of the subtext of all messages. There may be no direct reference to a source's motive in a message or conversation. But receivers will always make a side calculation of the message's value *in terms of the perceived motives of the source.* Put another way, the recipient of a persuasive message hears the message but also implicitly assigns reasons for the source's advocacy.[19] As a result, the theory guides persuaders to estimate likely attributed motives. For example, suppose you are a car salesperson and you begin a conversation with a potential customer by complimenting his or her clothing. How will the potential buyer interpret the compliment? It could be read as sincere admiration. But it is more likely to be interpreted as insincere—flattery to make a sale. The customer's attribution of the motive behind the compliment will affect the interpretation of all the communication that follows. The task for the would-be persuader is to calculate in advance the source motives likely to be assigned by the audience.

The process is deceptively complex; perceptions can vary and intentions are notoriously difficult to assign.[20] There are a multitude of variables that function dif-

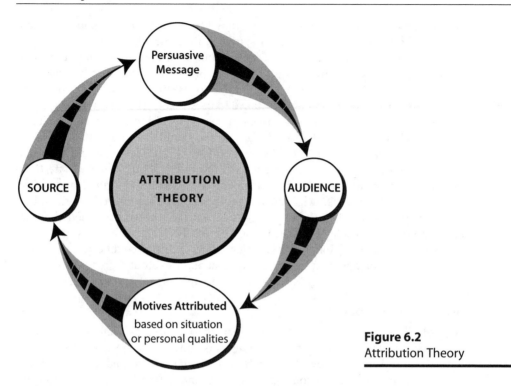

Figure 6.2
Attribution Theory

ferently depending on the individual. One person may praise a president for making a courageous defense of policy; another may condemn the very same effort as a collection of half-truths concealing a long-held bias.

There are two classifications of attributions: *situational* and *dispositional*.[21] *Situational attributions* focus on factors in the environment that might cause people to act in certain ways. Imagine that you are at a restaurant, and the experience is not a positive one. You waited a long time for the food, and it was cold when it arrived. The dish that was ordered turned out to be substantially different than what was described on the menu. A friend with you suggests that both of you leave a very small tip. He blames the server. But you note that the server seemed to do her job well. You think the kitchen is to blame. If so, an attribution of bad service would be incorrect. Situationally, there isn't much a server can do if a kitchen botches the order. "They did their best" or "That's what the job requires" are typical kinds of situational attributions.

Dispositional attributions identify internal, personal factors such as beliefs and attitudes that might affect people's behavior. A privileged individual with a lot of money might have little interest in addressing poverty because of a strong belief in the ability of everyone to work hard and get ahead. If we know a person well, we are usually confident that we can determine what motivates their thinking. As social creatures interacting with others, we do this all the time. Attribution theory reminds persuaders to consider likely audience attributions when designing a message.

Obviously, there is no certainty that we can formulate a correct or precise inter-pretation of an individual's motives or an audience's likely assignment of them. It is entirely possible that two individuals could attribute different motives to a single source. In such ambiguous situations, it is difficult to make predictions about how an event will play. For example, a friend has asked you to spend a weekend day working on a Habitat for Humanity building project. It makes a difference if you think his motives are altruistic: he wants to contribute to a good cause. The request looks different if less noble reasons can be attributed to your friend. Maybe he needs to solicit another volunteer to complete a service-learning requirement for graduation. But note that even if attributions can be ambiguous, the theory is not. It asserts that motives *will* be assigned that ultimately affect the salience of the message. Persuaders must make estimates of the most probable attributions.

The Boomerang Effect

When thrown correctly, the Australian boomerang follows an elliptical path and returns to the thrower. Most of us are not used to throwing an object and having it return on its own. The *boomerang effect* builds off this idea. It describes situations with unintended consequences—the persuasion attempt has *the reverse of its intended effect*, undermining the goals of the original message. The boomerang effect is one of the most interesting, frequent, and feared of all persuasive effects (see figure 6.3).

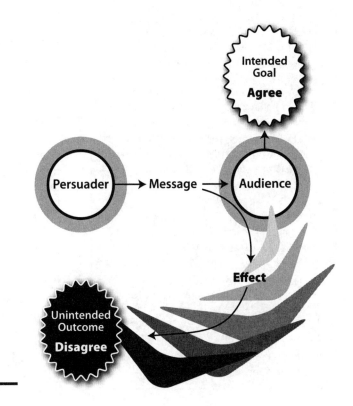

Figure 6.3
The Boomerang Effect

A study conducted several years ago at the University of Colorado at Boulder and the Children's Hospital in Boston found that teenagers who received pressure from peers and others to turn *down* the volume of their iPods actually turned them *up* instead. It was a reasonable assumption that peer-to-peer influence would produce a positive outcome. Peers would produce greater compliance with the request to listen at volume levels safe for the ear. But somehow peer pressure had the reverse of its intended effect.[22]

Message *boomerangs* are quite common. You might wonder who could be so ineffective as to trigger reactions 180 degrees from what they intended. In fact, all of us are sometimes winners of this unwanted prize. If you have ever found yourself saying, "I wish I hadn't said that," or "They looked at me like I was crazy," you probably experienced message boomerangs. In truth, it is not difficult to get mixed results from a message, which is why the model is useful. One message rarely fits all in a mixed audience. What works for some may have no effect on others and could alienate even more. As a student of persuasion, the author admits to some vicarious pleasure in watching the effect unfold on an unsuspecting advocate. When viewing an old or recent comedy film or series,[23] watch for messages that boomerang, leaving the character baffled by the consequences they never intended. But, of course, it's not fun if it happens to us.

Messages boomerang for many reasons: their designers have ignored needs or values of the target audience; they have offended audience attitudes; the source is unattractive; the advocate has picked the wrong words, arguments, or appeals.

The author lives along a narrow, single-lane road bordering a rural creek; at one time no speed limits were posted. In many spots, the bridges end in sharp

---

What Could Possibly Go Wrong?

Attempts to persuade are likely to produce unforeseen results. From a number of meta-studies we know that the odds of getting someone to alter their attitudes is probably no better than one in ten. Consider the following circumstances, all true.

- You show up to give an invited presentation to a group and (a) there is no screen for the PowerPoints you counted on, (b) none of the wall plugs in the room work, (c) there is no podium for your notes and (d) and a crew of ten men and nine machines are busy repaving the parking lot next to the room where you will speak. Under these circumstances, how effective do you think you will be?

- Your advertising agency has prepared a gay-friendly ad campaign that tested well and is now running on three national media outlets. Everyone on the creative team congratulated themselves on their progressive messages. Then a respected leader in the LGBTQ community criticizes the ads for "promoting old stereotypes." Condemnation of the campaign gains more attention than the inclusive message it attempted to convey.

- At a business lunch with a potential client you praise the good service you once got from a large national retailer, only to be chided for supporting a chain whose owners are "political reactionaries."

- You meet a new set of Michigan in-laws for the first time, not realizing that for this family of General Motors employees, your Ford parked in their driveway equates to a load of manure.

- You were promised a room full of people to hear your pitch, but there is a sea of empty chairs as you begin. Your contact notes afterword that the promise was only good for *last* month.

What we expect and what happens are not always the same things.

doglegs and can accommodate only one car at a time. The lane is also part of a regional trail. Walkers and cyclists share the space with cars, turkeys, deer, foxes, beavers and other slow-moving amphibians who live in the creek. The number of bridges and curves on the lane combined with the multiple users created the potential for accidents. The author thought that for everyone's safety, the township should post a maximum speed of 25 mph. He wrote letters documenting near misses and attended meetings. He defied the police to cross one narrow stone bridge doing more than just a few miles per hour. The outcome? The road is now littered with signs posting a significantly *higher* speed. The best intentions of even someone who has studied persuasion for years can go down in flames.

The effects of boomerangs are sometimes huge. Congress created the National Youth Anti-Drug Media Campaign in 1998. It appropriated almost $1 billion over six years for the campaign, which included TV and radio advertising. The targeted teen audience saw more than two advertisements per week discouraging them from initiating the use of illegal drugs, especially marijuana and inhalants.[24] To the surprise of all—and the embarrassment of the White House, which suppressed an evaluation report for two years[25]—the study found *increased* use of drug use among some teen groups exposed to the campaign's messages. The study concluded that some antidrug messages made teens more tolerant of drug use. What went wrong? The $43 million evaluation study found that higher exposure to messages leads to weaker antidrug norms.[26] The *more* antidrug messages from movie stars and others that the teens saw, the more they were likely to consider marijuana use as an identifying feature of their age group—a classic boomerang called *norming the problem*. The earnestness of the messages can seem sterile in relation to peer attitudes that celebrate degrees of rebellion.

Persuasion can be so difficult because it is hard to anticipate fully the meanings, associations, and effects of a given message. Most persuaders would be unhappy to learn that their messages had no effect on an audience. But at the boomerang effect reminds us that things can be worse. A result of little or no effect is more desirable than an audience in revolt.

Social Judgment Theory

Imagine that you have a friend who firmly believes that phases of the moon influence people's moods and how well they sleep. You may doubt their idea. But you may also discover that they are extremely committed to their attitude and that you will probably be unable to change it. **Social Judgment theory** is useful in such a setting. It helps to make estimates of how much change is possible, given what the theory calls an individual's "anchor position."

Social judgment theory grew out of the work of psychologist Muzafer Sherif,[27] who argues that people do not evaluate messages based on merit alone. People compare arguments with their current attitudes and then decide if they should accept the advocated position. The theory explores a key question: what is the *anchor position* for an individual, and how large is the anchor? It views attitudes and beliefs as existing on a continuum in which there is a range of acceptable positions, a range of neutral feelings, and a range of unacceptable positions. Ego involvement is a key variable. The more relevant an issue is to one's own world and self-image, the stronger the anchor opinion. When we perceive a contrast among attitudes, we see them as farther away from our anchor points. When we perceive attitudes as similar to ours, we assimilate them and view them as closer to our anchor points.

There are three important concepts to consider when analyzing how internal anchors affect attitude change: *latitudes of acceptance, rejection,* and *noncommitment* (see figure 6.4). On most issues, people can accept some variations from their own views—the *latitude of acceptance* describes the range of positions that would be approved. For example, many of those who are generally against abortion may favor exceptions in cases of rape, incest or protecting a mother's life. Persuasive messages that fall within the audience's latitude of acceptance are more likely to be successful. Messages that fall into the *latitude of noncommitment* are, by definition, not going to produce significant change. This may not be an exciting outcome, but it is realistic. With this category, the theory acknowledges resistance to change as a common effect. The most a persuader can hope is that, because of what Sherif calls the "assimilation effect," certain messages in this range may be perceived as similar to the anchor point. In contrast, the *latitude of rejection* is the cluster of positions that are objectionable. Messages in this category will not encourage attitude change; in fact, just the opposite often occurs. Messages that fall within this region may produce boomerangs.

It is important for persuaders to know where the latitude of acceptance ends and the latitude of rejection begins. For example, when does one person's free speech become another person's obscene language? When does one advocate's plea for equal opportunity employment become the receiver's perception of discriminatory preferences? If a person is highly ego-involved in an issue or topic, the latitude of rejection is quite large, and the latitude of noncommitment is small. Triggers against a willingness to change are activated when people who feel strongly about

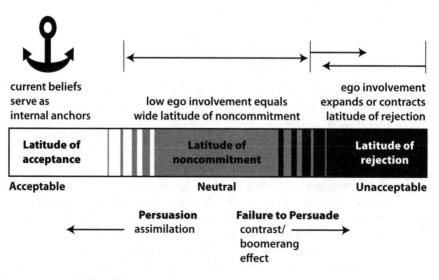

Figure 6.4 Social Judgment Theory

an issue hear a request that falls in their latitude of rejection. This is why people highly committed to one point of view are difficult to persuade.

According to Richard Perloff, this theory has special implications for politicians and political actors. Political communicators must moderate their messages for very diverse audiences, which can mean delivering an ambiguous message so that constituents are not offended.[28] Candidates are trying to gain support by sharing their views with the largest number of voters. In terms of social judgment theory, candidates want to encourage voters "to perceive that the candidate shares their position on the issue."[29] It is not surprising, therefore, that politicians so often straddle the fence on issues and appear to talk out of both sides of their mouths. From the perspective of social judgment theory, ambiguity and calculated vagueness may be a useful strategy. And not just for politicians. In the presence of others most of us temper our remarks on contentious issues. Moderation to stay in a peer group's latitude of acceptance is a kind of social glue. At its simplest, social judgment theory reminds us to look for and estimate the strength of anchor positions that exist in a setting. We can then judge the suitability of a message for its targeted audience.

Elaboration Likelihood Theory

Richard Petty and John Cacioppo developed a theory of persuasion that is both intuitive and absolutely essential for conceptualizing audience reactions to messages.[30] According to their *elaboration likelihood theory*, we process messages differently depending on how much mental energy we are willing to invest in the task of seeking understanding. Their model addresses questions about the levels of attention toward messages that receivers are willing to give. They defined two useful benchmarks along a continuum of personal interest ranging from *peripheral processing*, the low end of receiver involvement, to *central processing*, the high end (see figure 6.5) As Robert Cialdini states,

> You and I exist in an extraordinarily complicated environment; easily the most rapidly moving and complex that has ever existed on this planet. To deal with it, we need shortcuts. We can't be expected to recognize and analyze all the aspects in each person, event, and situation we encounter in even one day. We haven't the time, energy, or capacity for it. Instead, we must very often use our stereotypes, our rules of thumb, to classify things according to a few key features and then to respond without thinking when one or another of these trigger features is present.[31]

We process information in different ways, depending on our levels of interest or the amount of time available.

When a message is processed through peripheral routes, the receiver is not paying much attention and employs some simple decision rule to decide about the advocated position. The decision rule could be based on several variables: the relevance of the topic, communicator credibility or expertise, competition from other sources, and so on. In contrast, when a message is processed through the central processing route, the receiver is more interested and uses critical thinking skills to assess more aspects of the message. The central route involves extensive issue-relevant scrutiny; careful examination of the information contained in the message,

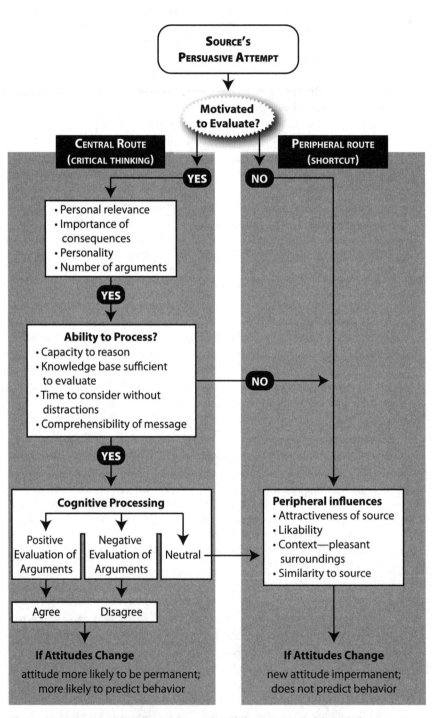

Figure 6.5   Central Peripheral Routes in Elaboration Likelihood Theory

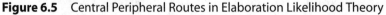

close reading of the message's arguments, consideration of the reliability of the source. Rather than testing whether the arguments presented in the message make sense (central route), those using the peripheral route tend to focus on characteristics of the speaker, such as likability or attractiveness.

The key element in the theory is contained in the word *elaboration*, which refers "to the extent to which a person scrutinizes the issue-relevant arguments contained in the persuasive communication."[32] Sometimes receivers will engage in extensive issue-relevant thinking, while at other times very little effort is extended. When conditions encourage people to engage in issue-relevant thinking, the likelihood of elaboration is high. Some of the factors include the receiver's mood, the degree to which the attitude is based on a mixture of positive and negative elements, the presence of multiple sources with multiple arguments, the personal relevance of the topic to the receiver, and the receiver's willingness to engage in critical thinking.[33]

Petty and Cacioppo argue that people want their attitudes to be consistent with behavior but also to be correct. We learn from our environment if our attitudes are right or wrong, acceptable or unacceptable. We must identify some standard for making judgments. For some, it may be a religious doctrine, political philosophy, or written documents. For many, acceptance results from comparing one's attitudes to those of others. We know, for example, that holding opinions like those held by a majority of others increases our confidence in the validity of our opinions.

Two key elements affect the probability of choosing one route over the other: ability and motivation.[34] The ability to elaborate is affected by our knowledge about the subject matter presented in the persuasive mes-

---

Our Noisy Lives

"Too much static on the line" might seem like a complaint whose time has passed. Digital media have eliminated the extraneous noise our grandparents used to complain about on their landlines. If we expand our definition of *static*, however, the very devices that freed us from bad connections have created a new category of noise. Various forms of digital devices assault us with more stimulation than we can accommodate. Thoughts become endangered species, easily overwhelmed by visual and aural noise. Talk to a friend while they are surfing the internet or texting someone, and you sense that there's definitely too much static on the line. A barrage of emails, cell messages, and tweets interrupt our powers of concentration at work and at home.

This has become a familiar and much-discussed issue, especially among older adults who see what they describe as the distractions and attention deficits of the young. To be sure, our children will survive, and no doubt help us tame the twin twenty-first century monsters of information overload and empathy fatigue. But it's also worth remembering that many enduring achievements in life tend to come in broad swaths of uninterrupted linear thinking. The mind works best when it has time to reflect about a challenge and to master its demands. We know this when we've finished reading a great novel, witnessed the performance of a sprawling but magnificent symphony, or absorbed the words of a provocative thinker. To reduce these efforts to anything less—because of a felt need to accommodate more truncated bits of information—produces mental static.

sage. Motivation is affected by our involvement with the issues presented—how important we believe the consequences of accepting the message will be to us. The number and variety of arguments presented also affect motivation. If we hear competing views, the central route may be the only means available to process and organize the information. One other factor influencing motivation is personality. Some people thrive on analyzing issues and weighing possibilities; others find the process stressful. The higher one's ability and motivation, the more likely the central route will be employed. If the issue is important but we don't feel qualified to assess the argument, we will seek more superficial cues from the situation.

We can also add one additional element that favors peripheral processing: time. It is an obvious but important point to remind ourselves that we generally have too many messages chasing us through a typical day. Numerous outlets and platforms want more attention than we have time to give. This problem grows every day, contributing to lives that are more distracted and less focused. We blame the pervasiveness of social media such as Twitter and Instagram for this time squeeze. But the problem is much larger than the growth of any single group of sources.[35] We exist in an *overcommunicated society*. Compared to prior generations, we have less patience to focus our attention on any one message for very long.[36]

Some issues will fall squarely in the central route while others will almost certainly be peripheral. For example, a parent of a teenager with a learner's permit could decide to search the internet for information about teenage driving. A parent who happens upon a website about cars going from 0 to 60 miles per hour in five seconds will probably process that information via the peripheral route (if at all). They are far more likely to use the central route to process information on a website that discusses the risks of serious injury for teens that drive without using seat belts.[37] By contrast, even responsible high schoolers may be inclined to process the warnings about seat belts peripherally, having been inoculated by previous exposure to many other safety messages.

Postulates from the theory include a number of important predicates for assessing how a message will be processed.

Postulates of the Elaboration Likelihood Theory of Persuasion

1. The underlying motivation of people is to hold correct attitudes.

2. People vary in the amount of issue-relevant elaboration in which they are willing or able to engage to evaluate a message.

3. Variables affect the amount of attitude change by (a) serving as persuasive arguments, (b) serving as peripheral cues, and/or (c) affecting the extent or direction of issue elaboration.

4. As motivation and/or ability to process argument decrease, peripheral cues become more important determinants of persuasion. Conversely, as argument scrutiny increases, peripheral cues become r less important determinants of persuasion.

5. Attitude changes that result mostly from central-route processing persist longer, more accurately predict behavior, and have greater resistance to counter-persuasion than attitude changes that result from peripheral processing.

Source: Richard Petty and John Cacioppo, *Communication and Persuasion: Central and Peripheral Routes to Attitude Change* (New York: Springer-Verlag, 1986), pp. 5–24.

As stated in postulate 5, the most consistent, powerful, long-term, and influential attitude change results from the central route of elaboration. This path is relatively permanent, resistant to counter-persuasion, and predictive of behavior. By contrast, under the peripheral route, attitude changes are more temporary, susceptible to counter-persuasion, and less predictive of behavior. Even so, especially in the cluttered and competitive environment of the mass media and internet, advocates may have no choice but to design messages for peripheral processors. Once a persuader begins to think in terms of this model, it becomes second nature to pause and wonder about how much motivation they can expect from a given audience.

The Motivated Sequence

Alan Monroe developed a sequential model to present psychologically satisfying message elements to an audience. The **motivated sequence** consists of five steps for organizing motivational appeals and supporting materials.[38] We think of it as a core model because there is otherwise little guidance for persuaders on how to sequence various message elements. In the motivated sequence, each step builds on the previous one, creating a series of consecutive stages that make a sensible whole.

The motivated sequence starts with *attention*. The first task of any persuader is to set the stage so that the audience is willing to focus on the issue or message. After gaining attention, the next step involves describing the *need* or problem, which is followed by *satisfaction* or solution of the need. These two stages are at the heart of the sequence. The two are linked by a core premise: the more we can convince others that a condition exists that needs a remedy, the more the persuasion will seem relevant and important. A proposal will languish unless it is preceded by a reminder of problems with the status quo. In the final two steps, the satisfaction stage is made concrete through *visualization*—framing the solution as it might work in the lives of audience members. A solution that seems to be a big step into the

ATTENTION — Attract audience interest

NEED — Show the need and describe the problem

SATISFACTION — Present the solution that satisfies the need

VISUALIZATION — Help audience see how they will benefit from the solution

ACTION — Request action as approval

Figure 6.6 Monroe's Motivated Sequence

unknown can be doable if we can visualize how it will work for us. The sequence closes by requesting *action*, asking the audience to take the first steps toward the suggested solution to the need.[39]

For example, a persuader might hope to convince members of an audience that their next pet should come from an animal shelter rather than from a pet store or breeder. Following the motivated sequence, the persuader would first get the audience interested in the topic. Pets not only create bonds with people, but our talk about them often forms bonds *between* people. Once the audience is focused on the topic, the next task is to explain the precarious existence of millions of dogs and cats living in shelters. There are more animals than potential rescuers, which results in many wonderful animals being euthanized. In a PSA from People for the Ethical Treatment of Animals, actress Charlize Theron points out a dilemma: "If you choose a dog from the mall, a dog you could have saved from the pound will die."[40] The statement efficiently links the need for change to its satisfaction, even for peripheral processors. The next stage is to help the target visualize how the adoption process works. Finding the right pet for the right family needs to be more than an impulse decision. On this topic, visualization might involve showing how a local shelter effectively matches animals to families. The final step in the sequence is the call to action. The action step seizes on changed attitudes or a new receptivity to the solution suggested, converting those attitudes into behaviors.

The motivated sequence is basic but useful because it can help identify why a message is sometimes not working very well. For example, the model tells us we will probably fail if we attempt to persuade an audience by proposing a solution and action without first showing a need for change. We tend to forget that problems that are real to us may be less apparent to others.

Theory of Motivated Reasoning

Leon Festinger developed the first of the theories we have considered here: cognitive dissonance theory. But Festinger also knew that predicting change in attitudes or behaviors was risky. He and his fellow researchers observed, "A man with a conviction is a hard man to change. Tell him you disagree and he turns away. Show him facts or figures and he questions your sources. Appeal to logic and he fails to see your point."[41] We close with a theory that addresses these circumstances.

The *theory of motivated reasoning* is essentially a model that explains one of the common psychological processes that produce resistance to change. The name of the theory suggests its premise: we search for validations of our current beliefs.[42] Our use of evidence is less for discovery than for confirmation.[43] People's preferences affect their beliefs, how evidence is gathered, how arguments are processed, and how memories are recalled. Our goals guide our reasoning to preferred conclusions. Threats to self-perception are a potent trigger to motivated reasoning. As the cultural critic Michael Bérubé has noted, "It is very difficult to get a man to understand something when his tribal identity depends on his not understanding it."[44]

The potential dissonance of *dis*confirming evidence is perhaps the most direct explanation for why we accept some examples and testimony and reject others. Motivation to reduce cognitive dissonance can lead to biased information processing. Hot weather in the summer confirms what most understand as rapid climate change. An

unusually cold winter discon-
firms it for climate change
skeptics. Of course climate science is more complicated than
either statement allows. Indeed, colder weather in a particular location may actually
indicate a warming planet.[45]

Psychologists sometimes
call this kind of thinking *confirmation bias*, the tendency for
people to accept information
that confirms their beliefs
while avoiding evidence that
contradicts them. Rhetoricians refer to *fantasy themes*
that are constructed by individuals to make sense of ambiguous or confusing realities.
As Earnest Bormann notes,
we create fantasies which involve "imaginative interpretations of events" that "satisfy
psychological or rhetorical
needs."[46] A person may believe Russian aircraft are infe-
rior to those made in the
West, latching on to examples
of airline accidents that confirm the fantasy. When we
talk about living in *information bubbles.* we are describ-

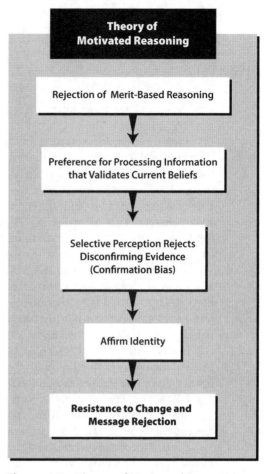

Figure 6.7   Theory of Motivated Reasoning

ing the effects of motivated reasoning. A consumer may favor Fox News or *The
Guardian* for a particular perspective on the news of the day that matches their
own. One of the civic challenges Americans face is that most of us have retreated to
sources that share our views. A neutral Associated Press story is likely to be less
prominent today than in mid-twentieth-century newspapers.

We are all susceptible to selective perception, to reasoning in the service of self-
interest. Humans are not cameras. Nor do we transfer information to others in the
ways that computers do: one file delivered to another unaltered and unchanged.
We are naturally inference makers and interpreters. Within those impulses there is
ample space to put a spin on a topic that conforms to the world as we need to see it.
A pattern of not seeing poses problems for the persuader, who may offer compelling ideas and evidence that are worthy of acceptance.

Motivated reasoning is a reminder of why persuasion is so difficult. Motivation
affects how receivers process information. If a proposal does not match a favored

position, they will not necessarily honor the rules of logic, science, or even common sense. Sometimes selective perception becomes a vehicle for self-deception.

SUMMARY

After exploring the nature of attitudes and behaviors that persuaders seek to alter, we highlighted models and theories that assist in making predictions about possible outcomes. Theories allow us to imagine the internal processes that take place when processing messages and appeals.

Among the most potent of the ten persuasion theories we considered are those that deal with consistency. Dissonance theory and its related cousin, the theory of induced discrepant behavior, assume that attitudes or behavior can change when it becomes apparent to an individual that there is an inconsistency in his or her attitudes. Dissonance is mental stress. We seek to reconstruct our attitudinal or behavioral selves when we become conscious of our inconsistencies.

Stimulus-response theory explores the fundamental idea of conditioning. Associations and connections that build up through systems of reward and repetition establish deep roots as core values and beliefs that lead to attitudes. Any single lifetime is governed by elaborate systems of rewards and conditioning. Schools, family, work, and peers all function as agents of socialization—reminding us that persuasion is intimately tied to the idea of learning itself.

Inoculation theory offers explanations for resistance to persuasion. Inoculation predicts failure or limited effects when others offer warnings that arm audiences against accepting subsequent messages. In the communication-saturated environment of modern life, many such counter-persuasive messages come our way, making us wary and more resistant. Attribution theory explains a related phenomenon: the desire to make sense of a message by calculating the intent or motivation of its source.

Several theories posit relationships in the ways we process information. Elaboration likelihood theory recognizes that we sometimes apply full reasoning powers to messages; other times we rely on automatic responses that have worked in the past. Social judgment theory alerts us to the anchors and reference points we use for analyzing how far we are willing to stretch to accommodate a new attitude or behavior. A persuader who pushes too far is likely to force a person beyond their latitude of acceptance, resulting in a failed attempt. Push much too far, and the result may be the boomerang effect: the interesting if sometimes frustrating phenomenon that can push audiences in the opposite direction from the persuader's goal.

The chapter closed with an overview of two useful frameworks for assessing messages. The motivated sequence offers a simple checklist of goals that—when combined in a single message—produce a psychologically satisfying series of message elements, where each step builds on the one before it. The theory of motivated reasoning explains why messages might not resonate with audiences. Selective perception can override the best efforts of persuaders.

These key ideas make us smarter analysts of messages. But they are by no means fully predictive. In the middle of our review of key models we introduced the idea of boomerangs—messages that do not work as intended or predicted. As Leon Festinger noted, people do not always react as we would expect they would.

A statement meant to produce cognitive dissonance could produce anger instead. An appeal designed to reassure a target regarding the goodwill of the source could—for reasons that are sometimes hard to fathom—make a person *more* suspect. Persuasion is sometimes like a poker game where the wildcard of a boomerang shows up at the least expected moment.

QUESTIONS AND PROJECTS FOR FURTHER STUDY

1. In describing the theory of motivated reasoning, the authors note that we "are not cameras." In light of the theory, what does this mean? Why do humans see more than the shutter captures?

2. Imagine that you are working on a health campaign with the goal of getting parents who smoke to never light up around their children. The risks of second-hand smoke are now well known. This task would seem to invite appeals producing dissonance that might create the behavior change you seek. Write out one of these appeals and explain why it may or may not work.

3. Attribution theory describes why assumed motives in an advocate matter. Cite an example where you think you can predict how an effort to persuade will be received based primarily on anticipated audience attributions of the source's motives.

4. We offer the following example of a boomerang in this chapter:

   > A study conducted several years ago at the University of Colorado at Boulder and the Children's Hospital in Boston found that teenagers who received pressure from peers and others to turn down the volume of their iPods actually turned them *up* instead. It was a reasonable assumption that peer-to-peer influence would produce a positive outcome: greater compliance with the request to listen at volume levels safe for the ear. But somehow peer pressure had the reverse of its intended effect.

   Account for some of the reasons the boomerang might have occurred.

5. Recall from your own experience a case of a message boomerang. What happened in the message that contributed to its failure?

6. Visit a university health center. Assess several of the brochures in the waiting room using the elaboration likelihood model. Would the messages work for peripheral processors? Do they provide enough detail and compelling reasons for central processors?

7. Inoculation is a common strategy when political candidates have engaged in embarrassing behavior that they must confess. Suppose a candidate for an important office had several convictions for "driving under the influence" when he was a college student. What might the candidate say about it? And what would be the theory's justification for "getting this on the record" many months before the election?

ADDITIONAL READING

Robert B. Cialdini, *Influence: Science and Practice*, 5th ed. (Boston: Allyn & Bacon, 2009).
Joel Cooper, *Cognitive Dissonance: Fifty Years of a Classic Theory* (Los Angeles: Sage, 2007).

James Price Dillard and Lijiang Shen (Eds.), *The Sage Handbook of Persuasion*, 2nd ed. (Los Angeles: Sage, 2013).

Martin Fishbein and Icek Ajzen, *Belief, Attitude, Intention, and Behavior* (Reading, MA: Addison-Wesley, 1975).

Robert Gass and John Seiter, *Persuasion, Social Influence, and Compliance Gaining*, 5th ed. (New York: Routledge, 2014).

Eric S. Knowles and Jay A. Linn (Eds.), *Resistance and Persuasion* (Mahwah, NJ: Erlbaum, 2004).

Stephen Littlejohn, Karen Foss, and John Oetzel, *Theories of Human Communication, Eleventh Edition* (Long Grove, Ill.: Waveland, 2017).

Richard Perloff, *The Dynamics of Persuasion*, 4th ed. (Hillside, NJ: Taylor & Francis, 2010).

Richard Petty and John Cacioppo, *Communication and Persuasion: Central and Peripheral Routes to Attitude Change* (New York: Springer-Verlag, 1986).

Notes

1. Quoted in Marten Vansteenkiste and Kennon Sheldon, "There's Nothing More Practical than a Good Theory: Integrating Motivational Interviewing and Self-Determination Theory," *British Journal of Clinical Psychology, 45*, 2006, p. 63.

2. Martin Fishbein and B. Raven, "The AB Scale: An Operational Definition of Belief and Attitude," *Human Relations, 15* (February 1962), p. 42.

3. Robert Gass and John Seiter, *Persuasion, Social Influence, and Compliance Gaining*, 5th ed. (New York: Routledge, 2014), p. 41–46.

4. Stephanie Rosenbloom, "Got Twitter? You've Been Scored," *The New York Times*, June 26, 2011, Week in Review, p. 5.

5. Russell Fazio and David Roskos-Ewoldsen, "Acting as We Feel" in Richard Petty and John Cacioppo (Eds.), *Communication and Persuasion* (New York: Springer-Verlag, 1986), pp. 74–82.

6. Richard Perloff, *The Dynamics of Persuasion*, 4th ed. (Hillsdale, NJ: Taylor & Francis, 2010), p. 85.

7. Leon Festinger, *A Theory of Cognitive Dissonance* (Evanston, IL: Row, Peterson, 1957), p. 3.

8. Cynthia Carr, "An American Secret," *New York Times Magazine*, February 26, 2006, p. 110.

9. Robert Gass and John Seiter identify several additional strategies for resolving apparent inconsistencies. One is called *bolstering*, which amounts to a rationalization of differences. A fish-eating "vegetarian" may believe that harvesting of fish is not as cruel as the slaughtering of cattle or fowl. The possible inconsistency is denied with an explanation they consider defensible. *Differentiation* is another kind of rationale where ideas are shown to be dissimilar. Thus, the fish eater may claim that most fish do not feel pain or are closer to plants than to possibly sentient animals like cows or pigs. Gass and Seiter, p. 59.

10. For a more nuanced view of dissonance theory, see Eddie Harmon-Jones, "A Cognitive Dissonance Theory Perspective on Persuasion," in James Dillard and Michael Pfau, eds, *The Persuasion Handbook: Developments in Theory and Practice, First Edition,* (Thousand Oaks CA: Sage, 2002), pp. 99–116.

11. See, for example, Duane Wegner, Richard Petty, Natalie Smoak, and Leandre Fabrigar, "Multiple Routes to Resisting Attitude Change," in Eric Knowles and Jay Linn (Eds.), *Resistance to Persuasion* (Mahwah, NJ: Lawrence Erlbaum, 2004), pp. 13–38.

12. *The Education of Shelby Knox*, video documentary by Marion Lipschutz and Rose Rosenblatt, InCite Pictures, 2005.

13. Michael Burgoon, Frank Hunsaker, and Edwin Dawson, *Human Communication*, 3rd ed. (Thousand Oaks, CA: Sage, 1994), p. 188.

14. Robert B. Cialdini, *Influence: Science and Practice*, 5th ed. (Boston: Allyn & Bacon, 2008), pp. 6–10.

15. For a detailed overview of the theory see Josh Compton, "Inoculation Theory" in James Price Dillard and Lijiang Shen (Eds.), *The Sage Handbook of Persuasion*, 2nd ed. (Los Angeles: Sage, 2013), pp. 220–236.

16. Ibid.

17. Fritz Heider, *The Psychology of Human Relations* (Hillsdale NJ: Erlbaum, 1958) pp. 79–124.

18. Kenneth Burke, *A Grammar of Motives* (Berkeley: University of California Press, 1969), p. xv–xvi.

19. See, for example, Kelly Shaver, *An Introduction to Attribution Processes* (Hillsdale, NJ: Lawrence Erlbaum Associates, 1983).

[20] See, for example, Gary C. Woodward, *The Rhetoric of Intention in Human Affairs* (Lanham, Md.: Lexington Books, 2013).

[21] Philip Zimbardo, Ebbe Ebbesen, and Christina Maslach, *Influencing Attitudes and Changing Behavior* (Reading, MA: Addison-Wesley Publishing, 1977), p. 74.

[22] "New iPod Listening Study Shows Surprising Behavior of Teens," *Insciences*, February 18, 2009, http://insciences.org/article.php?article_id=2517

[23] For examples, see *The Awful Truth* (1937) or *A Night at the Opera* (1935) or HBO's *Curb Your Enthusiasm*.

[24] Robert Hornik, Lela Jocobsohn, Robert Orwin, Andrea Piesse, and Graham Kalto, "Effects of the National Youth Anti-Drug Media Campaign on Youth," *American Journal of Public Health, 98*(12), December, 2008, pp. 2229–2236.

[25] Ryan Grim, "A White House Drug Deal Gone Bad," *Slate*, September 7, 2006, http://www.slate.com/articles/health_and_science/science/2006/09/a_white_house_drug_deal_gone_bad.html

[26] "Evaluation of the National Youth Anti-Drug Media Campaign: 2004 Report of Findings, Executive Summary," Department of Health and Human Services, June, 2006, http://archives.drugabuse.gov/initiatives/westat/NSPY2004Report/ExecSumVolume.pdf

[27] See Muzafer Sherif and Carl Hovland, *Social Judgment: Assimilation and Contrast Effects in Communication and Attitude Change* (New Haven, CT: Yale University Press, 1961).

[28] Perloff, p. 66.

[29] Ibid., p. 146.

[30] Richard Petty and John Cacioppo, "The Elaboration Likelihood Model of Persuasion," in *Communication and Persuasion* (New York: Springer-Verlag, 1986).

[31] Cialdini, p. 7.

[32] Petty and Cacioppo, p. 7.

[33] Daniel O'Keefe, *Persuasion: Theory and Research*, 3rd Edition (Thousand Oaks, CA: Sage, 2015), p. 148–170.

[34] Stephen Littlejohn, Karen Foss, and John Oetzel, *Theories of Human Communication*, 11th ed. (Long Grove, IL: Waveland, 2017).

[35] See, for example, Sherry Turkle, *Alone Together: Why We expect More from Technology and Less from Each Other* (New York: Basic Books, 2011), pp. 151–170.

[36] See Nicholas Carr, *The Shallows: What the Internet Is Doing to Our Brains* (New York: Norton, 2011), pp. 58–77.

[37] According to the National Highway Transportation Safety Administration, highway accidents are the largest single cause of death for teenagers, who are also less likely to use seat belts. http://www.nhtsa.gov/Driving+Safety/Teen+Drivers

[38] Kathleen M. German, Bruce Gronbeck, Douglas Ehninger, and Alan Monroe, *Principles of Public Speaking*, 18th ed. (Boston: Pearson, 2013), p. 222.

[39] Ibid., pp. 222–223.

[40] "Oscar Winner Charlize Theron Exposes Puppy-Mill Cruelty," People for the Ethical Treatment of Animals, YouTube, June 12, 2009, http://www.youtube.com/watch?v=NtS1gSBKyLw

[41] Leon Festinger, Henry W. Riecken, and Stanley Schachter, *When Prophecy Fails* (Wilder, 2011), p. 3.

[42] See, for example, Ziva Kunda, "The Case for Motivated Reasoning," *Psychological Bulletin, 108*(3), November, 1990, pp. 480–498.

[43] For further explorations of this idea in terms of current political attitudes, see Jonathan Haidt, *The Righteous Mind* (New York: Pantheon, 2012).

[44] Michael Bérubé quoted in Judith Warner, "Free Fact Science," *The New York Times Magazine*, February 25, 2011, http://www.nytimes.com/2011/02/27/magazine/27FOB-WWLN-t.html?_r=0

[45] See "Why Global Warming Can Mean Harsher Winter Weather," *Scientific American*, N.D., https://www.scientificamerican.com/article/earthtalks-global-warming-harsher-winter/

[46] Ernest Bormann, *The Force of Fantasy* (Carbondale: Southern Illinois Press, 1985), p. 5.

7

Persuasion, Audiences, and Social Learning

> True, the rhetorician may have to change an audience's opinion
> in one respect; but he can succeed only insofar as he yields
> to that audience's opinions in other respects.[1]
>
> —Kenneth Burke

The psychological explanations of persuasion discussed in the preceding chapter address the internal processes that occur within individuals when considering messages. But a different tradition in persuasion offers explanations with roots in *social* effects. Social theorists look at the power of community norms and values in shaping attitudes and behaviors. They start with the premise that we are largely what our contact with others has made us.

The sociologist Émile Durkheim noted that our world is made up of networks of formal and informal groups. Over a lifetime we acquire and share attitudes common to those groups.

> Sentiments born and developed in the group have a greater energy than purely individual sentiments. A man who experiences such sentiments feels himself dominated by outside forces that lead him and pervade his milieu. He feels himself in a world quite distinct from his own private existence. . . . Following the collectivity, the individual forgets himself for the common end and his conduct is oriented in terms of a standard outside himself.[2]

The familiar claim that we are social animals is thus basic to the study of persuasion. By nature we are learners, adaptors, and imitators. We accept what others model in their words and actions. And we like to think we have succeeded with others when our communication produces something approaching what John Durham Peters idealizes as the "direct sharing of consciousness."[3]

This chapter explores the multifaceted processes of identifying with and appealing to others, beginning with a reminder that many of our attitudes are inherited and modified through daily interaction. Most of our efforts here will focus on the calculations and risks of aggregating individuals into audiences, especially those on social media. As we shall see, there are many ways we can miss the mark. We conclude the chapter by considering several models that help conceptualize the varied relationships that can shape how individuals respond to appeals.

A Conceptual Baseline: Social Learning

Among the core principles common to almost all forms of persuasion is the idea of **social learning**, sometimes also called *peer influence* or *social proof*. It is deceptively simple but essential to an audience-centered approach to persuasion. The principle states that what we believe or do usually arises from learning the norms of others. We have a natural interest in conforming to what others expect, since the rewards for compliance are almost always greater than the costs of being an outsider. Robert Cialdini notes that "we view a behavior as correct in a given situation to the degree that we see others performing it."[4] Whether we are deciding if a topic is appropriate conversation in a restaurant, if we should laugh out loud in a movie theater, or if we should voice our opinion about a politician, we often take our cues from other people. We will make fewer mistakes and take fewer risks by acting in accord with social evidence than by behaving contrary to it. Culturally speaking, when a lot of people are doing something, it is almost by definition the right thing to do. We usually display attitudes and behaviors as confirmations of our membership in a community. We expect that our adherence to the norms of the group will keep us in good standing.

Social learning is often defined in negative terms, as when parents worry about the bad habits their children have picked up from their peers. But as Tina Rosenberg notes, positive peer pressure may be the most effective route to moving people to better choices and behaviors. She refers to the *social cure*—helping people obtain what they most care about: the respect of their peers. There may be no better route to persuasion than the immersion of an individual in a group with a commitment to the new attitude you want them to share.

> Identification with a new peer group can change people's behavior where strategies based on information or fear have failed. . . . The social cure is a natural solution to help people take care of their own health—to encourage them to accomplish the difficult tasks of avoiding risky sex; abstaining from cigarettes, alcohol, and drugs; losing weight; getting exercise and following doctors' orders. But it also has been successfully applied to problems in fields as diverse as political change, university education, organized religion, criminal justice, poor-country economic development, and the art of war.[5]

The point is obvious but important. The inability to learn the scripts of daily interaction—or our resistance against pressures to do so—usually results in social isolation. Novelists and screenwriters give us heroes and protagonists who push back against what they perceive as the oppressive conformity of adaption. Narratives of innovators like Steve Jobs, Jeff Bezos, and Alan Turing have often followed this path.[6] Characterizations of these kinds of individualists are appealing—perhaps because we can vicariously share their defiance of convention without having to pay the price of exclusion. But in everyday life deviance from any common social norm usually comes at a high price.

The socialization process is complex and sometimes contradictory, as illustrated by the role of alcohol in our society. Alcohol is used to celebrate life's various transitions and achievements, as a reward for a difficult day, or—in the case of many college students—a rite of passage sanctioned by their peers. At the same time, our society spends millions of dollars constructing messages that warn about the costly social effects of heavy alcohol use. Universities, for example, have hired people to help curb alcohol abuse, which in one study affected thirty-one percent of all undergraduate students.[7]

One of the most interesting approaches to the culture of drinking is to resocialize students by giving them statistical information on the actual attitudes and behaviors of other students. Called *social norms marketing,* the idea is to use real data in ads and posters that confirm most of their peers are only moderate drinkers and that binge drinking is aberrant, unusual, and potentially offensive. These campaigns seek to persuade students that they have overestimated the extent to which similar others consume alcohol. Inviting a group to reconsider the benchmarks of others' attitudes is a sound strategy, even though young adults are notoriously difficult to reach.

Social learning is also increasingly relevant today as the best explanation for what is driving the peer-to-peer influence built into most forms of social media. Outlets like Snapchat or Facebook make it easy to display our values, at least those we feel comfortable sharing with others. Similarly, the act of liking a person, product, or company publicizes potentially persuasive associations.

AUDIENCES: THE GENERATIVE FORCES OF PERSUASION

We can't forget the fact that persuasion must be oriented to others. Understanding the process of advocacy would be impossible without the idea of the audience. The earliest conceptions of persuasion assumed the presence of a well-understood group of receivers for whom appeals could be created.[8] We understand that persuasion is directed to someone and that its message must satisfy some of the needs and match the attitudes of a specific individual or a group of individuals. It is the rare individual who does not wonder if they have captured the interest of another, if their performance was good enough, and if they acted properly.

As we noted in the preface of this book, the twenty-first century has made the very idea of the audience problematic. It's a term that implies singularity: a defined and knowable group that will receive a message. The simple term, however, involves complex realities. Some understand it as indicating an imagined collection of receivers.[9] Others conceive of a universal audience: a group that has the potential to understand reasonable ideas and reasoned arguments.[10] Still others think in terms associated with commercial media: that audiences can be measured, quantified, and demographically known. There are huge markets for firms that provide metrics to businesses to help them reach target audiences.[11] For example, a prosecutor can hire a consulting firm to help with the jury selection process. If the defendant is a banker, the profile of the ideal juror who might vote for a conviction includes "someone who works in retail, makes less than $30,000 a year and, frequently changes employers." Those factors predict a distrust of financial institutions that might make it easier to get a conviction.[12] In a simpler vein, Gillette mails sample razors to men turning 18. The idea of reaching this target audience is a good one, but only if the mailing list is completely accurate. Instead, some older women and girls also receive the samples with a message that invites them to "become a man" with their first "real shave."[13]

The Challenge of Finding Homogenous Audiences

The concept of the audience assumes we can group individuals into cohesive units. We depend heavily on the idea of *homogeneity*—an expectation that individuals share some key attitudes and preferences and *demographic* similarities (age, sex, income, region of residence, interests, gay versus straight, and so on). Media outlets often sell their audiences to advertisers based on some of these features. And virtually every music, film, and television producer is convinced they know their niche or market. Even so, the concept rarely works as well in fact as it does in theory. Recall the conclusions from James Webster and Patricia Phalen cited in the first chapter: "audiences are not naturally occurring 'facts,' but social creations."[14]

If a group of people voluntarily gather in the same space at the same time, we might assume some aspects of homogeneity. However, the motives of those who self-select themselves into the same group can be surprisingly diverse. What common personality or demographic features would likely be present in a group gathered in a university theater to hear a retired U.N. Secretary General? We might make some guesses, but a survey of demographic features would likely reveal far more than our generalizations. In the case of the campus speaker, many come to support a leader they admire; others come as skeptics. Some may have tagged along with a friend, and some attend because of a requirement of one of their classes.

What are the common characteristics of a viewer of a YouTube video? It would be a huge mistake to assume that the billion-plus users *a day* are demographically similar.[15] The idea of the audience was born in a simpler period. Aristotle wrote his text, *Rhetoric*, with an eye on a few hundred citizens of a small city, meeting in the same place at the same time. In the late 1700s, participatory democracy was intended for a very restricted citizenry of white male landowners. Today, by contrast, audiences are sometimes defined in the millions, with wide demographic variations.

Structurally, the largest of our social and mass media made

> ### Digital Contagion
>
> One striking feature of modern life is how quickly millions of people can be connected to a local story filled with drama and emotion. In the first half of the last century, American radio and newspaper consumers voraciously devoured stories about children who had fallen down wells or suddenly disappeared. Today the digital media river makes it easy to link or re-post content that goes viral instantly, promoting feelings of anger and occasional sympathy. The empathy we feel for a victim is usually linked with disgust for the person seen as responsible. Proportionality is discarded in favor of expressing outrage in a simplified morality play.
>
> YouTube stories illustrate this kind of digital contagion, where the victims in two cases happened to be much-admired animals. In 2015 a Minnesota dentist paid $50,000 for a guided trophy-hunting safari in Zimbabwe, which ended in the killing of a well-known male lion name Cecil. A year later a zoo official in Cincinnati was forced to shoot Harambe, a silverback gorilla, to rescue a child who fell into the primate's habitat.
>
> World reaction to the dentist's behavior was swift and vicious, forcing him to close his practice and to go into hiding. Reactions to the death of Harambe were mostly directed at the mother, who momentarily lost sight of her young son before he fell. The woman received thousands of hate messages on social media sites, despite the fact that authorities declined to call the case anything more than an unfortunate accident. Both cases are reminders of the power of digital contagion in a world with an estimated 3.2 billion wired inhabitants.

diverse audiences a fact of life. Joshua Meyrowitz's study of modern media identifies surfing on the internet as a factor making it easy for individuals to eavesdrop on messages intended for others.[16] Cable and streaming facilitate access to messages intended for narrow demographic segments. For example, Lifetime television and other similar networks are billed as media for women. But they exist only one click away from very different television content. The result is that men consume them as well. This audience fluidity is even more obvious with social media, where it is possible for mass audiences to form and dissipate at rates that make the idea of a set schedule of television programs seem hopelessly "old school."

Even with these challenges, it is helpful to identify at least three distinct types of audiences: two that persuaders plan for and one that is sometimes beyond the ability of the persuader to control. *Primary audiences* are those that the advocate wishes to reach; for example, an inoculation campaign to discourage taking up smoking might target adolescents. *Secondary audiences* form an acceptable outer ring around the target audience; the message may be relevant for this group as well. An antismoking advocate may welcome the attention of parents to a message designed for teens. Eavesdropping extends the reach of the message, but in a useful way. The third type of audience is potentially more problematic for the advocate. An *unintended audience* is a group or community that may react negatively to the message and possibly undermine its effectiveness. Difficulties with unintended audiences arise typically when a message targeted to one group is reported via mass or social media to a second group with different sensibilities or expectations. They may take offense to what the message says.

The results that come with messages reaching unintended audiences may be humorous. In the classic farce *The Naked Gun* (1988), bumbling inspector Frank Drebin concludes a speech to a large gathering and then forgets to remove his wireless public-address microphone before visiting the restroom. But the results can also be very consequential. The massive computer hack into Sony and Columbia Pictures' computers at the end 2013 is one example. WikiLeaks compounded the problem by publishing 30,000 company documents that included health information about employees, their social security numbers, and their phone numbers as well as 173,000 employee emails.[17] WikiLeaks founder Julian Assange ignored the presumed confidentiality of communications of an organization outside of government. With more and more cases like this, documents leaked to unintended audiences have become a common source of news and a peculiar form of public entertainment. As we become voyeurs of stolen content fenced to the rest of us through eager-to-publish media, the goal of isolating audiences is less easily achieved.

Digital and Social Media Audiences

Digital media tend to make traditional persuader-persuadee roles more permeable. We are sometimes the advocate and sometimes the target. With peer-to-peer messaging, the roles can be easily switched and difficult for advocates to assess.[18]

To be sure, persuaders attempting to energize individuals or connect them to each other have enormous opportunities through the use of all forms of digital media. It is now easy for advocates with particular interests to find like-minded people who share their passions. Distance is no longer a crippling problem. Individuals anywhere can be mobilized and engaged through various outlets that are often checked daily and sometimes hourly. If you have recently joined a group intent on gathering members to work for any specific cause, you won't be surprised that the first items shared are email addresses and mobile phone numbers. Those are then linked to sites or listserves that can be the source of a chain of influence. As this is written, for example, the loose national movement Indivisible has organized groups in many states to push back against the political agenda of the Trump administration. Individual meet-ups of groups within the movement are maintained through specific social media messages.[19]

Political campaigns illustrate how careful strategists have become in delivering microtargeted messages that stay below the radar of the news media or unintended audiences who would be offended. Since Donald Trump won the presidency by working mostly outside of traditional political structures, the 2016 election may be an outlier. It's also possible that reality television and Twitter are now beachheads for someone intent on a national political career. We simply don't know how future electoral politics will unfold.

More conventional was the Obama campaign for the presidency in 2012, which used a traditional audience-building structure. The campaign created a megafile that merged information from pollsters, fund-raisers, field workers, consumer databases, social-media and mobile contacts, and voter files. The metric-driven campaign helped raise *$1 billion* by creating detailed models of voters that could be used to increase the effectiveness of everything from phone calls and door knocks to direct mailings, targeted TV ads, and the use of social media. The campaign used Facebook to help get out the vote. People who had downloaded an app were sent messages with pictures of their friends in swing states. They could click a button to urge those targeted voters to action—whether registering to vote, voting early, or going to the voting booth. About 20 percent of people contacted by a Facebook friend acted on the request, largely because the message came from someone they knew.[20]

Despite providing advantages in finding like-minded individuals, social media pose significant challenges. One is that most platforms are not exclusive to a specific set of intended receivers. As we have noted, ours is an age where individuals expect that they will be able to eavesdrop without difficulty on digital messages that straddle the line between public and private. Indeed, efforts by individual users to predict who will see their messages are often inaccurate. As Michael Bernstein and his research colleagues have noted:

> Our analysis indicates that social media users underestimate how many friends they reach by a factor of four. Many users who want larger audiences already have much larger audiences than they think. However, the actual audiences cannot be predicted in any straightforward way by the user from visible cues such as likes, comments, or friend count.[21]

In short, gathering an audience is easier than isolating an audience.

This problem can play out in ways that aren't always easy to predict. University graduates looking for work may be dismayed to discover that potential employers are using Facebook to research job candidates. One interviewer checked the Facebook entry of an applicant from Duke University. After seeing the photographs and summaries of sexual and drinking escapades, the interviewer was "shocked by the amount of stuff that she was willing to publicly display."[22] The scheduled interview was cancelled. The *public* nature varies depending on the specific site, but the unintended audiences of social media can seriously undermine an individual's or an advertiser's control of the message they want to deliver.[23]

More predictable are established websites that promote products, services, or ideas. The possibility of knowing a great deal about an audience exists for an online retailer mostly because many products are linked with certain demographic markers. Online behavioral tracking gathers the browsing histories and email interactions of web and mobile apps users. For example, if you purchase baby products, medical appliances, certain styles of music and so on, you become part of a database of collected information (zip code, sites visited, length of the visit, products viewed and purchased, articles read, etc.) that becomes part of your profile. Behavioral advertising consists of tracking online activities over time and delivering advertisements that match assumptions about the interests of the person tracked. The next time you type a search term, behavioral advertising triggers the display of links targeted to you. Because the pitch for the new product is based on information from a product you purchased or viewed, the pitch has an enormous advantage over random ads reaching an unmotivated audience. Interested readers are central processors. Tracking is common and effective,[24] even if sometimes off base (for example, if you purchased a product for someone else rather than yourself).

There is also increasing evidence of the same pattern in social media, but with an added problem: advertising messages that can easily become uncoupled from particular websites. With Google and other platforms, ads follow the user, sometimes creating unwanted associations. For example, when the department store Nordstrom advertises in a newspaper, it has a general sense of how that medium is perceived. But if Nordstrom advertises online, its banner ads may appear on sites with which it does not want to be associated. Nordstrom pulled its advertising from Google because the messages were following individuals to the right-wing and sometimes racist website, Breitbart. Similarly, banner ads from the *Guardian* newspaper appeared in YouTube videos from the Islamic State and on the websites of other racist groups. In both cases Google's automated ad placement put a company's message on a site with which they wanted no association.[25]

It is also increasingly common for audience research companies to buy information about users from retailers and social media sites. This *data mining* gathers personal details about users, which is then sold to political campaigns or others interested in microtargeting audience segments with messages that speak directly to their interests or concerns. For example, Facebook and Google came under harsh scrutiny in the spring of 2018 when it was revealed that a voter profiling company had made use of their user data without the knowledge of the users. The data was collected and sold to the Trump campaign, leading to an acknowledgment from Facebook's Mark Zuckerberg that selling personal data was "a breach of trust."[26] This case received a great deal of attention, but aside from differences over privacy issues it was not a singular event. There are many large-scale efforts at public persuasion that regularly use personal data from online sources to identify and target audiences for political and commercial purposes.

The gold standard for online advocacy is usually the **conversion rate** for a site as calculated by analytics services. This metric records the number of times per minute or day that a visitor to the site clicks through to make a specific purchase, a donation, or expression of interest.

Figure 7.1 Website
Audience Measurement

Common Audience Metrics for Internet Sites (calculated by hour, day, or week)	
Sessions	visits to the site
Average Session Duration . . .	minutes and seconds spent on the site
Page Views	number of pages seen
Bounce Rate	percentage of single-page visits
Conversions	percentage of purchasers or those who took a requested action

Is There a Common Center?

Regardless of an individual's political orientation, the 2016 presidential election illustrated that the United States was less united than perhaps at any other time since the Civil War. The growing political divide is an outgrowth of American individualism and our inherent suspicion of organizations, governments, and social movements. The fraying of a belief in a national community plays out daily in news stories dominated by oppositional messages and sometimes venomous attacks on those who see things differently. Americans can rightly ask if there are ideas and events that still unite us more than divide us. As a large and wealthy nation, are there shared core values that represent a common civic culture?[27] Some social theorists have noted that we are less a melting pot that dissolves our differences than a culture that simply accommodates them.[28] If that is the case, the idea of an audience of members sharing the same values and priorities may be easier to imagine than to achieve.

Even with these reservations, it is hard to think about persuasion very long without making estimates about how given groups exposed to the same message will respond. The idea of audiences with shared attitudes is still a necessary tool in the process of designing and measuring the effectiveness of appeals. But in the fluid informational climate that now dominates, persuaders must be cautious about making simplistic judgments about the features that audiences have in common.

THE AUDIENCE ANALYSIS PROCESS

Experienced persuaders usually try out their messages prior to the actual presentation. This auditioning may be informal, such as when we seek the reactions of friends to an upcoming presentation. Or it may be professionalized, as in the elaborate and expensive survey research and audience analysis studies that are commissioned by broadcasters, internet portals, content providers, and especially advertisers. At either end of the spectrum, the goals are generally the same: to identify the personal and demographic characteristics of targeted groups so that content will match their needs and interests. The benchmark for most advertisers is *cost per thousand* (CPM): the amount of money required to reach one thousand of the target audience via a specific media outlet. If the target is women between the ages of 16 and 25, and advertisement in *Cosmopolitan* will be a much better buy than an one in *Sports Illustrated*. If you are trying to sell pain relief products to seniors, CBS's *60 Minutes* will offer a lower CPM than NBC's *Saturday Night Live.*

Methods of testing messages and attitudes include phone interviews, internet questionnaires, *focus groups*, and *dial groups*. Focus groups are a small sample of a target audience (10 to 15 people) gathered together in one place to react to some form of persuasion. The goal is to get an honest assessment from the group about a product or planned pitch for it. A bonus feature of this method is that virtually every kind of persuader can afford to test messages in this way. Usually a neutral third-party group moderator convenes the group to keep the results from being skewed by the kinds of questions that are asked.

Various marketing, media, and testing organizations have refined this auditioning process with the use of dial groups. Screen Engine/ASI, for example, operates market research facilities in Hollywood designed to test audience responses to everything from television shows to game show hosts.[29] In a dial group test, a wide range of people are given free tickets to screenings. The participants begin their roles as audience members by completing questionnaires about their television-viewing and product-purchasing habits. They are then seated in the theater where each chair contains a ViewTrac control knob that can be turned to settings reflecting their opinions about the action unfolding on the screen (very good, good, normal, dull, and very dull). These controls are connected to a computer that provides a real-time graph of the audience's collective reaction to whatever is on the screen. A pilot for a new television series tests well if the collective response of the group is generally higher than the norm. Or, as is often the case, separate lines may indicate that men and women have different responses. In addition, the producers of a television pilot may learn that one character does not play well to the audience segment they want to reach.

Material that is already on the air or accessible via streaming services is measured by using phone surveys, black boxes attached to individual televisions, and household diaries that members agree to complete for several months. Newer systems can even track eye contact to determine if someone in a room is actually watching a given screen.[30]

Important as these varied tools are, the heart of the study of audiences from a persuasive point of view is the process for finding routes around potential resistance. We can analyze how messages are tested, but the most important strategies are those that aid in the design of messages.

The Principle of Identification

Not all communicators are persuaders, because some communication is not intended to win over audiences. For example, some writers and musicians may work to please only themselves or to achieve a private aesthetic goal. In such cases, self-expression may be its own reward. Even though most art *is* rhetorical (that is, those who produce it actively court receptive audiences), it is plausible that a given artist of some form might say "I like it, and that is all that's important." Persuaders, however, *must* always go further; they must construct messages that narrow the gap between their attitudes and those of their audiences. In ways not demanded of other manipulators of words and images, they need to reconcile topic-relevant differences with those they seek to influence. Identification is the primary tool for achieving this goal.

The *principle of identification* may be the most universal of all the elements of communication. We seek connections with others and resonance with their ideas or experiences. Music would lose one of its most appealing aspects if it did not transport us back to a time or place with which we identify. Imagine a film, television drama, or novel where the story deliberately *denied* our psychological alignment with any character—chances are good that we would lose any interest in what happens next.

Reaching an audience is rooted in an advocate's ability to understand the collective beliefs of the members of the audience: what they like and dislike, what they take for granted, and what they are likely to challenge. St. Augustine noted that a person is persuaded if he "embraces what you commend, regrets whatever you build up as regrettable, rejoices at what you say is cause for rejoicing"—in short, when the person thinks as you do.[31] Persuasion may be described as a process that uses the familiar to gain acceptance for the unfamiliar.

These opportunities for identification are enormously important and more varied than one might first suppose.[32] In our casual usage of the term, we often observe that identification is the product of various forms of similarity, for instance: *ideological* ("I agree"), *demographic* ("We are both men"), or shared circumstances ("Both of us grew up in Colorado"). What more intensive study reveals, however, is our remarkable capacity to extend our empathy to people and situations even when there seem to be no obvious analogies. Given the inclination to do so, humans are surprisingly adept at "standing in another person's shoes."

We can establish identification with others on many different levels. Our manner of dress and style of delivery can communicate physical similarity, while expressions and examples we use can reassure an audience that we share similar experiences. This method can be seen in the seminal work of Tony Schwartz, who became a legend in the history of radio and television commercials. Schwartz believed that the most effective persuasion triggers beliefs and feelings that already exist *within* a person. Effective advocacy depends as much on calling forth what individuals already believe or know as on advancing new ideas. Schwartz noted that an audience is the persuader's workforce. A persuader, "must deeply understand the kinds of information and experiences stored in his audience, the patterning of this information, and the interactive . . . process whereby stimuli evoke this stored information."[33] Identification is the sharing of this common information; it is achieved when listeners and readers sense that what is being said expresses their own attitudes.

Commonplaces

Identification flows from a sense that advocate and audience share the same cultural beliefs. Known as *commonplaces*, these beliefs represent the core thoughts and ways of thinking that characterize a society. According to the French social theorist Jacques Ellul, a *commonplace* "serves everyone as a touchstone, an instrument of recognition. It is rarely quoted, but it is constantly present; it is behind thought and speech; it is behind conversation. It is the common standard that enables people to understand one another."[34]

The earliest compilers of commonplaces were Greek and Roman rhetoricians, notably Aristotle and Cicero.[35] Both identified habitual patterns of thought common to segments of their societies. Anthropologists, sociologists, and communications analysts have used commonplaces through the ages to map the ideological landscape of a tribe, nation, or culture. In 1935 researchers Robert and Helen Lynd studied a city (Muncie, Indiana) dubbed Middletown with an interest in discovering the attitudes shared by members of the community. They catalogued the essential commonplaces of the city—"the things that one does and feels and says so naturally that mentioning them in Middletown implies an 'of course.'"[36] A sampling from their list of attitudes on the general subject of the proper roles for government illustrates that many are still active.

- The government should leave things to private initiative.
- The American democratic form of government is the ideal form of government.
- The Constitution should not be fundamentally changed.
- Americans are the freest people in the world.[37]

The Pew Research Center looks for generational, political, and demographic differences.[38] However, they often find attitude similarities across the culture that span specific groups. Some commonplaces that have a greater than 60 percent acceptance include the following:

- It is sometimes necessary to use military force to maintain order in the world.
- The freedom to pursue life's goals without state interference is important.
- Religion is important in American lives.[39]
- The living standards separating the rich and poor have widened.
- Success is deserved when it comes from hard work.
- Cheating to get unearned government benefits is wrong.
- Americans can still work together to solve most of their problems.
- People who work hard will get ahead.[40]

Not every individual would accept all of these commonplaces, nor do they always remain unchanged from generation to generation.[41] They are universal in the sense that they reflect mainstream public opinion at a specific time and in a specific society. We can isolate them as the building blocks of persuasion because they are readily accepted by so many within a culture. Locating the right commonplaces is vital in initiating a sequence of persuasive appeals that can move an audience toward agreement.

When the woman who organized the Consumer Finance Protection Bureau spoke at the annual US Chamber of Commerce conference to about 300 executives, she expected that they would oppose many of her initiatives to regulate the banking industry. But Senator Elizabeth Warren reached for a commonplace that they could all endorse: "I do not consider myself in hostile territory right now because I believe we share a point of principle." Then came the commonplace: "Competitive markets are good for consumers and for businesses." She rightly assumed her audience would find no quarrel with that statement, using it to make her ultimate point that markets don't work as they should "unless there are some well-enforced rules."[42]

Four recent presidents addressed another highly regarded commonplace: *personal responsibility.* In his 1992 address, Bill Clinton stated:

> It is time to break the bad habit of expecting something for nothing from our government or from each other. Let us all take more responsibility, not only for ourselves and our families, but for our communities and our country.[43]

George W. Bush repeated the theme in 2001:

> America, at its best, is a place where personal responsibility is valued and expected.[44]

Barack Obama's 2012 address continued to emphasize personal responsibility.

> Our celebration of initiative and enterprise, our insistence on hard work and personal responsibility, these are constants in our character.[45]

In 2016 a newly inaugurated President Trump offered a variation that inverted the wording but kept the principle:

> We will get our people off of welfare and back to work—rebuilding our country with American hands and American labor.[46]

Precisely because these statements are unremarkable, they provide useful paths to persuasion. Getting someone to agree with you is not usually about confronting them with foreign or new ideas. Instead, it is often about finding existing and shared ideas, then *using these points of agreement to leverage change toward the persuader's ideas.*

Audience-Specific Norms

There is a second level of beliefs that work as commonplaces. *Audience-specific norms* differ from commonplaces by appealing to groups or communities within a society, but not necessarily to all. Earlier we discussed the potency of the group in shaping its members' attitudes. Aristotle understood audience-specific norms as a key process in persuading others. He devoted many pages of his study of persuasion to a distinction pollsters continue to explore: the different beliefs that divide the young from the old.[47]

Contemporary advocates attach special importance to a person's membership in real or virtual communities of people with shared concerns. Subjects such as legal abortion, the death penalty, and gay marriage are so significant to many individuals that they can be fairly described as *identity issues:* positions that may be crucial in defining their personal affinity groups. Beyond this high-intensity inner ring are other rings of attitudes that indicate alliance with others.

American society consists of thousands of organizations and coalitions—some formal and some informal; others intensely personal, religious, or political. These groups are defined by their shared attitudes, some of which place supporters in the mainstream of public opinion or in a minority with others who think differently. When we are swimming against the tide of public opinion on deeply held beliefs, we learn how important group norms can be. Pew's research on attitudes found Americans deeply divided over why the American Civil War was fought and whether leaders today should honor Confederate leaders or display the Confederate flag. Skin color, region of the country, and education all play a role in predicting what views an individual will endorse. Not surprisingly, white Southerners were the most positive about praising the war and its leaders. Northern African Americans, followed by northern whites, expressed very different opinions.[48]

We could describe many other attitudes linked with specific organizations, for example: Handgun Control Incorporated ("Handguns are too abundant in the United States"), the National Rifle Association ("The Second Amendment protects the private ownership of firearms"), People for the Ethical Treatment of Animals ("Animals have rights that should not be ignored"), or Planned Parenthood ("Health care needs to be accessible to all American women").[49] Being a supporter of a group or organization can become a badge of honor and a way to construct our own identity. "Make Love, Not War," "Save the Whales" and "Jesus Saves" may be old bumper stickers, but they and their Twitter counterparts indicate our willingness to display our membership in a community of shared values. Norms that are accepted by others confer legitimacy within a specific group, even while sometimes creating tensions in the larger society.

Research has identified two types of norms. *Descriptive norms* tell us what a group believes, *injunctive norms* indicate a group's approval or disapproval of specific behaviors. Descriptive norms remind us what our peers think. Injunctive norms tell us how our peers believe we should act.

Robert Cialdini and his researchers discovered that injunctive norms can be especially effective in controlling out-of-norm behavior in public places. They studied the rate of thefts of small fossil pieces in Arizona's Petrified Forest National Park, finding that signs around the park taking the injunctive form, "Please don't remove petrified wood from the park" were more effective than signs with the descriptive norm, "Many past visitors have removed the petrified wood from the park, changing the state of the Petrified Forest." The latter signs seemed to actually *encourage* theft, probably by *norming the problem*—theft—that they sought to change. The unintended implication of the sign is that "everybody does it." The more direct injunction "Don't remove" implied the behavior was unacceptable.[50]

Using the same logic, public television and radio fund-raisers should avoid stating that very few listeners or viewers donate. Staffers at a local affiliate in Philadelphia sometimes note "only 1 in 10 users actually contribute." Such statements are norming what they intend to communicate as a significant problem. We suspect they would be better off using the injunctive form that talks about the friends and neighbors like you who contribute.

There are generally two ways to locate audience norms. One is to test for attitudes by surveying a sample audience. As we noted earlier, dial groups represent these efforts. A second way is to consider the demographics of a group to arrive at reasonable inferences about what they currently believe. We can sometimes predict attitudes based on attributes such as age, occupation, and religious affiliation.

Variations within any group can be broad, but some collections of individuals show greater similarities than differences. Radio stations and their advertisers, for example, generally find that preferences for musical formats correlate with particular kinds of listeners (teens, older adults, suburban adults, young urban men, and so on).[51] Similarly, cable and television networks and commercial websites attempt to show prospective advertisers that their content reaches lucrative segments of the population, such as adult women who make a high percentage of all household purchases.

Making inferences involves using known facts to arrive at conclusions about probable beliefs. Although such inferences are inexact, it is advantageous to make estimations about the attitudes of people based on what is known about their personal and social situations. Audiences with heavy concentrations of farmers need to be addressed differently than audiences of small business owners, retirees, union members, or college seniors. Persuaders addressing a specific group work backwards from general traits to conclusions about probable attitudes and values that group could be expected to endorse or condemn. For example, we might judge union members as more likely to share norms with the Democratic Party than with the Republican Party, favoring governmental spending on health care, a higher federal minimum wage, and so on. Of course, one might be close to the mark for the group as a whole, but probably wrong about some norms for any single individual. In 2016 Hillary Clinton bested Republican Donald Trump in union households only by eight percentage points.[52] Such is the uncertain nature of inference making about anyone's beliefs: the law of averages means we can project tendencies in groups better than for any single individual.

As briefly referenced earlier, jury selection in trials remains one of the most interesting forms of inference making about audiences. Defense attorneys and prosecutors seek every advantage to select sympathetic jurors, often hiring firms that specialize in identifying characteristics of jurors. Television's *Dr Phil*, for example, had an earlier career as a litigation consultant. His Courtroom Sciences Incorporated helped Oprah Winfrey overcome a lawsuit brought by the American cattle industry that charged she had caused beef prices to fall by making disparaging remarks about beef on her popular talk show.[53] *Jury consultants* played significant roles in the trials of Martha Stewart, Enron's Jeffrey Skilling, and Casey Anthony (the young mother who was acquitted in 2011 of murdering her child).[54] In what is now considered a benchmark case on the art of jury selection, lawyers defending O. J. Simpson against charges of murdering his ex-wife and her friend looked for male jurors rather than women, older rather than younger jurors, African Americans, and football buffs rather than football widows.[55]

ADVOCATES, MESSAGES, AND AUDIENCES

One useful approach to understanding audiences is to play out the possible relationships that can exist among three essential variables. For persuasion to occur, there must be an *advocate* (someone or some group with a viewpoint to express), a *message* (the action the advocate wants listeners to accept), and an *audience* (listeners, viewers, or readers). Our three-sided model of this process presented in figure 7.2 is based on the work of researchers attempting to look at how people maintain and change their attitudes.

Imagine that for any persuasive setting the relationship between any two of the three variables can be positive (**+**) or negative (**–**). A positive sign indicates approval; a negative sign indicates disapproval. The model predicts resistance or agreement on the critical variables of *acceptance of the advocate* and *acceptance of the message*. Its six different configurations depict the possibilities that can flow from two key questions about any persuasive encounter: Does the audience like the advocate? Does the audience share the advocate's point of view? Taken together, the model's different scenarios offer some revealing conclusions about what may need to happen in an individual setting to alter an audience's attitudes.

The most difficult form of persuasion is diagrammed in scenario 6. The audience has negative feelings toward the persuader *as well as* his or her ideas—a common circumstance in our current political environment. Before exploring this difficult circum-

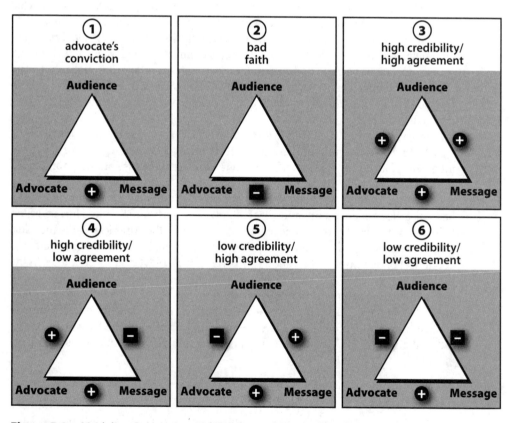

Figure 7.2   Modeling Persuasion Challenges and Opportunities

stance and other possible combinations, we'll start with the *baseline* precondition: *the only relationship that should be a constant* (scenario 1), *but occasionally is not* (scenario 2).

Believing in Our Words

Boxes 1 and 2 set up two preconditions for all of the other scenarios. Although what an audience thinks about a topic may range from approval to disapproval, the audience rightly assumes that expressions of support for an idea are sincere. We expect advocates to believe what they say; the *advocate's conviction* in Box 1 is the default expectation for person-based persuasion, represented by the plus between the message and the source. Assuming no coercion, people are not likely to argue for what they do not believe. If we learn the reverse—that a persuader supports a position he or she does not accept—we may feel used. The minus sign in box 2 indicates that a speaker is saying one thing but believing another, which represents *bad faith communication*.

To be sure, there are times when people are required to front for someone else's viewpoints. *Fronting* typically happens when individuals must represent the views of organizations to which they are attached, but with which they privately disagree. Many people face the challenge of loyalty (or continued employment) over honesty, either as retail or service workers or in defenses we feel obligated to make on behalf of family and friends. Beyond a limited range of professional and personal loyalties, we will assume that individuals will be authentic in their expressed support for an idea— that what a person professes is what they believe.

> ### The Strange Business of Fronting for Others
>
> David Sedaris is a bestselling author and humorist heard frequently on National Public Radio. His audience loves his sardonic wit, especially when he retells his well-known story about the season he spent working as a department store elf in Macy's New York store. The job requires elves to put up with overstimulated children and demanding parents. It's funny in part because we know that it cannot be easy for a sarcastic middle-aged man to put on green tights and prance around in fake snow. For fans of Sedaris, there is a yawning and hilarious gap between the small and prickly writer and the fantasy of simple innocence required of Santa's elves.
>
> This imperative to perform a noncongruent role has a name: fronting. It's a handy term because it identifies one cause of the angst we experience when a communication task seems daunting. Fronting with apparent conviction is often a lie, made worse if we have learned to recognize our own hypocrisies.
>
> Fronting is the requirement to represent in speech and body language the interests of others. It's the primary job skill for work in customer service, sales, teaching, and lawyering. Professors front for their disciplines and colleagues to students or deans. Lawyers front for their clients, even when they have significant doubts about their claims. Servers front for the restaurant even when they are aware that their optimism about the food may not be accurate. Airline attendants front for airlines, remaining upbeat in the face of passenger resentment over perceived injustices. Look carefully, and you might see them straining to keep their frustrations hidden. It can be stressful to serve the interests of an organization like an airline with declining popularity.

High Credibility/High Agreement Persuasion

The ideal communication environment is one in which the audience is positive about both the message and its presenter (box 3)—enthusiastic supporters gather to hear a popular leader recite esteemed beliefs. Democratic Party campaign speeches given to Democratic audiences and Mormon sermons given to Mormon congregations are two examples of "preaching to the converted." Audiences attentive to a candidate appearing on television or face-to-face are usually populated by people who already appreciate the source and the message. Basic persuasion research suggests that "people pay attention primarily to content that already interests them and is congenial to their point of view."[56]

High credibility/high agreement persuasion may seem unnecessary. However, it is a mistake to overlook the need for reinforcing communication. Rhetoric that matches an existing attitude is extremely satisfying; it fulfills our need for membership in communities and it involves practically no risk. Such reinforcement may seem empty and ritualistic, but organizations and movements must periodically remind believers of the tenets basic to their faith. Speeches, websites, and rallies prolong the enthusiasm of members who need occasional psychological renewal.

Persuasion for reinforcement sometimes also benefits from mass media exposure, which allows it to reach secondary audiences who are not already in agreement. In some instances, a message that seems to be intended for people who are already true believers may be designed to use their enthusiasm to infect a larger and previously indifferent mass media audience. The primary audience's support becomes part of the persuasive message, generating fervor to impress those witnessing the event second-hand. This explains the laugh tracks on situation comedies that tell us others find the material hilarious. Political conventions similarly exploit this dual audience arrangement. They know that potential voters watching on television may be influenced by the zeal on the convention floor. A presidential candidate addressing like-minded party members who can barely contain their excitement may influence the undecided 5 or 6 percent who could make the difference between electoral success and failure.

High Credibility/Low Agreement Persuasion

High credibility/low agreement persuasion (box 4) occurs when an advocate has earned the goodwill of the audience but tests their approval by arguing the merits of an unpopular idea. Political leaders sometimes push against the views of their most ardent supporters by advocating ideas many of them may not like.

In 2006, for example, former President Jimmy Carter disappointed some admirers with a new book that accused the Israelis of inhumane practices in their occupation of Palestine. *Palestine Peace Not Apartheid* triggered resignations from the board of directors of the Carter Center and accusations that Nobel Peace Prize winner Carter was anti-Semitic. But even unlikely audiences like students and faculty at Brandeis University gave the president a respectful hearing.[57] Likewise, many African American clergy—traditional supporters of Barack Obama—initially took issue with his announced support for gay marriage in 2012.[58]

Two very different approaches seem well suited to the high credibility/low agreement setting. One is to intensify audience identification with the favorable public image of the advocate ("If such a terrific person believes this, maybe my opinion is wrong). With this approach, more time is spent focusing on the advocate's acceptance with an audience. Most celebrity endorsements of products function this way. In advertisements very little is said about the product itself; the emphasis is on its association with a person we admire.

A second strategy is basic common sense: make the best case possible. The advocate's reputation is sufficient to guarantee that an audience will listen to a reasoned presentation making a convincing case for a problematic issue.

Low Credibility/High Agreement Persuasion

The situation represented in box 5 is the exact reverse of the one discussed above. The audience in *low credibility/high agreement persuasion* fundamentally *agrees* with the *ideas* being expressed but does not approve of the advocate. A persuader might analyze this situation and conclude, "Why bother? I'm content to do nothing if the audience already agrees with me." This is a reasonable concern based on the idea of the boomerang effect. The association of a popular idea with an unpopular advocate could possibly sour some of the audience on the message.

But an advocate with effective presentation skills can find at least one major reason for using low credibility/high agreement persuasion: the *opportunity to increase personal credibility.* By exploiting the audience's agreement on an issue, he or she may be able to reverse some negative feelings. Like the chameleon that blends in with the colors of a landscape, the advocate may gain protection against an audience's hostility by carefully cultivating shared ideas (commonplaces, norms and ultimate terms) as a vindication of his or her own suspect character. Ideas serve as membership cards to groups that would otherwise reject the low credibility speaker.

President Trump struggled to win over more than half of America's voters in the first six months of his presidency. Even so, a broader group liked his "America first" ideas and his hostility to "liberal elites." By all accounts they approved of the message more than the messenger.[59]

President Bill Clinton gave one of the most interesting addresses of any modern presidency in 1993. The short Memorial Day address was given at Washington's Vietnam Veterans Memorial. To many of the veterans and military leaders who had gathered, Clinton did not have the required credentials to be a Veterans Day speaker. His reputation as a draft dodger had endured beyond the bitter 1992 campaign. Like many other college students of his day, he avoided service in Vietnam and protested the continuance of the war. When he began to speak, he was greeted with both applause and boos, but he persisted with ideas that resonated with his audience. He was eloquent in identifying common ground and in making a plea to put the negative feelings generated by Vietnam in the past.

> Let us continue to disagree, if we must, about the war, but let us not let it divide us as a people any longer. No one has come here today to disagree about the heroism of those whom we honor, but the only way we can really honor their memory is to resolve to live and serve today and tomorrow as best we can. . . . Surely that is what we owe to all those whose names are etched in this beautiful memorial.[60]

Common belief in the message's idea is the potential agent for creating more goodwill toward the source. We may enjoy the music of a musician but disagree with their politics, but the cultural products they produce can soften perceptions of *who* they are.

Low Credibility/Low Agreement Persuasion

We return now to the persuasive situation that carries the heaviest burdens—but is also the most interesting to study (especially if someone other than ourselves is confronting the difficult situation). *Low credibility/low agreement* in box 6 exists when the audience is hostile to *both* the persuader *and* his or her ideas. The two minuses signify large obstacles to overcome. Not unexpectedly, most people do not tackle such an arrangement joyfully. Indeed, more than a few students have suggested that a persuader should come to this setting only with bodyguards and a familiarity with possible escape routes! Gary Sherman, the head of the Recording Industry Association of America, addressed the Personal Democracy Forum, a group that disagrees vehemently with the Association's prosecution of music file sharers.[61] Sherman tackled the difficult task of winning over an audience that included a lot of committed file sharers.

As discussed in chapter 2, universities are frequently challenged to protect the appearances of unpopular advocates on their campuses. These situations illustrate the tough dynamics in box 6. Former Iranian President Mohammad Khatami was invited to address Harvard's Institute of Politics on the eve of the fifth anniversary of the 9/11 attacks on New York and Washington. The date was a coincidence. About 200 demonstrators gathered outside the Kennedy School of Government chanting "Shame on Harvard," but the audience inside listened politely and then asked a range of questions about human rights in Iran and other issues.

Like most speakers facing a hostile audience, the reform-minded Iranian president could find common ground with many in the audience, eventually winning grudging acceptance. Noted one Harvard student, he was "more evenhanded" than she expected.[62] Khatami condemned the hated Osama bin Laden, who was still at large. He also condemned his successor's oft-quoted wish that Israel be "wiped off the map." Listed below are some of his credibility-establishing statements.

- I stand before you to once again express my deepest sympathy with the families of the victims [of Sept. 11] and with all the great American people.

- One cannot, and ought not, be engaged in violence in the name of any religions. Just as one cannot and ought not turn the world into one's military camp in the name of human rights and democracy.

- The East ought to choose democracy as the most fitting method of collective life and progress.[63]

As our national political life has become more polarized, members of Congress and occasionally members of the Trump administration have faced hostile audiences regarding the issues of immigration reform, medical insurance reform, and deregulation of banking and other interests. Some members meet open groups as little as possible. President Trump prefers social media over open and extended exchanges with the national press. But some in Congress relish the chance to explain their views and votes to angry constituents.[64] This type of persuasion requires a committed, hardy, and resolute advocate. The challenge of overcoming both low agreement and low credibility is daunting. Both tasks must be undertaken simultaneously. It is essential to find commonplaces or norms that can be initial stepping stones to agreement and building credibility.

Are There Limits to Adaptation?

Plato called excessive attention to audience beliefs *pandering* and claimed that it was a common if unfortunate feature of persuasion as taught by most of his peers. He worried that the presence of the audience and its cherished norms put enormous burdens on a persuader to ignore the truth.[65] Anybody who has witnessed someone reject long-held beliefs to win someone else's approval can understand what Plato feared.

This simple but common complaint can obscure a false dilemma. The idea of pandering requires accepting the supposition that communication is *not* naturally audience based—that when we are alone with our thoughts, we are somehow truer to our authentic selves. That is certainly possible. But the reactions of others not only *do* matter, they *should* matter, functioning as essential reference points in our quests to prosper within groups and communities. Social learning is not just an adaptive strategy but a learning and survival strategy as well. The admonishment to "not to worry about what others think" sounds romantic and perhaps heroic, but it denies the essential sociality of human communication. We are defined by our interactions with others. We cannot escape the influences and judgments of individuals within our orbit.

There may be times when we praise the idea of acting and speaking without compromising with the feelings of others. Luckily, we have melodramas, comics, rappers, and film stars who can act as surrogates for our fantasies of living as defiant outsiders. But the broader reality is that most of us enjoy belonging to a communal world of friends, families, and communities

Even so, an ethical line *is* crossed when adaptation extends beyond the natural process of mediation and reaches into the denial of core values or beliefs. The bad-faith persuader who deliberately ignores beliefs for the sake of performance violates the acceptable threshold of accommodation. It can be unethical to sacrifice personal feelings for the sake of winning over others. However, it is reasonable and shrewd to build on audience values. Anyone who seeks change from a group of people by giving their beliefs serious consideration should not be accused of pandering.

SUMMARY

The central theme of this chapter is that successful persuasion must be measured against the necessity to adapt to specific audiences. We naturally access our strengths and weaknesses in relation to those we want to influence. Sometimes our strengths lie in who we *are*; in many instances, they reside in the specific *ideas we advocate*. In either case, we assume persuaders will maximize their leverage over an audience by finding common ground to establish effective connections. This is the primary dynamic of adaptive persuasion. There are few other communication skills that matter as much as the ability to link one's persuasive message to relevant audience beliefs or values.

This chapter is also meant to be a reminder that the idea of the audience is not as simple as it used to be. Social media and the ease we now possess to connect with others makes the idea of a well-defined target less stable and more fluid. Nonetheless, core ideas related to strategic thinking about audiences are still important. These include the usefulness of finding sources of audience identification, anticipating effects of intended and unintended audiences, the importance of building messages using shared commonplaces and norms, and assessing the acceptability of a persuader's credibility and ideas with a given group.

Persuasion is an ongoing dialogue with an audience. Outwardly it appears as if the audience is asked to do most of the giving. The persuader's intention to transform the attitudes or behaviors of a group of people implicitly says, "*Give me* both your attention and the benefit of your agreement." But if the audience is truly the generative source of a message's ideas, the persuader who adapts enters into a process that compliments the audience.

QUESTIONS AND PROJECTS FOR FURTHER STUDY

1. Look for commonplaces within an article in a mass-market magazine or its online equivalent. Locate more specialized group norms in a media outlet with a narrower audience such as *Maxim* or *Cosmopolitan*. Describe how some of these elements function as appeals to the audience.

2. Using the online resource, Nielsen Wire (http://blog.nielsen.com/nielsenwire/), identify some current audience analysis trends in media use. Consider some of the findings in terms of the chapter's discussion of the challenges of thinking about modern audiences.

3. Identify a social media platform or online retailer that you use. What features and patterns in these media are most effective in influencing what you see, believe or buy?

4. At one point in the chapter, the authors note that an ethical presumption that goes with all forms of persuasion is that persuaders should believe in what they want others to accept. To do otherwise is bad faith. Publicly representing an organization's position about which one has doubts is also called fronting. Cite an instance of fronting that involved you, or cite some situations where fronting is common and perhaps necessary. Do any of these situations suggest that fronting may be ethical?

5. Using recent news items, interviews, blogs, or personal experiences, illustrate what is meant by the following terms used in the last two chapters:
   - Boomerang Effect
   - High Credibility/Low Agreement Persuasion
   - Using commonplaces to find common ground
   - Identity Issues
   - Norming the Problem

6. View Bill Clinton's short address to vets at the Vietnam Veterans Memorial (YouTube: https://www.youtube.com/watch?v=qr-_Oi_qHYI). Identify commonplaces used to try to win over this hostile audience.

7. Pick an issue or position on which you hold strong views. Given your position on the chosen question (i.e., defending a politician, a controversial policy, or group), identify an organization that would hold contrary or different attitudes. Imagine that you were invited by this organization to explain your convictions online or face to face. After giving your invitation some thought. Describe the norms you think the hypothetical audience holds and how you would build bridges to increase their support or understanding of your point of view.

8. We have noted that peer pressure (social proof) is a significant form of influence. Using your own experiences or an example with which you are familiar, illustrate Tina Rosenberg's idea of the "social cure" at work. Where have others clearly been persuaded by a strong group norm that affected the thinking of a new member of the group?

ADDITIONAL READING

Alessandro Acquisti and Ralph Gross, "Imagined Communities: Awareness, Information Sharing, and Privacy on the Facebook," in George Danezis and Philippe Golle (Eds.) *Privacy Enhancing Technologies*, (Berlin: Springer, 2006), pp. 36-58.

Robert Cialdini, *Influence: Science and Practice*, 5th ed. (New York: Longman, 2009).

Robert Cialdini, Linda Demaine, Brad Sagarin, Daniel Barrett, Kelton Rhoads, and Patricia Winter, "Managing Social Norms for Persuasive Impact," *Social Influence*, March, 2006, 3–15.

Anja Bechmann and Stine Lomorg, "Mapping Actor Roles in Social Media: Different Perspectives on Value Creation in Theories of User Participation, *New Media and Society*, August, 2013, Sage Journals Online.

William McGuire, "Attitudes and Attitude Change," in Gardner Lindzey and Elliot Aronson (Eds.), *Handbook of Social Psychology*, Vol. II, 3rd ed. (New York: Random House, 1985), pp. 233–346.

James E. Porter, *Audience and Rhetoric: An Archaeological Composition of the Discourse Community* (Englewood Cliffs, NJ: Prentice Hall, 1992).

Tina Rosenberg, *Join the Crowd: How Peer Pressure Can Transform the World* (New York: Norton, 2011).

James Webster and Patricia Phalen, *The Mass Audience: Rediscovering the Dominant Model* (Mahwah, NJ: Lawrence Erlbaum, 1997).

NOTES

[1] Kenneth Burke, *A Rhetoric of Motives* (New York: Prentice Hall, 1963), p. 56.

[2] Émile Durkheim quoted in Hugh Dalziel Duncan, *Symbols and Social Theory* (New York: Oxford, 1969), pp. 152–153.

[3] John Durham Peters, *Speaking into the Air* (Chicago: University of Chicago Press, 1999), p. 4.

[4] Robert Cialdini, *Influence: Science and Practice*, 5th ed. (New York: Longman, 2009), p. 99.

[5] Tina Rosenberg, *Join the Club: How Peer Pressure Can Transform the World* (New York: Norton, 2011), p. xxi.

[6] See, for example, Morten Tyldum's *The Imitation Game* (2014) about Alan Turing, or Danny Boyle's 2015 film, *Steve Jobs*.

[7] "College Drinking: Changing the Culture," National Institute on Alcohol Abuse and Alcoholism, March 3, 2013, http://www.collegedrinkingprevention.gov/statssummaries/snapshot.aspx

[8] James Jasinski, *Sourcebook on Rhetoric* (Thousand Oaks, CA.: Sage, 2001), p. 68.

[9] Alessandro Acquisti and Ralph Gross, "Imagined Communities: Awareness, Information Sharing, and Privacy on the Facebook," in George Danezis and Philippe Golle (Eds.), *Privacy Enhancing Technologies* (Berlin: Springer, 2006), pp. 36–58.

10 See, for example, James E. Porter, *Audience and Rhetoric: An Archaeological Composition of the Discourse Community* (Englewood Cliffs, NJ: Prentice Hall, 1992), pp. 51–61.

11 Jack Marshall, "Marketers Question Quality of Ad Targeting Data Providers," *The Wall Street Journal*, February 23, 2015. http://blogs.wsj.com/cmo/2015/02/23/marketerspquestion-quality-of-ad-targeting-data-providers/

12 Malia Wollan, "How to Be Selected for a Jury," *The New York Times Magazine*, July 30, 2017, p. 21.

13 Sapna Maheshwari, "Welcome to Manhood, Gillette Told the Woman, 50," *New York Times*, July 17, 2017, pp. B1, B6.

14 James Webster and Patricia Phalen, *The Mass Audience: Rediscovering the Dominant Model* (Mahwah, NJ: Lawrence Erlbaum, 1997), p. xiii.

15 YouTube Pressroom, "Statistics," February 24, 2017, https://www.youtube.com/yt/press/en-GB/statistics.html

16 Joshua Meyrowitz, *No Sense of Place* (New York: Oxford University Press, 1985), pp. 73–92.

17 Zetter, Kim, "Sony Got Hacked Hard: What We Know and Don't Know So Far," *Wired*, December 3, 2014. https://www.wired.com/2014/12/sony-hack-what-we-know/

18 Anja Bechmann and Stine Lomorg, "Mapping Actor Roles in Social Media: Different Perspectives on Value Creation in Theories of User Participation, *New Media and Society*, August, 2013, Sage Journals Online.

19 Elana Schor and Rachael Bade, "Inside the Protest Movement that Has Republicans Reeling," *Politico*, February 10, 2017, http://www.politico.com/story/2017/02/protest-movement-republicans-234863

20 Michael Scherer, "How Obama's Data Crunchers Helped Him Win," November 8, 2012, http://www.cnn.com/2012/11/07/tech/web/obama-campaign-tech-team/index.html

21 Michael Bernstein, et al., "Quantifying the Invisible Audience in Social Networks," Proceedings of the SIGCHI Conference on Human Factors in Computer Systems (New York ACM Digital Library, 2013), pp. 27–28.

22 Alan Finder, "When a Risqué Online Persona Undermines a Chance for a Job," *The New York Times*, June 11, 2006, pp. A1, A30.

23 For examples of two recent ad campaigns that ran into a backlash generated through social media see Stuart Elliot, "Milk Campaign Ended amid Social Media Firestorm," *The New York Times*, July 22, 2011, B3.

24 Stephen Baker, "Can Social Media Sell Soap?" *New York Times*, January 6, 2013, p. SR1.

25 Sapna Maheshwari, Publishers Retreat From the Risks of Google-YouTube Advertising," *New York Times*, March 27, 2012, p. B5; Sapna Maheshwari, "Breitbart, Blacklisted, Still Hosts Brands' Ads," *The New York Times*, March 27, 2017, pp. B1, B5.

26 David Streitfeld, Natasha Singer and Steven Erlinger, "Call for Privacy Hands a Crisis to Tech Giants," *New York Times*, March 25, 2018, pp. 1, 26.

27 For a discussion of this question see Robert N. Bellah et al., *Habits of the Heart*, updated ed. (Berkeley: University of California Press, 1996), pp. 275–307.

28 Todd Gitlin, *The Twilight of Common Dreams: Why America is Wracked by Culture Wars* (New York: Henry Holt, 1995), p. 203.

29 See their website at http://www.screenenginellc.com/

30 Sapna Maheshwari: "For Marketers, TVs Act as Priceless Sets of Eyes," *The New York Times*, February 26, 2017, pp. A1, A13.

31 Augustine quoted in Kenneth Burke, *A Rhetoric of Motives* (Berkeley: University of California Press, 1969), p. 50.

32 For a more detailed discussion see Gary C. Woodward, *The Idea of Identification* (Albany: State University of New York Press, 2003), pp. 1–43.

33 Tony Schwartz, *The Responsive Chord* (New York: Anchor, 1974), p. 25.

34 Jacques Ellul, *A Critique of the New Commonplaces*, trans. by Helen Weaver (New York: Knopf, 1968), p. 13.

35 See, for example, Aristotle, *Rhetoric*, Book I, Chapters 5–7, trans. by W. Rhys Roberts (Mineola, New York: Dover Thrift Editions, 2004); Cicero, *De inventione; De optimo genere oratorum; Topica,* trans. by H. M. Hubbell. (Cambridge, MA: Harvard University Press, 1949).

36 Robert S. Lynd and Helen Merrell Lynd, *Middletown in Transition: A Study in Cultural Conflicts* (New York: Harvest, 1937), p. 402.

37 Ibid., pp. 413–15, 418.

38 See, for example, Katie Reilly, "A Generational Gap in American Patriotism," *Pew Center for the People and the Press*, July 3, 2013, http://www.pewresearch.org/fact-tank/2013/07/03/a-generational-gap-in-american-patriotism/

39 "The American-Western European Values Gap," *Pew Research Center*, February 29, 2012, http://www.pewglobal.org/2011/11/17/the-american-western-european-values-gap/

40 "Partisan Polarization Surges in Bush, Obama Years, Section 3: Values About Economic Inequality and Individual Opportunity," *Pew Research Center*, June 4, 2012, http://www.people-press.org/2012/06/04/section-3-values-about-economic-inequality-and-individual-opportunity/

41 Some commonplaces in the Lynds' study have become antiques, for example, "a married woman's place is first of all in the home and any other activities should be secondary to 'making a good home for her husband and children'" and "married people owe it to society to have children." Lynd and Lynd, p. 410.

42 "Entering the Lion's Den," *The New York Times*, April 3, 2011, Week in Review, p. 2.

43 Bill Clinton Inaugural Address, in Michael Osborn and Suzanne Osborn (Eds.), *Public Speaking*, 3rd ed. (Boston: Houghton Mifflin, 1994), p. B24.

44 "President George W. Bush Inaugural Address," *The San Diego Union-Tribune*, January 21, 2001, p. A8.

45 Barack Obama's Inaugural Address, January 21, 2013, http://www.whitehouse.gov/the-press-office/2013/01/21/inaugural-address-president-barack-obama

46 Donald Trump, Inaugural Address, Friday, January 20, 2017, Washington, D.C., https://www.whitehouse.gov/inaugural-address

47 Aristotle, *Rhetoric*, Book II, Chapter 12.

48 "Civil War at 150: Still Relevant, Still Divisive," Pew Research Center for the People and the Press, April 8, 2011, http://pewresearch.org/pubs/1958/civil-war-still-relevant-and-divisive-praise-confederate-leaders-flag 2011

49 Readers interested in norms-based persuasion related to health issues can find many interesting studies on the National Social Norms Institute website, http://www.socialnorms.org/Research/articles13.php

50 Robert B. Cialdini et al., "Managing Social Norms for Persuasive Impact," *Social Influence*, March, 2006, pp. 3–15.

51 See, for example, "Radio Today 2013: How America Listens to Radio," *Arbitron*, 2013, http://www.arbitron.com/downloads/Radio_Today_2013_execsum.pdf

52 Philip Bump, "Donald Trump Got Reagan-like Support from Union Households," *The Washington Post*, November 10, 2016, https://www.washingtonpost.com/news/the-fix/wp/2016/11/10/donald-trump-got-reagan-like-support-from-union-households/?utm_term=.abc25009fb30

53 Gary C. Woodward, *Center Stage: Media and the Performance of Politics* (Lanham, MD: Rowman and Littlefield, 2007), pp. 119–120.

54 Mimi Swartz, "Enron Multiple Choice," *The New Yorker*, February 6, 2006, pp. 35–36; Sylvia Hsieh, "On Murder and Social Media: Casey Anthony's Jury Consultant Speaks," *Lawyers USA*, July 5, 2011. http://lawyersusaonline.com/blog/2011/07/05/on-murder-and-social-media-casey-anthony%E2%80%99s-jury-consultant-speaks/

55 David Margolick, "Ideal Jury for O. J. Simpson: Football Fan Who Can Listen," *The New York Times*, September 23, 1994, p. A1.

56 Kurt Lang and Gladys Engle Lang, *Politics and Television* (New York: Quadrangle, 1968), p. 16.

57 About half of the students at Brandeis are Jewish. See Michael Powell, "Jimmy Carter's Peace Mission to Brandeis," *The Washington Post*, January 24, 2007, C1.

58 Peter Baker and Rachel Swarns, "After Obama's Decision on Marriage, Call to Pastors," *The New York Times*, May 13, 2012, p. A1.

59 "How Unpopular Is President Trump?" *FiveThirtyEight*, July 17, 2017, https://projects.fivethirtyeight.com/trump-approval-ratings/

60 Bill Clinton, Memorial Day Address, May 3, 1993. http://www.youtube.com/watch?v=qr-_Oi_qHYI

61 See the YouTube video of his 2012 speech at https://www.youtube.com/watch?v=mSUsiVnvS2w

62 "Khatami Urges US, Iran to use Restraint," *Boston Globe*, September 11, 2006, NewsBank, Access World News.

63 Ibid., and "Controversial Visitor," *Harvard Magazine*, November–December 2006, http://harvardmagazine.com/2006/11/controversial-visitor.htm

64 Trip Gabriel, Thomas Kaplan, Lizette Alvarez, and Emmarie Huetteman, "At Town Halls, Doses of Fury and a Bottle of Tums," *The New York Times*, February 21, 2017, p. A1.

65 See chapter 2 for a more extended discussion of Plato's concerns.

PART III

Persuasion Settings

8

Contexts
of Persuasion

The permanent campaign is the political ideology of our age.[1]

—Sidney Blumenthal

The goal of this chapter is to highlight unique attributes that define four common settings for persuasion. After looking at interpersonal persuasion, we focus on social marketing and advertising campaigns and conclude with persuasion campaigns in the political world. In the last three areas, persuasion only makes sense when considered as a series of sustained and repeated attempts at influence, usually using various media platforms. Interpersonal communication is, by definition, more intimate. But as we shall see, interpersonal style is also an integral part of most campaigns, ranging from politics to advertising. Video content, for example, projects an aura of face-to-face intimacy. Understanding the unique features of each setting provides important details that advocates need to consider.

DIMENSIONS OF INTERPERSONAL PERSUASION

We live in an age where the most overt persuasion comes to us via a media source: paper, broadcast advertising, internet sites, or social media and all their evolving mutations. Yet we would miss one of the chief assets of persuasion if we ignored the importance of messages delivered in real space and time. Sometimes there is no substitute for being within four or five feet of the individuals we seek to influence. Airports and hotels are congested because the economy depends on employees who travel extensively to be in the same room with a client. Men and women involved in business-to-business transactions understand that they can't phone in their pitches. Most have an appreciation of the logistics of gaining attention, holding interest, and bargaining a pathway to agreement. And many believe it will only happen with extensive face-to-face contact.

The necessity is clearly evident in other interpersonal interactions—from birthdays to graduations to marriages to funerals. If a person doubts the value of interpersonal contact, they need only look at films depicting modern American life. Few of us go to movies or plays to watch a character text their friends, send emails, or talk on the phone. Screenplays emphasize the vibrant and transformative moments that happen between people in the same space.

Within the interpersonal context, persuasive efforts may be characterized as:

- *Dynamic*—participants send and receive signals continually and simultaneously.

- *Interactive*—participants influence each other; they are interdependent. Each person is constantly aware of the other and assumes the roles of both sender and receiver, which involves continual adaptation and adjustment.

- *Proactive*—A message to persuade involves the total person. Attitudes, values, social background, and previous transactions all influence the nature of the interaction.

- *Based on Reciprocal Obligations*—we are compelled to give more attention to a person who has made a gesture of good will in our presence.

- *Involving*—conversations in real time rarely let us function as mere spectators. Participation and commitment come with being in another's presence.

The scenario of selling your old car depicts some of the basic dimensions of interpersonal persuasion. If a potential buyer is a stranger, the first part of the interaction involves establishing trust and building identification. You must persuade the person that you are honest and have nothing to hide; the potential buyer must convince you that he or she intends to buy the car and has the funds to pay for it. You might emphasize similarities and commonalities between you and the prospect (such as mutual interests or experiences). The process becomes transactional and interactive.

Even in this simple exchange it is easy to see three obvious differences with online or video selling. First, in interpersonal contact there is continuous and instantaneous *feedback*. Set the car price too high and you will instantly recognize the buyer's hesitation, even if they say nothing. The feedback loop of interpersonal communication is far more dynamic than is possible with even the most interactive digital systems. Second, there is a system of *mutual obligation* that exists in most interpersonal encounters that is missing in mass communication. Demonstrating a degree of interest when talking with another person is one

Sleepwalking Through a Conference Call

One of the author's good friends regularly commutes to the West Coast, Asia, and Europe to meet with clients and other members of his firm. By all accounts, he's very good at what he does. On those rare occasions when he is back in town, friends invariably ask him if he could save a lot of wear and tear by Skyping or connecting via a conference call. He usually responds with a half-smile, asking the questioner what *they* do when they are in a long meeting that requires listening to a disembodied voice through a speaker phone. The truthful answer for most of us is that we go into the human equivalent of a digital device's airplane mode. We are present, but we aren't really connecting.

There are a number of elements that degrade the conference call experience. Because we can't see the face and body language of the other person, it's tough to judge the intensity of their interest and their ability to hold eye contact. Seeing someone gives us clues to their state of mind. In addition, conference calls tend to disrupt accustomed rhythms of listening and responding to one another. We can't judge when the unseen person has finished a thought or whether they are sending cues that indicate agreement or puzzlement. As interpersonal researchers might put it, there is no true synchronicity. Moreover, most of us are now so device dependent that an extended conversation with the unseen is an open invitation to move on to other tasks: cleaning out the in-box of our email, sending texts, or counting the minutes until we can leave.

Of course being in the *same space* is not always rewarded. Meeting face-to-face with an angry client can be taxing. And the logistics of flying long distances are now more challenging than ever. Even so, our frequent-flyer friend regularly endures a juggernaut of 10-hour flights and airport transfers to meet with clients and coworkers. He knows that being within four feet of a person gives him leverage for his point of view.

of the obligations. Eye contact usually follows, and nods of agreement or acceptance are often expected and given. This nonverbal data helps communicators assess where they stand in relation to the other person. And third, direct contact makes it possible for the target in a persuasive transaction to offer comments and sometimes counter-persuasive ideas. Even the simplest exchange empowers the audience, an element that is missing from media-based persuasion. Both verbal and nonverbal pathways are available to advocates sharing the same space as their audience.

Verbal Characteristics

We select our verbal behaviors largely based on interactions that were successful in the past. We repeat those that created satisfying exchanges and eliminate the ones that were ineffective.

A person's personality and how they use language shapes their verbal communication style. Many patterns are possible. A *dominant* verbal style consists of intense, direct, and opinionated language. This style leaves the impression of control, competence, confidence, forcefulness, and competitiveness. A *dramatic* style uses very vivid language, sarcasm, satire, and anecdotes that enhance interpersonal attentiveness, attractiveness, and popularity. A *contentious* style uses factual and logical messages to challenge others. This can easily lead to impressions of a quarrelsome, rude, or aggressive communicator. The *attentive* style uses messages that paraphrase statements of others and to show appreciation for what others are saying. People using this mode project feelings of warmth, friendliness, caring, and empathy. We often think of such communicators as good listeners. An *open* verbal style is more conversational, informal, and disclosing—expressing experiences and feelings that give us reasons to have trust. A *precise* verbal style uses very careful, direct, concise, and concrete messages. It suggests a person who is credible and competent.[2]

Of course, we use a combination of different styles across contexts and relationships. For example, patients prefer physicians to be attentive or dramatic, but not dominant or contentious. Students prefer teachers to be attentive, dramatic, and friendly.[3] In most cases receivers also warm to another person who uses pronouns like *we, our,* or *us,* reinforced with head nods, smiles, and touch. Confidence and expressiveness help generate trust and involvement. Effective advocates avoid using confusing terms, overgeneralizations, and stereotyped or sexist language.

We tend to develop and maintain interpersonal relationships that provide more rewards than costs. The most satisfying are those where both parties share these outcomes. Conscious efforts to provide positive rewards in daily interactions strengthen relationships. These can include simple behaviors such as thanking someone, inquiring how people are feeling, or acknowledging the efforts of others.

Nonverbal Characteristics

Nonverbal communication is an essential part of all human communication. Some scholars argue that the meaning we get from interactions comes primarily from the nonverbal dimensions of message exchange.[4] While the importance of nonverbal elements can be oversold, they clearly do accentuate messages in a multitude of ways. A certain look, gesture, or increase in volume may provide clues about the attitudes or emotions of the communicator. Nonverbal messages may complement or contradict what is stated verbally. In addition to emphasis, nonverbal behaviors also regulate the flow of interactions. From certain nonverbal cues, we learn when it is our turn to speak or when someone wishes to interrupt. Nonverbal messages also substitute for verbal messages. A simple nod of the head or shaking of a finger can provide a reply to some questions.

There are numerous channels for nonverbal communication. *Body communication* refers to the various messages sent by our physical presence, such as gestures, posture, movements, and appearance. *Facial and eye communication* include smiles, frowns, raised eyebrows, scowls, winks, and eye movements such as eye contact and pupil dilation. *Artifactual communication* includes all the material objects accumulated by people, such as pens, clothing, and cars. Artifacts communicate social class, status, or success. There are often expectations of style and dress, for example, associated with many professions. Most research indicates that certain artifacts, especially clothing, can influence compliance and persuasiveness. The concept of *paralanguage* refers to the sounds and the meanings associated with *how* words are spoken. Vocal rate, pitch, volume, and pauses all affect the meaning communicated in our verbal messages. These simple categories are useful reminders that there is much more visual data that is being given to us than we may fully appreciate. If you doubt it, ask a television director what matters in putting a scene on tape. More attention will be spent making sure the eyes of the actors are lit and shot in close-up. Facial characteristics provide important cues revealing the feelings and concerns of another person.

People who are aware of nonverbal encoding (sending) and decoding (receiving) variables are more successful in interpersonal relations and influence. Nonverbal behavior can create powerful persuasive outcomes. Peter Andersen notes that nonverbal immediacy behaviors communicate power, attention, warmth, and liking and have a substantial impact on compliance (often stronger than verbal message variables).[5] Judee Burgoon and Gregory Hoobler argue that nonverbal communication is just as much a skill set as oral or verbal communication, and highlight some of the findings of contemporary studies.[6]

- The facility for nonverbal expressiveness is greater among those who are extroverted, expressive, high in self-esteem, persuasive, and physically attractive.

- Nonverbally skilled individuals are more successful in deceiving and influencing others.

- Females have greater nonverbal skills. Women tend to be more accurate interpreters of nonverbal cues than men.

- Age, occupation, and training are related to skills of nonverbal fluency, but race, education, and intelligence are not. It is also no surprise that those with better nonverbal skills are more inclined toward people-oriented occupations.

Scholars have reported other findings about eye contact, facial expression, and body movements. Eye movement can gain attention, signal desire to speak, or show support and empathy. Eye movement can also enhance trust and credibility, whereas looking down or blinking frequently may signal deception. Strong leaders tend to maintain direct eye contact, while those who view themselves as weak tend to avoid eye contact and look away from others.[7]

In general, interpersonal advocates who are dynamic are more persuasive. Specific examples of dynamic behavior include frequent gesturing, hand movements, head nodding, smiling, and high levels of energy. Of course, these activities must appear natural, genuine, and sincere. Body movements and gestures also reveal likes and dislikes.[8] Leaning forward, orienting one's body and head directly toward a person, affirmative head nods, and smiling are nonverbal behaviors indicating liking—while an absence of gestures and a rigid body posture are signs of tension and dislike. The audience also uses body movements and gestures to assess assertiveness, power, and status. A relaxed posture, dynamic gestures, and varied vocal inflections communicate confidence and power, while hunched shoulders, vocal fillers such as "uh," and nervous hand movements communicate powerlessness.

Interpersonal touch is probably one of the oldest forms of human communication. Research shows that touch communicates emotions such as anger, fear, love, sympathy, and gratitude, to name a few.[9] We learn appropriate touching behavior in specific contexts through social interaction. The rules regarding touch behaviors vary greatly by culture. In the United States, there are clear sex differences in touching behavior. For men and women, touch by close friends is positive and reinforces feelings of agreement, support, and empathy.

Touching can also be a powerful tool of reinforcement for compliance. For example, studies revealed that almost any touch increases likelihood of compliance of a request ranging from signing petitions, to purchasing items, to leaving higher tips.[10] While touching tends to stimulate feelings of liking, trust, and interpersonal involvement, there are cultural norms and limitations to such behavior. In making a request, a slight touch on the arm may increase compliance. However, a sustained touch may increase anxiety and stress. The person touched will interpret the meaning of the nonverbal behavior.[11] How well you know the participant in the interaction is, therefore, crucial in deciding how and when to touch someone.

The same is true when considering the distance of interaction. Standing close to the persuadee is usually more likely to gain compliance in cultures where proximity to others indicates liking. If, however, someone feels that his or her personal space has been invaded, there may be a perception of intimidation. The persuader may be perceived as demanding, desperate, or needful. Mediterranean, Middle Eastern, or Latin cultures tend to interact at closer distances. Italians maintain less distance than do Germans or Americans. In the United States, intimate distance of interaction has historically been up to 18 inches, personal distance between 18 inches and 4 feet, social distance between 4 feet to 12 feet, and public distance greater than 12 feet.[12]

Even with its advantages, we close this brief review of interpersonal persuasion with three cautions. First, sometimes what may look like direct interpersonal influence can actually be something else: the gaining of compliance through a *power advantage* held by one side. In most organizations there is a hierarchical structure that separates bosses and employees, superiors and subordinates. These divisions are often functional; employees, students, patients and others usually want clear direction from whomever is in charge. But we sometimes fail to notice people in the same physical space may not be equals. Differences in power are often downplayed in interests of organizational harmony. Companies and other organizations will often define groups of workers as teams, masking the power advantage of the leader who is higher on the organizational chart. But there should be no mistake here. The dynamics of these arrangements mean that employees, students, and others usually *must* comply. And, strictly speaking, compliance is not the same thing as assent freely given.

We will briefly touch on a second caveat about the nature of interpersonal persuasion Recent research indicates that younger Americans are losing some of their interest in face-to-face exchanges.[13] This is surely an effect of the now ubiquitous use of phones and other devices for managing both big and small personal matters. And that is worrying. Interpersonal communication includes the full self. Other media forms always take something away. A mediated message adds a layer that acts as a filter, sometimes creating unwanted distance or simple confusion.

And finally, our enthusiasm for unmediated messaging notwithstanding, it is important to acknowledge that direct encounters with others will not always settle conflicts, produce a sales order, or bring people closer together. The odds for a positive result are better than when using disembodied media, but there are no guarantees. Even when we meet in the same space, conflicts can sometimes escalate, boomerangs may still happen, and egos can be bruised.[14]

The remainder of this chapter focuses on media-based persuasion campaigns. But as we shall see, retaining some features of the interpersonal style usually increases the effectiveness of media messages.

PUBLIC PERSUASION CAMPAIGNS

At the very heart of democracy is public discussion. The quality of that public communication directly impacts the quality of our society. Mitchell McKinney, Lynda Lee Kaid, and Dianne Bystrom see "the fundamental nature of a democracy as that of a *civic dialogue*, an ongoing conversation."[15] At their simplest, mass persuasion campaigns involve *extended attempts* to influence the conversation. This is constant across very different settings.

Media-based campaigns of all types usually include the following defining features.

- *The development of consistent messages, repeated for positive effect.* The repetition aspect is crucial. Well-funded campaigns will often assure that their messages are seen by the target several times in a given week. And since any single message often shows only minimal effects, the use of a group of messages with the same objective builds accumulated effects that can move the target closer to the desired action.

- *A firm start and end date.* Campaigns are usually not ongoing but specific to a given time frame. This helps all concerned focus on achieving measurable effects. If change in behavior or attitudes is not seen, a new campaign will be created and launched.

- *The identification of a target audience.* No campaign targets everyone. Persuasion gains traction by designing messages that speak to a market segment most able act on the message or in need of change.

- *The use of market or audience research to improve message effectiveness.* As noted in chapter 5, there are many ways to test messages, including the use of the old standby of focus-group testing. This testing with a small sample of a target audience helps expose flaws and other problems in the planned messages.

- *The development of a well-defined goal.* Every campaign needs to define what success looks like. For health campaigns, for example, meta-studies indicate a change rate of 5 to 10 percent.[16]

- *When necessary, the inclusion of messages calculated to minimize success of the opposition.* Campaigns sometimes gain traction by making unfavorable comparisons to the groups or individuals that will offer counter-persuasive claims. In politics this means the use of attack ads paid for by opponents. In cases where tobacco use is discouraged, tobacco industries are named and their point-of-sale displays referenced.

SOCIAL MARKETING CAMPAIGNS

Social marketing campaigns encompass numerous issues and social causes: from public health and safety to protecting the environment to pushing for broader human rights protections. They share many techniques and strategies with their commercial and political counterparts.[17] In health campaigns the goal is usually to address a segment of the population (smokers, drug abusers, young parents, senior citizens, etc.) to alter a personal choice that produces negative health or social consequences. A prime example is *The Truth Campaign* which attempts to inoculate adolescents and teens against becoming smokers.[18]

Campaign efforts are considered **outbound** if they employ traditional advertising tools to target audiences. Advertising on cable and network television is an outbound form, as are billboards and various pitches that show up online based on search behavior. **Inbound** *marketing* integrates a message *into* entertainment or informational media content, such as a quasi-news story. For example, *The Daily Beast* in 2016 published what could have been mistaken for an article written by its staff comparing weight loss programs. In reality, Nutrisystem paid for the narrative. Unsurprisingly, the story recommended Nutrisystem. Similarly, raves for a product or service that show up in a movie (i.e., *The Lego Movie*, in 2014) are examples of inbound campaigns.[19] Film revenue targeting kids is often predicated on selling licensed products built around the story.

Top-Down Campaigns

The traditional outbound model for a social marketing campaign is **top down**, where professionals have created and placed messages to engage potential users or supporters. The goal is to develop and deliver messages through a wide range of media platforms and types: television and internet advertising, direct mail, display advertising, and even warnings printed on product packages. For example, we have new research that suggests that a warning on a package of cigarettes that includes a graphic visual image (i.e., a smoker with a TEP, or throat hole) slightly increases the chances a smoker will quit, up to 40 percent for at least seven days of cessation, compared to 34 percent for the text only group.[20] Like most campaigns, those seeking change often rely on various forms of information dissemination: press events, press releases, video news releases, public service announcements (especially for radio, cable and broadcast operations), and advertising. Think of social marketing efforts to increase rates of trash recycling, to encourage families to eat meals together (a factor important in reducing childhood obesity), or to eliminate distracted driving. Since 2010, AT&T claims that it has signed up more than 6.5 million drivers to its "It can wait" campaign to not text and drive.[21]

Bottom-Up Campaigns

A *bottom up* campaign gets most of its energy from volunteers or citizens who seek changes in local ordinances, regional laws, or community attitudes. Citizens lobbying school boards, homeowners hoping to stop real estate developers, or students lobbying for tougher gun laws are examples of bottom-up campaigns. Organizing, marching, raising money, and writing letters are common grassroots efforts, which are sometimes joined by nonprofit groups that typically employ top-down campaigns.

There are many impressive examples of social media seeding interest in a group or a cause. The 2017 Women's March on Washington—perhaps the biggest protest ever in the nation's capital—started as a Facebook post. The ALS (Lou Gehrig's disease) cold water bucket challenge (friends and associates photographed pouring buckets of cold water on each other) in July and August in 2014 went viral on social media, raising $114 million for research into the disease. The group Black Lives Matter continues to sustain interest and support around the country through frequent social media posts and events.[22] After a gunman killed 17 students at Marjory Stoneman Douglas High School on Valentine's Day in 2018, five media savvy teens at the school immediately organized an activist movement (#NeverAgain), convinced the governor of Florida to sign legislation mandating stricter background checks, and planned a nationwide protest, "March for Our Lives" for March 24. The teens attracted a $500,000 donation from George and Amal Clooney, soon matched by Oprah Winfrey, Steven Spielberg and Kate Capshaw, and Jeffrey and Marilyn Katzenberg. The Clooneys and the Katzenbergs were among the estimated 300,000 marchers in Washington, DC.[23]

It is easy to romanticize grassroots activism, particularly today when many social media messages (somewhere between one-quarter to one-half) are generated by *social bots* (automated software to create posts on social media that appear to be from human users) programmed by commercial or political interests.[24] Even so, individual efforts have impressed seasoned marketing professionals. A tweet from a celebrity can hijack attitudes toward a political candidate in the early moments of a 90-minute television debate.[25] Similarly Lynda Obst, a legendary Hollywood producer, notes that marketing a film works only until opening day. Then the buzz of social media opinion-makers takes over.

> A thousand people will each tell a thousand people what they think of a movie opening in three thousand theaters simultaneously. They will BBM it, tweet it, Facebook it, and before you know it, it's around the world in sixty seconds. No matter how many TV spots feature the three good reviews, word of mouth from your six closest friends always wins.[26]

The features of inbound and outbound forms of conveying messages apply equally to other campaign forms, especially advertising. And, of course, the durable idea of grassroots campaigns—the bottom up approach we just described—retains its place in assessing political campaigns.

ADVERTISING CAMPAIGNS

Obst's observations about marketing films is a fitting introduction to *advertising campaigns*. Advertising is a pervasive campaign form in our society. In the 1970s, people were exposed to about 500 advertisements per day; today the number ranges from 4,000 to 10,000.[27] An hour of prime-time network programming contains almost 17 minutes of advertising, with cable and daytime programs exceeding 20 minutes per hour. One-third of daytime television is taken up by commercials.[28] Sixty percent of newspaper space is advertising, with online revenue beginning to surpass hard copy sales. By the time Americans reach the age of 65, they will have been exposed to nearly 140 million advertisements across all media and will have watched 2 million television commercials.[29]

In 2018, 26 percent of American adults reported that they go online almost constantly (up from 21 percent in 2015); another 43 percent go online several times a day.[30] Such extensive use explains the explosive growth of internet advertising. In 2000, internet advertising in the United States was $8.1 billion; in 2010, it was $26 billion; in 2016 it was $72.5 billion.[31] Millions go to YouTube to watch ads daily. In 2017, the top five ads watched were: Samsung India Services (150.3 million views), Clash Royale (110.7 views), Ping Pong Shots sponsored by Oreo (90.6 million views), Miss Dior (43 million views), and Budweiser Super Bowl Commercial (28.5 million views).[32] In 2016, $191.2 billion was spent on advertising; TV and the internet had almost equal shares of $152.3 billion; the remaining $38.9 billion was for radio, print, and outdoor advertising.[33] Digital ad revenue is projected to hit $116 billion in the United States by the end of 2021.

A common feature of the ad world today is *cross-selling*, a variation of inbound marketing. In 1937, Disney was the first studio to merchandize films by selling toys and items linked with *Snow White and the Seven Dwarfs*. The proliferation of cross-selling has grown exponentially since then and includes license merchandizing, product placement, and cross-promotion with fast-food restaurants. Consider the placement of products in television and films. In 1982 sales of Reese's Pieces increased 300 percent when E.T. ate the candy. After Tom Cruise wore Ray-Ban aviator sunglasses in *Top Gun*, sales increased by 40 percent.[34] And Manolo Blahnik became a much more popular brand of shoe after its affiliation with HBO's *Sex and the City*.[35]

Jean Kilbourne argues that "magazines, newspapers, and radio and television programs round us up, rather like cattle, and producers and publishers then sell us to advertisers."[36] The various types of media become devices to deliver audiences that meet the specific criteria advertisers consider important for the purchase, support, and acceptance of their products or services. *Narrowcasting* is the term used for reaching very specific markets. The explosion of cable channels has resulted in many programs designed for very particular interests. For example, business executives are likely to watch CNBC, while teenagers and young adults tune in to MTV. In addition, cable subscribers are younger, more affluent, and better educated with greater purchasing power. The specialized programming on cable that reaches specific markets appeals to advertisers.[37] As Juliann Sivulka notes, "No single institution has played a greater role in both reflecting and shaping American life. . . . Advertising both mirrors a society and creates a society."[38]

Although advertising is mediated, a well-crafted message functions much like an interpersonal message. It's worded in personal terms and suggests a connection with the receiver. Successful appeals are tailored *demographically* (by age, income, etc.) and *psychographically* (appealing to the passions of a social sub group). Indeed, successful advertising sometimes results in the audience responding to advertising characters. For example, we think of the droll actor J. K. Simmons as the face of Farmers Insurance.

Evolving Ad Strategies

With some exceptions, advertising prior to the mid-1950s focused mostly on a strategy of selling products based on their specific features and characteristics. A *rational-reasons approach* to marketing might tout apparel as durable, spot resistant, or rugged. In the past, patent medicines were sold with dubious claims about their curing powers. Early advertising in the 1860s promoted a product called Egyptian Regulator Tea. The advertisement was three pages long and claimed an almost unlimited list of curative characteristics.

A good-reasons-to-buy approach is no longer the dominant style of advertising today. By the end of the 1950s, the medium of television and its capabilities influenced a change in approach to branding products for recognition and prestige. Messages took a *positioning approach*—touting what owning a product could say about the owner. Positioning is a result of the evolution of advertising messages from what a product *does* to what a product *says* about who we *are*. The primary strategy of positioning is to offer a satisfied need as a reward for using a product. In short, brand personality became more important than brand performance. Sexy jeans have a stronger appeal than long-lasting jeans. A stylish, designer watch is favored over an accurate one. Clothes are worn for self-identity rather than warmth; they reflect our social values and good judgment. Products are portrayed as having unique and evocative associations. Look at contemporary ads for products as diverse as Omega watches or Lincoln automobiles and you will find more attention paid to image (sports legend or film spokespersons) than any advertising copy devoted to the features of the product. Clearly branded sunglasses, handbags, and clothing are similarly meant to represent something about the aspirations of the owners.

Creating Demand

There are four basic functions of advertising.[39] The most simple and basic is *precipitation*; the persuasive goals are brand awareness and knowledge. The second function is *persuasion*; the messages appeal to human feelings and attempt to induce a sale. The third function is *reinforcement*; the goal is to legitimize existing purchases and to validate previous purchase decisions. *Reminder* is the final function; the goal is to reinforce brand loyalty. For example, most McDonald's ads are designed to keep top-of-mind awareness rather than to describe product attributes.

We purchase some products simply because we recall the ads from television and just want to try them. We may then like the product and will form a favorable attitude. In other cases, the advertising causes an attitude to form without ever experiencing the product, as in the belief that Mercedes are superior automobiles. We attach significance to the products (status or prestige, for example) before any purchase takes place. In this sequence, we start with an attitude change, develop a positive attitude toward the product, and then, if circumstances allow, purchase the car.

One school of thought is that likability enhances persuasion; however, many well-liked ads have no impact on sales. Conversely, advertisements that consumers find aggravating can generate sales. Others claim that commercials that are less overtly manipulative are liked more. The basis of this hypothesis is that well-liked ads provide information, work better without celebrity endorsers, and tell us something we didn't previously know.[40] Finally, it is thought that liking an ad evokes a gratitude response. While perhaps a stretch, it is thought that part of consumer behavior is based on the pleasure produced by consuming the advertising itself.[41] Think of the Super Bowl, where the ads are sometimes better than the game.

Creating demand sometimes involves planting unrealistic expectations in a consumer's head that can then be solved by purchasing a product. Advertising perpetuates a cycle of images that can create dissatisfaction. Consider all the ads that target young and middle-aged women, where the predicate of the ad is that a condition exists—whether dry skin, exposed roots, facial wrinkles, acne, or cellulite—that needs to be fixed. Happiness with one's self-image is destabilized by messages that create concern about appearance. Social critiques of advertising note that its most damning features are messages that include body-shaming to personal products. In her landmark study of cultural pressures on adolescent girls, Mary Pipher observed: "Advertising teaches that pain can be handled by buying and consuming products. There's big money to be made in creating wants and then encouraging consumers that these wants are needs, even rights. We are encouraged that if it feels right, it is right."[42]

Assessing Ads

Advertisements transform statements about things into statements of significance to people. For example, if a characteristic of a car is high gas mileage, then this characteristic is translated into beliefs about economy and rationality. The key is to transform the language of objects into the language of people.

As a critic, a person should look at the textual relationships between the parts of the message and the meaning created. Through ads, diamonds are equated with love—a transformation beyond mineral and rock to a purely human emotion. In some ads, objects become the symbols for human messages (e.g., "say it with flowers" or "gold says I love you"). In other ads, people are identified with the objects that project significance (e.g., "I'm a Pepper" or "become part of the Pepsi generation").

The visual image created plays a very important part of the meaning created. In fact, the more prominent the central image in an ad, the greater the potential impact. In a now famous television ad for Apple computers reminiscent of George

Orwell's *1984*, an athletic woman hurls a sledgehammer through the video screen that hundreds have been watching in a trance. The spot was a media sensation and won several creative awards; it relied entirely on the visual image for its power. The clear implication was that the new Apple Macintosh computer was a breakthrough for individual creativity and freedom, releasing us from the world of domination and control by "big brother." Another highly visual campaign was the original campaign for Infiniti automobiles. The first two years of the television and print campaigns used a positioning approach. The car was never shown: owning one was an experience beyond the simple goal of transporting oneself from point A to point B. The visuals were of sweeping landscapes, accompanied by poetic descriptions.

When analyzing advertising, look for patterns of similarities and differences. For example, how are people portrayed in print ads—as housewives or executives, smart or dumb, fat or thin? How frequently are certain roles portrayed? What are the sex roles and models for expected behavior? This approach to viewing ads reveals cultural roles and stereotypes. First, focus on the attributes, claims, and promises of the product. Next, analyze the images, stereotypes, and placement/positions of the visuals. Finally, and mostly importantly, consider audience needs that are satisfied if the ad leads to the purchase of a product or service. Listed below are common *need appeals* in advertisements.

- *Self-esteem*. How does product positioning translate into a greater sense of self worth?
- *Prestige*. What tribe has the purchaser of a unique product joined?
- *Control*. How does the product or service promise greater freedom or personal choice?
- *Acceptance*. How does the product promise greater approval or support from others?
- *Self-Reward*. How is the product sold as something the buyer deserves?
- *Convenience*. How will a service or product make my life easier?
- Keep these questions in mind when assessing advertisements.
- What was the first thing that caught your attention?
- What is the target audience of the ad? How can you tell?
- What benefits does the ad promise the product will provide?
- What does the ad not say?
- How do the visuals model the audience or their aspirations?
- Are any rational reasons offered?
- How is the ad selling more than the product? (For example, a Mercedes is more than transportation; we buy the world that it represents.)
- Does the ad illustrate how we can be recruited to participate in our own persuasion?

A reasonable assessment considers whether an ad works; is it effective? If we take the long view, advertising is important in feeding demand for the consumer economy, which is roughly 70 percent of all economic activity. In general terms, advertising provides some of the fuel for many forms of business activity. At the level of specific messages, the question is harder to answer. Consumers respond more positively to ads that are authentic; for example, reviews by previous purchasers as seen on various online retailer sites.[43] Even so, individual Americans do not believe advertising influences their buying decisions.[44] In a telephone survey, only 14 percent of the respondents said they were influenced by advertising. Interestingly, however, respondents believed that women, young people, and people in low-income groups were more affected by advertising than other groups. Individuals from those groups disagreed. In addition, anyone immersed in even a small portion of the media platforms spread across the culture can realize that *clutter*— the industry term for too many competing ad messages in one location or time frame—can dull our awareness.

Overall, any answer about the effectiveness of advertising is surprisingly complicated, partly because those within the industry usually put the most optimistic face on their efforts. To be sure, product campaigns specifically intended to increase market share need to show some success. How much is usually a closely guarded metric. Advertising agencies will often lose an account if sales are flat after an expensive campaign. There is clearer evidence that ads do help maintain a brand's market position, perhaps not changing buying habits as much as reinforcing existing customer loyalties. Even so, we occasionally do see evidence of surprisingly *minimal effects.* In 2017 J.P. Morgan/Chase had internet ads running on 400,000 different websites before deciding to limit messages to just 5000 sites. Like other advertisers using Google and YouTube, they became disturbed about the content of the some of the sites where their ads appeared. (Internet advertising follows specific buyers across the various platforms they use, so if they visit a site that is racist or offensive, the ad then appears on that site.) The usual online click-through rate indicating that someone did more than simply see an ad is about 3 percent. But even with their dramatic cutback in the number of sites where the ads were seen, Chase saw no difference in their business.[45] The safest conclusion is that ads are best at generating and maintaining top-of mind awareness. Converting new buyers is rarely easy.

POLITICAL PERSUASION

We have established that persuasion is a process of altering or strengthening beliefs or attitudes to elicit a desired behavior. Although the types of political messages and the forms they take are limitless, there are commonalities among them. The most general characteristics of *political persuasion* include: an orientation toward the short term, interest in obtaining one specific objective, and an emphasis on being responsive to the target audience.[46]

The Immediacy of Politics

Political life is preoccupied with transitory issues and limited time frames. Messages are typically planned, prepared, and delivered with an eye to *immediate* outcomes. The limited and specific time frames for political campaigns are rather obvious—the campaign ends once votes are cast or a decision is made.

According to Lloyd Bitzer, most political messages occur in specific historical situations that structure possible responses.

> Political speakers find themselves in situations that present problems, crises, obstacles, or other kinds of exigencies which they seek to modify by addressing messages to mediating audiences—that is, to audiences which have sufficient power to modify the exigencies.[47]

After an issue or problem has been identified (often as the result of a targeted campaign), some type of action will likely occur. The action could be a new law, a court ruling, a national or state referendum, or a designated investigation.

The political talk of campaigns, of legislation, and of public discourse is carefully molded, crafted, and sometimes tested to insure an intended effect. Sound bites are created, answers to anticipated questions are rehearsed, and messages are targeted to very specific audiences of essential constituents. Communication is *directive* and intentional. Because political communication seeks to induce individual or collective action, it is founded squarely on the principles of persuasion. All practical communication is audience centered. However, political discourse is especially audience sensitive. Politicians and government officials are motivated by the desire to gain the support of specific constituencies. Political messages are not neutral; they are created with a targeted audience in mind.

Robert Denton and Jim Kuypers define political communication as the "public discussion about the allocation of public resources (revenues), official authority (who is given control; i.e., the power to make legal, legislative, and executive decisions), official sanctions (what the state rewards or punishes), and social meaning (what does it mean to be an American, the role of the citizen, implications of social policy, etc.)".[48] How revenue is generated and allocated are clear matters of political discussion, debate, and policy. The Affordable Care Act dominated much of President Obama's first term and the 2012 campaign; attempts to repeal and replace it dominated the first 100 days of the Trump Administration four years later. Political campaigns are official exercises in granting authority to elected officials to represent citizens or to implement policies advocated during the electoral contest. There are all types of sanctions beyond legal compliance. Tax policies, for example, sanction very specific types of behavior; the public debate over same-sex marriage is another example. The final consideration, social meaning, acknowledges that political communication is much more than the enacting of legislation and the election of officials. Public debate expresses our beliefs and values as a nation. Our debates over abortion, gun control, affirmative action, or charter schools all reflect firmly held beliefs. Thus, how individual policies are treated have a significant impact on the degree to which we feel acknowledged by the culture.

Levels of Interaction

Silvo Lenart investigated three levels of interpersonal political processes: person-to-person, group-to-person, and opinion climate-to-person.[49] The person-to-person level comes from the two-step flow model (see chapter 5) of political influence. Opinion leaders are similar to the individuals they influence in terms of attitudes and beliefs. They tend to belong to the same primary groups (e.g., family, friends, or coworkers). Most studies show this to be the most powerful mode of influence, although being in the echo chamber (a context of similar opinions and beliefs) with friends (who may not be opinion leaders) has an equally strong influence. The role of the media is secondary to the role of interpersonal influence.

Studies investigating group influence on individuals come primarily from network-analysis and social-context research. This perspective views individuals as highly interdependent with others in homogeneous groups where members conform to group goals and identity through peer pressure. The interpersonal relationships provide networks of communication and anchor points for individual attitudes and beliefs. The more cohesive the group, the higher the level of individual satisfaction and the greater the tendency to influence and to be influenced by others.[50] Through interaction with group members (direct or via social media), individuals learn which attitudes are acceptable and thus have the potential for positive reinforcement and social approval.

Many believe that the mass media function as opinion climates. Research dating back to the 1950s demonstrates that many people eventually agree with what they perceive to be the majority point of view. Prominent German pollster Elisabeth Noelle-Neumann introduced the spiral of silence in 1974.[51] Her concept provides insight into why people think the media have such strong influence when, empirically, studies find very minimal direct effects. She posits that we are constantly surveying our social environment for cues about what is popular and what is in disfavor. On issues of political or social importance, we assess and form an impression among various viewpoints that seem to have the most public support. We make such evaluations, according to Noelle-Neumann, because we do not want to be perceived as ill informed and risk being isolated by others. If our opinions or viewpoints are not those of the majority, then we suppress our opinions. Rather than voicing our opposing views, we simply keep quiet. Thus, "the spiral of silence holds that (a) those in the minority will curb the expression of their views, with (b) the result that the impression of public opinion resulting from the tripartite of personal experience—others, events, and media—will be distorted toward an overestimate of support for the majority and an underestimate of support for the minority."[52]

Contexts of Political Persuasion

We usually think of politics in terms of election campaigns. In this section, we address that topic as well as other important contexts.

Administrative Persuasion. For presidents, mayors, and officers of corporations, *administrative persuasion* is a necessity. The formal powers of most governmental leaders rarely fall in the category of unilateral orders that are carried out swiftly. Despite being elected president for four terms (1932 until his death in 1945) and steering the country through the Great Depression and World War II, Franklin Delano Roosevelt thought he had very little power, once telling an amused gathering of reporters,

> The Treasury is so large and far-flung and ingrained in its practices that I find it almost impossible to get the action and results I want. . . . But the Treasury is not to be compared with the State Department. You should go through the experi-

ence of trying to get any changes in the thinking, policy, and action of the career diplomats and then you'd know what a real problem was. . . . [And the Navy?] To change anything in the Na-a-vy is like punching a feather bed.[53]

Although topping the organizational chart, governmental leaders recognize that authority is not sufficient. To be an effective leader, they must cultivate their persuasive skills. A judge in a court of law renders decisions and sentences, but others know that they cannot govern by decree only. The need to win the allegiance of their own bureaucracies (not to mention the support of members of Congress and the mass media) dictates the necessity for constant attention to the techniques of persuasion. While prime minister of Great Britain in 2008, Gordon Brown described the world as at a tipping point where opportunities to eradicate poverty and to establish social justice vied with the struggles of people to adapt to many new challenges. One reporter suggested that to accomplish his goal of reforming international institutions, "he will have to acquire a skill he has never perfected—the ability to communicate and persuade."[54] Some of the same criticisms have been leveled against President Trump.[55]

Over the last quarter century, we have seen the convergence of the activities, skills and demands of political and corporate leadership. Many members of the business community enter politics, and long-term politicians enter the corporate and academic arenas. We look to leaders for more than the daily management of governmental affairs. We expect their actions and words to embrace our goals and values; leaders are simultaneously symbols and symbol makers. The success that any single leader enjoys is partly a function of skill in evoking a public sense of participation. Broadly speaking, administrative persuasion sets the public agenda, builds coalitions, and channels public attitudes into a workable course of action.

One measure of any leader's success is how well he or she can focus attention on a common problem and dramatize its significance. At any given time, public attention is limited to a relatively small number of issues that dominate newspaper headlines and evening news broadcasts. A governor with an eye on shaping a state's agenda may repeatedly focus on a limited number of urgent issues to orchestrate news coverage that will alter public opinion. This is sometimes called "staying on message," or "managing the news agenda."

The Reagan administration in the early 1980s was highly successful in managing the news agenda. Reagan combined his considerable personal charm with a unique ability to stay on message. Access to the president was limited, and advisers kept the press busy with at least one message of the day and one photo opportunity. As one unhappy journalist noted, "Together they sold the official myths of Reagan's presidency to the American public by developing a sophisticated new model for manipulating the press."[56]

Barack Obama's 2012 convention nomination address was written in seven-minute segments that made it ideal for YouTube presentation. Syracuse University media scholar Robert Thompson said the address was "made for use by the Democrats for social media."[57] More than 36 million people watched the acceptance address and generated 4 million tweets. The Obama campaign not only managed the news agenda but also successfully challenged what had become an accepted way of thinking about how the news is presented.

The essence of political leadership is coalition building. Finding ways to get groups with different goals to work together is a powerful skill. Effective leaders know when to make alliances and when to end them. Bill Clinton used a strategy of triangulation between Republicans and Democrats to put together coalitions on a range of issues including free trade, family leave, and welfare reform. Ted Sorensen, former speechwriter for John F. Kennedy, compared Barack Obama's historic primary campaign in 2008 to the efforts of Kennedy, the first Catholic president. He remarked that Kennedy's victory in Protestant West Virginia electrified the country. Of Obama, he said, "At the root of all this is his remarkable ability to transcend traditional politics and reach across lines—regional, political, racial—just as John F. Kennedy did."[58]

Early presidents rarely addressed Congress or the public in person, but their modern counterparts are expected to express the collective grief, anger, joy, and resolve of their constituents. Theodore Roosevelt declared the White House a "bully pulpit," and each succeeding leader has understood the role of president as encompassing an important public dimension. We expect the president to be, in Mary Stuckey's words, our "interpreter in chief." As she notes, the holder of the highest office in the land has become "the nation's chief storyteller," offering narratives of "what sort of people we are, [and] how we are constituted as a community."[59] George W. Bush's first address to Congress after the terrorist attacks on New York and Washington and Ronald Reagan's eulogy for the crew lost in the explosion of the space shuttle *Challenger* gave voice to the feelings of most Americans, expressing both national resolve and grief.

Legislative Persuasion. Members of Congress spend their time shuttling between Washington DC and their home state—between governing and campaigning. In a routine day, a senator or representative may meet with constituents in the morning, lunch with a lobbyist at noon, question an expert witness in an afternoon committee meeting, and receive an evening phone call from a cabinet official soliciting support on an upcoming vote. In between these events, members may consult with a dozen colleagues, plan strategy on the introduction of a piece of legislation, tape a radio report to constituents back home, and review the schedule for a busy weekend of campaigning. The time spent studying legislation is slim.

We tend to judge our representatives by their communication with the citizens of their district, the way they deal with constituents, and the services they provide for the district. Constituent service includes voicing concerns of the state or district, solving individual problems that citizens have with the government, and making sure that the district gets its share of federal money and assistance. Most of the constituent work is done by district staff members.[60] The currency of legislative life is communication with staff members, constituents, and peers.

When it comes to legislating, there is less discussion and deliberation than we might think. In the 112th Congress, the House introduced 6,711 bills and the Senate 3,695, yet only 283 were enacted. Since 2000, less than 5 percent of all bills introduced are voted into law.[61] One of the most potent forums for *legislative persuasion* of both the U.S. public and individual legislators is the committee hearing. This venue is where much of the work of legislating and negotiating is done. In 1973, the three major commercial networks devoted over 235 hours to the presentation of Senate hearings into the Watergate affair.[62] The political and cultural history of the United States could be partly written from the minutes of the legislative hearings that have taken place in the nation's capital—ranging from Joseph McCarthy's attempts in 1954 to find Communists in the State Department to the testimony of tobacco executives in 1998. More recently, former FBI Director James Comey gave testimony in 2017 regarding his meetings with Donald Trump as an investigation of Russian involvement in American campaigns began. Millions of Americans become transfixed by the theater of these high-visibility proceedings.

Hearings are conducted by the members of committees who have jurisdiction over specific types of proposed legislation. They present an ideal setting for supporters and opponents of legislation to dramatize their concerns. Victims, experts, and lobbyists regularly appear before committees that consider early drafts of proposed legislation. Committee members often count on the presence of the press—especially television cameras—to place issues of concern before the general public. Hearings have an inherent drama—whether a heated exchange between a committee member and someone called for questioning or the prepared statements of those who have suffered a loss. The testimony of victims is often graphic and dramatic; the narratives highlight innocent victims and the villains who have harmed them. For example, the Enron employees who lost their jobs and their pensions fueled public anger against the company executives called by House and Senate committees to explain their accounting practices.[63] Committee leadership can orchestrate hearings to sway public opinion and to make a convincing case for new legislation.

Members of legislatures are also the recipients of influence *from* constituents and colleagues. In a representative democracy, messages from constituents receive attention, although action is not always taken. Letters, faxes, phone calls, and email from a legislator's district can all be factors in determining how he or she will vote on a pending question. Office holders and interest groups rely on the internet to maintain and extend electoral support and to bring public pressure for or against individual bills.[64] Individuals and groups are empowered by email, internet blogging, text messaging, and other online communication—adding their voices to campaigns.[65] The new voices represent both opportunities and challenges for congressional members.

A loose confederation of concerned citizens formed Indivisible after the 2016 general election. Echoing the work of abolitionists and suffragettes in the first half of the nineteenth Century and the Tea Party's emphasis on defense rather than offense in local activism, members met in churches and homes to identify ways to influence local members of Congress.[66] Social media provided the glue for interested individuals to keep informed about specific events. For example, in New Jersey's Seventh Congressional District, motivated citizens who connected through social media packed two meetings held by Representative Leonard Lance. Most urged the moderate Republican to vote against early attempts to repeal the Affordable Care Act. In a crucial first attempt on medical reform in March of 2017, Lance became a key "no" vote that contributed to the initial defeat of the legislation.

Another source of influence is the party. Political parties are less dominant than they once were, but they are still important. Parties in Washington and the state capitals used to be able to deliver the votes of their members with great regularity. Prior to the 1950s, the act of going against one's party was a risky business. Powerful leaders like Lyndon Johnson in the Senate and Sam Rayburn in the House of Representatives headed well-drilled teams of floor managers and whips who would regularly deliver the votes of members on questions that had been defined as party issues. In terms of general voting, most legislatures follow the will or direction of their party. However, in controversial votes or issues, they may well rely on personal beliefs or clear preferences of key constituencies. Sometimes, individual legislators are influenced by colleagues who are friends or by a norm reciprocity that requires returning a favor by supporting a colleague's legislation.[67]

Social Action Campaign Persuasion. As noted earlier in the chapter, some campaigns are designed to mobilize citizens and voters on a wide array of issues. Politics is always more than elections. Indeed, if we want to find evidence of the health of our democracy, we are perhaps most likely to sense its pulse in the daily output of citizen's groups and other nongovernmental organizations that seek to influence public opinion and the legislative and executive branches.[68] Much of the office space in the nation's capital is taken by organizations that lobby to influence state and federal legislators and agencies. This is a core goal of *social action campaigns.* They seek to mobilize the grassroots, frequently with help from organizations like the Sierra Club, the National Rifle Association, the American Association of Retired Persons, or the Me Too Movement.

Sometimes a specific issue matters less for how it might evolve into legislative proposals than for what our position on it says about who we are. In his interesting discussion of what he calls *status politics,* sociologist Joseph Gusfield notes that we tend to combine our attitudes toward specific issues with stereotyped attitudes about certain kinds of people.[69] A concern becomes a *status issue* when a group collectively makes the judgment that *where* other people stand on a question demonstrates their superiority or inferiority. In short, status issues are linked to identity— to our sense that we are acknowledged and valued by the rest of society. For example, how should the western expansion of the United States be portrayed in school history books? Was government negotiation with Native Americans fair? Did government policy serve the nation or enforce harsh terms on indigenous people with prior claims on the land? Story lines for history books are hotly debated by many school boards in many states.[70]

Policies perceived as hostile or friendly to LGBTQ people, veterans, African American men, the disabled, women protected under Title IX, or Medicaid recipients are among the many flash points for various groups seeking acknowledgment from the culture that they have a voice. When statements are made that confirm the prestige of groups with which we identify, our own self-esteem is confirmed. A victory for the group is a victory for us as well. The concept of status politics is a potent reminder that political persuasion is not only about objective changes in policy but also about our sense of solidarity or estrangement from others.

Electoral Campaign Persuasion. We tend to forget that there are nearly 500,000 elective offices in the United States, most too local to employ the television advertising and campaign consultants that dominate elections for national positions. A person in Alameda County, California, for example, will not only vote for members of Congress and a president, but also long slates of individuals representing the County Board of Supervisors, members of the water district, the park district, the state assembly, superior court judges, the State's Superintendent of Public Instruction, and about 50 additional people.[71] Local office seekers often rely on old-school approaches, including direct mail. In smaller states, voters may expect to meet a candidate or hear them speak at a local school or municipal building. Campaigns at the local level remain largely retail, with candidates spending a great deal of time trying to meet as many voters as they can. *Canvassing* (campaigning door to door) whether by the candidate or supporters remains a common technique.

We often seek leaders who can bring about change in every corner of the nation, which explains our fascination with campaigning and governing at the national level. According to longtime political operative Ed Rollins:

> The modern campaign . . . is a high-tech, high-maintenance, high-anxiety, high-concept monstrosity where response time is instant. The candidate may have never held office. The manager is a professional political consultant who may be juggling three other races. The pollster samples public opinion every night for weeks. The press is frantically looking for dirt on the candidate and his or her every relative, dead or alive. The television budget may be larger than the gross national product of Niger. And if your ads don't slash and burn, you'll lose.[72]

There still are true citizen-politicians at the state and local level; however, there is an increasing professionalization of political campaigns, even at the local levels. As Daniel Shea and Michael Burton note:

> The Internet, which found its political footing in the 21st century, has wrought fundamental change. Every position paper, every advertisement, every news release, can now be personalized to voters across the World Wide Web. In the new millennium, the local knowledge once monopolized by local political workers who knew constituents by name or at least by reputation is being supplanted by computer-generated voter lists that serve much the same function.[73]

Increasingly, campaign workers and money come from outside the geographic area of the race. Money rules the day in terms of staff, advertising, and the use of campaign technology—the most far reaching of which now includes *data mining*. Online giants like Google and Facebook have troves of data about their users, some of which can end up being used by a campaign to microtarget voters. Express opinions about abortion access in Facebook, and you may find you are receiving ads in your feed from a member of Congress sympathetic with your expressed view.[74]

With regard to money, it has always been the lifeblood of politics. In the 1960 presidential campaign, John F. Kennedy spent $70 million ($2.05 per vote received). Each campaign becomes more expensive and breaks previous spending records. In 2008, John McCain was limited to spending just $85 million for the general election because of his participation in the public financing system. In contrast, the Obama campaign spent $750 million. In 2012, Mitt Romney spent $992 million, while Obama spent $1.07 billion.[75] The 2016 campaign was somewhat different. Trump spent about half of Hilary Clinton's nearly billion dollars, largely by gaining a great deal of free media coverage.[76]

According to Shea and Burton, it is essential for every campaign to have a theme. "A good theme is a carefully crafted merger of what the voters want, what the candi-

What Are Political Campaigns For?

Journalists seem fascinated with the strategy and tactics of political campaigns; their endless analysis far exceeds what most of us want to know. The antiquated system of state primaries dominates presidential politics. The largest states wait for primaries in smaller ones like Iowa and New Hampshire. A crazy quilt of organizational needs and commercial opportunities play out in repetitive loops over many months.

In their book, *Spiral of Cynicism*, communication researchers Kathleen Jamieson and Joe Cappella assert that *process reporting* contributes to the chaos. Process stories tell us very little about what the candidates will *do* should they get the opportunity to govern; they tell us much more about what the campaigns are *planning* as they do battle with their opponents. *Substantive* coverage includes stories on what a candidate thinks: how he or she would govern and lead, and what policies they would propose. By contrast, the process frame of reference focuses on political polling and the strategies of individual campaigns to win votes. Why is a candidate spending so much time in a particular swing state? Why did they show up at this location? Whose decision was it to keep the candidate away from interviewers from *The Washington Post*? The lists of strategic questions are endless and often trivial. But as is true for color commentators broadcasting professional sports, we seem to have an endless reservoir of curiosity about the backstories of individual players. The journalists at cable news outlets, in particular, would be enfeebled without constant commentary about campaign mechanics.

Years ago the iconic journalist I.F. Stone often noted that journalists would do better to stay away from the campaign trail and write stories based on the public record: the policy positions of governments or the position papers of candidates who want to run them. He knew that when we are consumed with the sideshows of the campaigns, we are also sacrificing the opportunity to find safe passage through the thorny tasks of governing that lie ahead.

date has to offer, and what the opponent brings to the table."[77] Public opinion polling helps candidates develop a theme that sums up voter concerns. Challengers have more latitude in theme selection. Incumbents are more restricted because they have a record to defend or exploit and prior rhetorical postures from which deviation is difficult. Campaign themes are most effective for voters who make their choice of which candidate to support for reasons other than party affiliation or incumbent status. Campaign themes try to be as inclusive and broad as possible. Consistency and repetition of the campaign theme are critical considerations. Themes can include the economy, peace, prosperity, participation, hope, leadership, and change.

Campaign slogans often reflect campaign themes. Examples include: "Vote yourself a farm" (Abraham Lincoln); "Peace and prosperity" (Dwight D. Eisenhower); "The stakes are too high for you to stay home" (Lyndon B. Johnson); "It's morning in America" (Ronald Reagan); "Change we can believe in" (Barack Obama, 2008), "Forward" (Barack Obama, 2012); and "Make America Great Again" (Donald Trump).[78] Many interpreted the results of the 2016 presidential campaign as a reaction against newly enfranchised groups (transgender Americans, undocumented workers, environmental activists, and so on). The pushback came mostly from working-class Americans caught in a web of wage stagnation, underemployment, and a shrinking white majority. The nationalist "America first" appeals of candidate Trump expressed many of those grievances.[79]

Politicians increasingly use marketing techniques and research tools to plan effective campaigns. Joe McGinniss wrote *The Selling of the President* after learning that both presidential candidates in 1968, Richard Nixon and Hubert Humphrey, had hired advertising agencies "to package them like products and sell them to the American people."[80] Television changed how candidates campaigned. Nixon's image adviser stated bluntly, "the response is to the image, not to the man. . . . It's not what's there that counts, it's what's projected."[81]

The Sawyer Miller Group in the 1970s "married Madison Avenue with Pennsylvania Avenue, selling candidates like consumer goods in an electronic democracy."[82] The political consulting group very successfully "wrapped intellectual voter appeals in emotional clothes." By the time it dissolved in the early 1990s, its victorious clients included four senators, six governors, Vaclav Havel, and Israel's Shimon Peres. Its techniques included constant polling, sloganeering, and attack ads. James Harding's *Alpha Dogs* traces the spread of the very effective techniques nationally and internationally. As he notes, "we now live in a tactical age, not an ideological one. Managers, speechwriters, pollsters and get-out-the-vote specialists have more power than we'd like to admit."[83] Lisa Spiller and Jeff Bergner similarly argue that, following contemporary marketing theory, "the task is to *begin with what people want, and to shape the image of a candidate to fit these wants. We have moved altogether beyond a product-centric marketing approach to an approach that is completely customer centered.*"[84]

In marketing terms, the political party is viewed as the company, and the vote is the purchase. Instead of analyzing political parties from the perspective of their history, ideology, or policy platforms, political marketing considers them in terms of their market standing or competitive position.[85] Are they market leaders, challengers, followers, or nichers? When a political party is the market leader, strategies focus on expanding the total market as well as maintaining current market share and working to extend it. Of course, the market leader is always under attack. The problem of increasing market share involves balancing the appearance of stability and dominance with that of being innovative and open to new ideas and constituencies. Achieving this delicate balance requires a blend of product (policies) and promotion (communication). The primary strategy is to maintain market share by reinforcing the existing image among supporters as well as reminding them of reasons for remaining loyal to the party.

Every campaign needs a strategy or a blueprint for winning an election. A strategy is how to position the candidate and allocate resources to maximize the candidate's strengths and to minimize the candidate's weaknesses. The simplest way to think of strategies is in terms of incumbent approaches and challenger approaches. An incumbent generally uses a rhetoric of reassurance, noting that their leadership has helped things get better. A challenger almost always runs as an outsider, favoring a reputation as an insurgent, ready to make big changes. This was largely the message of Donald Trump in 2016. Supporters liked his vague but evocative promise to "drain the swamp of Washington" and "Make America great again."

Shea and Burton designate three main goals for campaign strategy: reinforcement, persuasion, and conversion. Reinforcement is keeping core or base voters committed to the campaign. Persuasion is gaining the support of swing or undecided voters. Conversion is bringing opponent supporters over to your side. Generally, campaigns use messages to reinforce their own partisans, persuade the swing voters, and convert partisans of the opposition. Of course, it is easier to reinforce voters than to convert them.[86]

Message strategies may be based on the personal virtues or vices of the candidates (e.g., (in)experience, (in)competence, integrity or lack thereof, compassion, and so forth); ideological or partisan differences (e.g., liberal, conservative, libertarian, etc.); or some combination of the two. The main point is that the campaign message must draw a line of distinction between the candidate and the opposition by framing a clear choice for voters.[87]

Priming and framing are two pivotal concepts that focus on how the placement or deletion of story details can alter audience attitudes about political agents. *Priming* is a technique involving the placement of information. For example, if a certain piece of information is introduced first, it can affect perceptions of everything else that follows. Priming theorists Shanto Iyengar and Donald Kinder note:

> Political persuasion is difficult to achieve, but agenda setting and priming are apparently pervasive. According to our results, television news clearly and decisively influences the priorities that people attach to various national problems, and the considerations they take into account as they evaluate political leaders or choose between candidates for public office.[88]

It is possible to dramatically alter an audience's judgment about the competence and integrity of a politician by altering the *sequence* of details presented. If a campaign story about a candidate starts with a negative fact about him or her, that fact will loom as a significant measure of the candidate for the rest of the story. It is notoriously difficult to induce attitude change from a television or a news story, but it is comparatively easy to use television news or ads to build a sense of importance for a topic.

Framing is like priming, but more general. It represents a persistent pattern for structuring stories, always reminding us that "the devil is in the details." Frame analysts do not necessarily argue that the media employ a secret tool to smuggle attitudes into ostensibly objective reporting. However, all stories must start from a specific perspective—and that perspective dictates what facts and details will be relevant.[89] It is useful to think of a media frame as a window with a limited view of the terrain outside. Other windows in different locations might offer a very different perspective. The press chooses the window from which we look at the territory.

The internet presents framing and priming problems as well. Unsubstantiated facts that frame an unflattering portrait of a candidate or his/her stance on issues spread virally—a simple copy and paste is all that is required to disseminate a story. Videos on the internet have a much longer shelf life than a newspaper story; televised or audio stories can be captured and posted. Audience opinions may be primed months after the original airing. Electronic rumors about Barack Obama included false reports that he was a Muslim and that he could not produce his birth certificate. During both the 2008 and 2012 presidential elections, his campaign dedicated websites to counter this falsehood.[90] In 2016 Trump had his own framing issues that were mostly self-inflicted. He tweeted demeaning comments about women, competing candidates, journalists, and others. News organizations increasingly framed him as a bully based on these behaviors and included the information early in narratives to prime voters to be hostile to Trump.

Campaigns at the state and national level are now a new form of the Wild West. Money feeds many of these bids for public office. And there has been a surge of coverage from nontraditional media. Tom Rosenstiel, director of the Pew Project for Excellence in Journalism, commented, "With bloggers and talk radio and the more partisan media in full flower, the norms of what's a story and what's not a story have been broadened. It is a given now that everything is fair game."[91] There is a bewildering array of websites offering information that ranges from highly reliable, nonpartisan, and fair reporting to highly partisan opinions, character assassination, and rumor mongering. "Many websites and blogs perform valuable civic service, while others practice guerilla warfare."[92] Online expert Michael Cornfield describes the internet as "Part deliberative town square, part raucous debating society, part research library, part instant news source, and part political comedy club."[93]

Expressive Political Persuasion. Thus far, we have primarily described political persuasion in instrumental terms—the use of persuasion to achieve specific goals. However, we close by noting that politics also has dramatic and ***expressive functions*** in any society. Like all the popular arts, political symbols sometimes exist more for the emotional lift they give participants than for the specific effects they produce in the nation's governmental and civil life.[94] A Memorial Day tribute—with music, flags, and soldiers—hardly lends itself to a discussion of the foreign policy decisions that caused the deaths of those being honored. The cross, the flag, and their verbal counterparts are not instruments of discussion as much as expressive symbols of affirmation. Think of shows like Broadway's *Hamilton*, Lee Daniel's film, *The Butler* (2013), or the docudrama *Hidden Figures* (2017) about women mathematicians breaking the color barrier at NASA. Politics in settings like these play to the kinds of status needs mentioned earlier in the chapter. They function as political narratives about our deepest aspirations.

SUMMARY

This chapter provided an overview of four related but distinct settings for persuasion. *Interpersonal persuasion* is vital; direct contact with target groups is generally more effective than mediated messages. The interpersonal route trades limited impact with many people for higher impact with fewer. Even so, as we have shown here, social media and specific forms of campaigns—especially electoral campaigns—include several variations of direct contact. The ideal of interpersonal connection needs to be replicated even in primarily one-way communication with various media.

Social marketing campaigns focus on influencing specific targets to change harmful or destructive habits, often to benefit their personal health or the health of their communities. Some are driven by leadership in organizations; others arise from grassroots efforts that today can expand to reach much larger audiences through social media. These campaigns contribute to positive changes that persuaders and communities feel good about, providing excellent examples for advocates engaged in other contexts for persuasion.

Advertising campaigns share the goal of changing behaviors—in this context, convincing consumers to buy products or services. A key strategy in most ads is positioning, which promotes what a product can say about us or our aspirations. We may grow weary of the daily inundation of sales pitches, but advertising is vital to an American economy largely driven by consumer spending.

The final context was political persuasion and covered legislative, executive, social action, electoral, and expressive forms. Deliberative bodies and political leaders—presidents, governors and mayors—are engaged in endless efforts to build coalitions and to find ways to move public opinion. Elected officials make extensive use of intense persuasion, as do ordinary citizens who seek to influence those in power. We reviewed some of the strategies and challenges of running for public office. Running for any of the thousands of public offices requires a panorama of skills to use social media, traditional media, and conventional person-to-person campaigning effectively. However imperfect, the noisy public sphere is the nation's birthright—a place for civic discourse to elect representatives to engage in the process of governing.

Questions and Projects for Further Study

1. Describe three nonverbal cues you watch for in interactions with friends, acquaintances, and employers.

2. If you work for a business, how would you describe its values and climate? With whom do you interact the most on the job? Do you feel free to make suggestions for job improvement to superiors? Are peers and managers good at handling tricky interpersonal tasks such as job-performance reviews?

3. The Truth Campaign is the work of the Truth Initiative®. Profile this public advocacy group. Who is their target? What assumptions do they make about the target? What makes their videos vivid and memorable?

4. Think about the items you have purchased in the last two weeks. How did you learn about them? Why did you buy one brand rather than another? What medium (including interpersonal connection) was critical in helping you make the purchase?

5. Select one product category and one print magazine (for example, automobiles and *Time* magazine or cosmetics and *Cosmopolitan*). Using a local library or an online archive, find back issues of the publication and see how the advertising for the product has changed for each decade since 1940.

6. Attend a city council meeting, a session of the state assembly, legislative hearings, or an address given by a prominent political leader. After observing one of these events, compare your overall impressions with the coverage provided by newspapers, radio, or television stations in your area. Did framing or priming occur? Was the coverage focused on strategy or messages? How well was the public served by the news story?

7. Plan a group viewing of the classic campaign film, *The War Room*. This documentary traces the work of advisers George Stephanopoulos and James Carville in the 1992 presidential campaign of Bill Clinton. While campaigns have

changed because of social media, the documentary nonetheless provides an interesting look at daily activities and strategies. After the film, compare your impressions. Specific questions to discuss might include:

- Does the film explain why the Clinton campaign was successful in 1992?
- What personal characteristics worked for or against Carville as an advocate for his candidate?
- What is the most interesting persuasive strategy you observed?
- How would you like to see political campaigns change?
- Which of the settings (political commercials, television news reports, rallies, and debates) offered the best opportunity for reaching and persuading voters?

8. Read and discuss *Shattered: Inside Hillary Clinton's Doomed Campaign* by Jonathan Allen and Amie Parnes. If time is limited, read several reviews of the book. What were some of the mistakes of the campaign? How did social media help or hurt her efforts? We tend to think of campaigns as just about the candidates. How does the book enlarge our view? Why was Clinton's relationship with her staff so problematic?

ADDITIONAL READING

Michael Burton and Daniel Shea, *Campaign Craft*, 4th ed. (Santa Barbara, CA: Praeger, 2010).

Robert E. Denton, Jr., and Jim A. Kuypers, Politics and Communication in America: Campaigns, Media, and Governing in the 21st Century (Long Grove, IL: Waveland Press, 2008).

Andrew Essex, *The End of Advertising* (New York: Spiegel & Grau, 2017.

Paul Herrnson, Christopher Deering, and Clyde Wilcox, *Interest Groups Unleashed* (Los Angeles, CA: Congressional Quarterly Press, 2013).

Marieke de Mooij, Global Marketing and Advertising: Understanding Cultural Paradoxes, 4th ed. (Thousand Oaks, CA: Sage, 2013).

Timothy Mottet, Sally Vogl-Bauer, and Marian Houser, *Your Interpersonal Communication* (Boston: Pearson, 2012).

Carol Pardun (Ed.), *Advertising and Society: An Introduction*, 2nd ed. (Hoboken, NJ: Wiley-Blackwell, 2013).

Robert Shapiro and Lawrence Jacobs, *The Oxford Handbook of Public Opinion and the Media* (Oxford, England: University of Oxford Press, 2011).

David Stewart, Ed. *The Handbook of Persuasion and Social Marketing Vol. 3*, (Santa Barbara, Ca.: Praeger, 2015).

Judith Trent, Robert Friedenberg, and Robert E. Denton, Jr., *Political Campaign Communication*, 7th ed. (Lanham, MD: Rowman & Littlefield, 2012).

Sherry Turkle, Reclaiming Conversation: The Power of Talk in a Digital Age (New York: Penguin, 2015).

NOTES

[1] Sydney Blumenthal, *The Permanent Campaign: Inside the World of Political Operatives* (Boston: Beacon Press, 1980), p. 7.

[2] Timothy Mottet, Sally Vogl-Bauer, and Marian Houser, *Your Interpersonal Communication* (Boston: Pearson, 2012), pp. 94–95.

[3] Ibid, p. 94.

[4] Laura K. Guerrero and Michael L. Hecht, *The Nonverbal Communication Reader: Classic and Contemporary Readings*, 3rd ed. (Long Grove, IL: Waveland Press, 2008), p. 4–5.

[5] Peter A. Andersen, *Nonverbal Communication: Forms and Functions*, 2nd ed. (Long Grove, IL: Waveland Press, 2008), pp. 256–257.

[6] Judee Burgoon and Gregory Hoobler, "Nonverbal Signals" in Mark Knapp and John Daly (Eds.), *Handbook of Interpersonal Communication*, 3rd ed. (Thousand Oaks, CA: Sage, 2002), pp. 240–242.

[7] Timothy Borchers, *Persuasion in the Media Age*, 3rd ed. (Long Grove, IL: Waveland Press, 2013), p. 257.

[8] Ibid., p. 258.

[9] David Matsumoto and Hyi Sung Hwang, "Body and Gestures" in David Matsumoto, Mark Frank, and Hyi Sung Hwang (Eds.), *Nonverbal Communication: Science and Applications* (Los Angeles: Sage, 2013), pp. 86–87.

[10] Ibid., p. 87.

[11] Kathryn Sue Young and Howard Paul Travis, *Communicating Nonverbally: A Practical Guide to Presenting Yourself More Effectively* (Long Grove, IL: Waveland Press, 2008), p. 81.

[12] Matsumoto and Hwang, pp. 84–85.

[13] See, for example, Sherry Turkle, *Reclaiming Conversation: The Power of Talk in a Digital Age* (New York: Penguin, 2015), pp. 19–56.

[14] For examples, see some of the research reported in William Cupach and Brian Spitzberg, (Eds.), *The Dark Side of Close Relationships II* (New York: Routledge, 2011).

[15] Mitchell McKinney, Lynda Lee Kaid, and Dianne Bystrom, "The Role of Communication in Civic Engagement," in Mitchell McKinney, Lynda Lee Kaid, Dianne Bystrom and Diana Carlin (Eds.), *Communicating Politics: Engaging the Public in Democratic Life* (New York: Peter Lang, 2005), p. 4.

[16] Charles Atkin, "Promising Strategies for Media Health Campaigns," in William Crano and Michael Burgoon (Eds.), *Mass Media and Drug Prevention* (Hillsdale, NJ: Erlbaum, 2002), p. 37.

[17] David Stewart, "Introduction," in David Stewart (Ed.), *The Handbook of Persuasion and Social Marketing Vol. 3* (Santa Barbara, CA: Praeger, 2015), p. 2.

[18] See one of the Truth websites at https://www.thetruth.com/articles/videos/ squadless?source=ASMSEARCH&gclid=COjdgJrUtdICFZpLDQodrk8HdQ.

[19] See, for example, Andrew Essex, *The End of Advertising* (New York: Spiegel & Grau, 2017), 171–174.

[20] Nicholas Bakalar, "Pictures Do Deter Smokers," *The New York Times*, June 14, 2016, p. D4.

[21] "Smartphone Use While Driving Grows beyond Texting to Social Media, Web Surfing, Selfies, Video Chatting," *ATT Newsroom*, May 5, 2015, http://about.att.com/story/smartphone_use_while_ driving_grows_beyond_texting.html

[22] Hilary Woodward, "Using Social Media for Advocacy and Public Education," Brown Bag Lecture, The College of New Jersey, April 7, 2017.

[23] Maane Khatchatourian, "Clooneys, Spielbergs, Katzenbergs, Oprah Donate to Parkland Students' March for Our Lives," *Variety*, February 20, 2018.

[24] A.J. Vicens, "Twitter Has a Serious Problem," *Mother Jones*, April 14, 2017, http://www.motherjones.com/ politics/2017/04/what-twitter-going-do-about-disinformation-campaigns/

[25] Alex Halperin, "Dan Balz: 'Being in Power Doesn't Mean You Have Real Power,'" *Salon*, August 7, 2013, http://www.salon.com/2013/08/07/dan_balz_being_in_power_doesn%E2%80%99t_ mean_you_have_real_power/

[26] Lynda Obst, *Sleepless in Hollywood: Tales from the New Abnormal in the Movie Business* (Boston: Simon and Shuster, 2013), p. 102.

[27] Ron Marshall, "How Many Ads Do You See in One Day?", Red Crow Marketing, Inc., September 10, 2015, https://www.redcrowmarketing.com/2015/09/10/many-ads-see-one-day/

[28] "Limit Commercialism," *Changing the Channels*, http://changingchannels.org/pages/parents/ commercialism.php

[29] George E. Belch and Michael A. Belch, *Advertising and Promotion: An Integrated Marketing Communications Perspective*, 9th ed. (Boston: McGraw-Hill Irwin, 2012), p. 120.

[30] Andrew Perrin and Jingjing Jiang, "About a Quarter of US Adults Say They Are 'Almost Constantly' Online," Pew Research Center, March 14, 2018.

[31] "Online Advertising Revenue in the United States from 2000 to 2016," 2018.

[32] Tim Nudd, "The 10 Most Watched Ads on YouTube in 2017," *Adweek*, December 6, 2017, http:// www.adweek.com/creativity/the-10-most-watched-ads-on-youtube-in-2017/

33 Zach Brooke, "Digital Ad Spending Expected to Near $250 Billion by 2019," *American Marketing Association*, September 15, 2017.

34 "Franchise Fever!" *Newsweek*, April 22, 2002, p. 58.

35 Lindsay Kolowich, "From Ray-Bans to Reese's Pieces: 13 Unforgettable Examples of Product Placement," *Hubspot*, November 12, 2015, https://blog.hubspot.com/marketing/product-placement-examples#sm.0000wgh2iyl5oe9tt9y1dbark5z9b

36 Jean Kilbourne, *Deadly Persuasion* (New York: The Free Press, 1999), p. 34.

37 Belch and Belch, p. 382.

38 Juliann Sivulka, *Soap, Sex, and Cigarettes* (Belmont, CA: Wadsworth, 1998), p. 425.

39 Kim Rotzoll and James Haefner, *Advertising in Contemporary Society*, 3rd ed. (Champaign: University of Illinois Press, 1996), pp. 114–115.

40 Zach Schonbrun, "Savvy Consumers May Be More Trusting of Ads Than Marketers Expect, *The New York Times*, July 31, 2017, p. B3.

41 Alexander Biel, "Likability: Why Advertising That Is Well Liked Sells Well," in Joe Jones (Ed.), *How Advertising Works* (Thousand Oaks, CA: Sage, 1998), pp. 111–120.

42 Mary Pipher, *Reviving Ophelia: Saving the Selves of Adolescent Girls* (New York: Riverhead Books, 1994), p. 202.

43 Schonbrun.

44 Marieke de Mooij, *Global Marketing and Advertising: Understanding Cultural Paradoxes*, 4th ed. (Thousand Oaks, CA: Sage, 2013).

45 Sapna Maheshwari, "A Bank Had Ads on 400,000 sites. Then Just 5000. Same Results," *The New York Times*, March 30, 2017, pp. B1–B2.

46 Robert E. Denton, Jr. and Jim Kuypers, *Politics and Communication in America* (Long Grove, IL: Waveland Press, 2008), pp. 5–12.

47 Lloyd Bitzer, "Political Rhetoric," in David Swanson and Dan Nimmo (Eds.), *New Directions in Political Communication* (Newbury Park, CA: Sage, 1990), p. 239.

48 Denton and Kuypers, p. 15.

49 See Silvo Lenart, *Shaping Political Attitudes* (Thousand Oaks, CA: Sage, 1994), pp. 18–34.

50 Ibid., pp. 20–22.

51 See Elisabeth Noelle-Neumann, *The Spiral of Silence*, 2nd ed. (Chicago: University of Chicago Press, 1993).

52 In George Comstock and Erica Scharrer, *The Psychology of Media and Politics* (San Diego: Elsevier/Academic Press, 2005), p. 13.

53 Roosevelt quoted in Emmet John Hughes, *The Living Presidency* (New York: Coward, McCann and Geoghegan, 1972), p. 184.

54 Catherine Mayer, "Voyager to the West, *Time*, April 28, 2008, p. 37.

55 See Matthew Miller, Donald the Weak, *Politico*, February 12, 2017, http://www.politico.com/magazine/story/2017/02/donald-the-weak-214771

56 Mark Hertsgaard, *On Bended Knee: The Press and the Reagan Presidency* (New York: Schocken, 1988), p. 345.

57 Reuters, "Obama Draws Biggest Convention TV Audience, Twitter Record," September 7, 2012. http://www.reuters.com/article/2012/09/07/us-usa-campaign-media-idUSBRE88619220120907

58 Christi Parsons and John McCormick, "Obama's Formula: It's the Network," *Chicago Tribune*, May 25, 2008, p. 6.

59 Mary Stuckey, *The President as Interpreter in Chief* (Chatham, NJ: Chatham House, 1991), p. 1.

60 Roger Davidson, Walker Oleszek, Frances Lee, and Eric Schickler, *Congress and Its Members*, 15th ed. (Thousand Oaks, CA: CQ Press, 2015), pp. 105–110.

61 Josh Tauberer, "How Many Bills Are There? How Many Are Enacted?" Govtrack.us, August 4, 2011. http://www.govtrack.us/blog/2011/08/04/kill-bill-how-many-bills-are-there-how-many-are-enacted/; Thomas, "List of Bills Introduced in the 112th Congress," http://thomas.loc.gov/home/LegislativeData.php?&n=BillText&c=112

62 Stephen Hess, *The Ultimate Insiders: U.S. Senators in the National Media* (Washington, DC: Brookings, 1986), p. 38.

63 Richard Oppel, Jr., and Richard Stevenson, "Enron's Many Strands: The Overview," *The New York Times*, February 27, 2002, p. A1.

64 Joseph Cooper, "The Modern Congress," in Lawrence C. Dodd and Bruce I. Oppenheimer (Eds.), *Congress Reconsidered*, 10th ed. (Thousand Oaks, CA: CQ Press, 2013), p. 408.

65 Dennis Johnson, *No Place for Amateurs: How Political Consultants are Reshaping American Democracy*, 2nd ed. (New York: Routledge, 2007), p. 15.

66 See Charles Bethea, "The Crowd Sourced Guide to Fighting Trump's Agenda," *The New Yorker*, December 16, 2016, http://www.newyorker.com/news/news-desk/the-crowd-sourced-guide-to-fighting-trumps-agenda

67 Larry Powell and Joseph Cowart, *Political Campaign Communication: Inside and Out*, 2nd ed. (Boston: Pearson, 2013), p. 230.

68 For one view see Yascha Mounk, "Democracy Has Stood Up to Trump," *Slate*, April 9, 2017, http://www.slate.com/articles/news_and_politics/the_good_fight/2017/04/democracy_has_been_remarkably_resilient_in_the_face_of_trump_s_assaults.html

69 Joseph R. Gusfield, *Symbolic Crusade: Status Politics and the American Temperance Movement* (Urbana: University of Illinois Press, 1963), pp. 1–22.

70 Todd Gitlin, *Twilight of Common Dreams* (New York: Metropolitan Books, 1995), pp. 7–36.

71 Alameda County Calif, *Voter Guide, 2016 General Election*, http://www.acgov.org/rov/documents/CandidateGuide2016-11-08.pdf

72 Johnson, *No Place for Amateurs*, p. 15.

73 Daniel M. Shea and Michael J. Burton, *Campaign Craft*, 4th ed. (Westport, CT: Praeger, 2010), p. 4.

74 See, for example, Karen Tumulty, "Maybe We Should Be High-Fiving Facebook," *Chicago Tribune*, March 21, 2018, p. 25.

75 "The 2012 Money Race," *The New York Times*, November 26, 2012. http://elections.nytimes.com/2012/campaign-finance

76 Jeremy W. Peters and Rachel Shorey, "Trump Spent Far Less Than Clinton, but Paid His Companies Well," *The New York Times*, December 6, 2016, https://www.nytimes.com/2016/12/09/us/politics/campaign-spending-donald-trump-hillary-clinton.html

77 Shea and Burton, *Campaign Craft*, pp. 130–134.

78 Presidential Campaign Slogans. (n.d.). http://www.presidentsusa.net/campaignslogans.html

79 For an interesting representation of this view see J. D. Vance, *Hillbilly Elegy: A Memoir of Family and Culture in Crisis* (New York: HarperCollins, 2016).

80 Joe McGinniss, "The Selling of a President," *Parade*, April 27, 2008, p. 12.

81 Ibid.

82 Tony Dokoupil, "How Global Politics Got Starbucked," *Newsweek*, May 19, 2008, p. 8.

83 Ibid.

84 Lisa Spiller and Jeff Bergner, *Branding the Candidate* (Santa Barbara, CA: Praeger, 2011), p. 7.

85 Neil Collins and Patrick Butler, "Considerations on Market Analysis for Political Parties," in Nicholas O'Shaughnessy (Ed.), *The Idea of Political Marketing* (Westport, CT: Praeger, 2002), pp. 1–18.

86 Shea and Burton, p. 116.

87 Ron Faucheux, "Strategies that Win!" *Campaigns and Elections*, 18(10), (1998), p. 25.

88 Shanto Iyengar and Donald Kinder, *News That Matters* (Chicago: University of Chicago Press, 1987), p. 117.

89 Paul D'Angelo and Jim Kuypers, "Introduction: Doing News Framing Analysis" in Paul D'Angelo and Jim Kuypers (Eds.), *Doing News Framing Analysis* (New York: Routledge, 2010), pp. 1–14.

90 Daniel Strauss, "Obama Campaign Launches Website to Fight Misinformation," *The Hill*, September 13, 2011. http://thehill.com/blogs/blog-briefing-room/news/181301-obama-campaign-launches-website-to-fight-misinformation

91 Dick Polman, "Those Aren't Rumors," *Smithsonian Magazine*, April, 2008, p. 118.

92 Johnson, *No Place for Amateurs*, p. 74.

93 Ibid., p. 27.

94 For a broad discussion of this perspective see Jack M. McLeod and Lee B. Becker, "The Uses and Gratifications Approach," in Dan Nimmo and Keith Sanders, *Handbook of Political Communication* (Newbury Park, CA: Sage, 1981), pp. 67–99. A less technical discussion of this perspective is also developed in Murray Edelman, *The Symbolic Uses of Politics* (Urbana: University of Illinois Press, 1967), pp. 1–43.

9

Visual Persuasion in the Design of Social Marketing Messages

> Form is the creation of an appetite in the mind of the auditor,
> and the adequate satisfying of that appetite.[1]
>
> —Kenneth Burke

Every instance of influence has a particular sequential logic—finding the best elements and putting them in the most effective order. For example, a new car salesperson knows that when a customer pulls onto a lot, the sales sequence should unfold in an expected order. The customer must typically be coaxed through the just-looking phase to describe what he or she wants. The next step is to check the inventory at the dealership to see if there is a match. If it's a good day, taking a test drive soon follows. It puts the prospect in a specific automobile and moves them one step closer to making the decision to purchase.[2]

The rule that every message has its own natural form even applies to creating music, which is perhaps the ideal model for understanding how form satisfies our expectations. Traditionally, the easiest way to think about a pop hit is it will probably adhere to what is usually known as the 32-measure A-A-B-A structure. This includes two eight-measure statements of the melody, followed by a modulated refrain or bridge that offers a contrasting musical hook, before concluding with a final eight-bar restatement of the first theme. By the time we've heard a third repeat of a good melody, it won't be easily erased from our minds.[3]

The pace of modern life often means that advocates must adapt messages to work in *nondiscursive* media where time and space are at a premium. Longer *discursive messages* like a set speech or an extended discussion with another person may have better chances of changing attitudes and behaviors, but that is a luxury not always available. Nondiscursive messages include online banner ads, magazine and television ads, billboards, posters, tri-fold flyers and short videos. They are a type of continuous wallpaper that lines the informational paths we travel. These

Knowing by Seeing

The idea that some people are visual learners is an old one. But it has special relevance in an age where media content is often designed as an image rather than information to read. Screens are a pervasive daily presence that have contributed to making us *ocularcentric*—oriented to visual content. The shift began with television in the 1950s. The new screen in the living room changed family life forever. A second milestone in moving toward the visual was Steve Jobs use of a graphical interface for computers. Video recording, DVDs and digital cameras facilitated construction of visual messages.

The transition to visual orientation has not been seamless. Messages can still produce boomerangs. For example, a 2017 Pepsi campaign portrayed a woman on the scene of an encounter between police and protesters. She broke through the line to offer a policeman a Pepsi, reminding many in the audience of Black Lives Matter activists protesting the deaths of innocent black men at the hands of police officers. The ad was widely criticized and quickly withdrawn because it proved to be an awkward misappropriation of a significant cultural meme.

short pitches are well suited to our more *ocularcentric world*, where what we know is often determined by what we can see.[4] This chapter explores important techniques of nondiscursive message design.

WHAT WE LEARN FROM DESIGN GUIDELINES

What does it take to be a good critic or analyst of visual design? There's a reasonable school of thought that a film critic, for example, is better equipped for the job if they have worked in the film industry. The critic is a better observer of visual storytelling if they have tried their hand as a screenwriter or actor. Music criticism benefits from knowledge of what it takes to compose or perform. An outsider to the process may still have interesting things to say, but the basis of their understanding will always be from the outside, not as a participant.

We can apply the same logic to persuasion analysis. Preparing persuasive messages in any medium is harder than it looks. What to say and how to say it are not ideas that announce themselves. We get an insider's perspective by gaining an understanding of the skills and sensibilities that contribute to effective messages. The Roman rhetorician Cicero notably included the practical processes of invention and arrangement (*inventio* and *dispositio*) as two of the cornerstones of persuasion.[5] The Greeks and Romans understood that a working knowledge of the skills needed to discover and execute messages was essential in grasping their limits and possibilities.

Our emphasis in this chapter is mostly on the representative category of *social marketing* messages and product advertising that combine verbal and visual elements. Social marketing campaigns work to change attitudes about lifestyle choices, health choices or contributions to organizations that contribute to the public good.[6] Think of posters, print ads and their home page counterparts as typical. Groups that sponsor these kinds of messages are spread across American culture, ranging from the Centers for Disease Control to the Truth antismoking campaign. Our attention to them here has three purposes: to appreciate what persuasion looks like when executing a short message, to gain some insight into how visual elements—photos, fonts, color, and other design elements—can help sell a specific action, and to notice the challenges of commanding the attention of a target audience that will spend only seconds consuming a message. Social marketing messages are good test cases for exploring the challenges advertisers and other types of persuaders face in reaching modern audiences.

STRATEGIC CONSIDERATIONS FOR NONDISCURSIVE PERSUASION

Nondiscursive media depend on the instant connections made by visual information because they usually have less time to make their point. Complex relationships and statistical data are usually given graphic representations or visual reference points that are easy to follow.[7] Text headlines must communicate an attitude (not just a topic) clearly and directly. Implications of danger or safety, threat or reassurance, approval or rejection often must be communicated in the familiar iconography of the culture.

The challenge of constructing nondiscursive messages is to stand out against the clutter of competing messages. *Clutter* is the advertising industry's term for too

Figure 9.1

many other appeals competing for attention in the same space. In the language of the elaboration likelihood model discussed in chapter 6, we usually process messages peripherally especially when they are one of many messages swirling around us. An image or key phrase must be memorable or the message will not draw our attention. In the realm of the internet, for example, the length of time an average user spends on a page is under a minute. Researchers refer to screen-based reading behaviors of scanning, keyword spotting, and nonlinear reading as power browsing.[8] Amplifying text is often ignored. There is only time for an impression. Persuaders need finely honed skills to make their messages memorable. The remainder of the chapter provides a concise design checklist.

Setting Realistic Goals

In direct one-on-one oral communication with another person, the chances of producing agreement can be relatively high. But it is far less likely that any brief encounter with a nondiscursive message will have a dramatic effect on attitudes and behavior. A message may capture attention, but usually to a lesser degree than a friend's direct plea. In addition, an hour of commercial television, as one example, contains about 40 commercials, billboards (brief announcements, usually 3, 5, or 10 seconds in length), or public service announcements (PSAs)—fostering impatience and inattention. Watching anyone peruse a magazine or an online news site also reveals the problem in attracting notice. A full-page ad may get little more than a glance as it competes for attention with photographs, human interest stories, editorials, headlines, and other advertising. Our level of involvement with advertising is less than in most forms of interpersonal contact.[9] To offset this handicap, audiences must repeatedly be exposed to the same messages. A successful direct-mail campaign, for example, may generate a response rate of 4.4 percent, while emails and online appeals typically get response rates barely higher than zero (.12 percent).[10] Online retailers have the most success; they can convert browsers into buyers at rates that range from 1 to 4 percent.[11] Advocates with sufficient cash may buy billboard space directly under a Google query, now considered "the most valuable real estate" on the internet.[12] We click through to these sites with much more frequency than to sites that appear down the list. Social marketing campaigns rarely have the resources of an Amazon.com or other online retailers. But many can still be effective in creating awareness about subjects that are socially or personally significant. Many of them allow persuaders to feel positive about the changes they are asking from others.

Targeting and Voicing

Targeting an identifiable audience is essential in every campaign. Finding the audience that will bring a persuasion campaign the success it seeks ranges from placing messages where they may be seen to buying access (via data-mining services that collect emails, preferences, and buying habits) for the best exposure. If you've distributed posters for an event, you know what the low-tech form of the first guideline looks like. The digital counterpart may involve posting an item on a blog, posting messages on social media, or purchasing an email or social media listserve. Many online content providers and merchants sell access to their users, most of which have identified key interests through their browsing habits.

Voicing a message requires deciding *who* the implied source of a message will be. It is important to remember that all messages have an actual or implied source. Of course, commercials make the brand the source, possibly adding a celebrity endorser as well. In social marketing campaigns, the brand may be the organization. Video PSAs need to select the source carefully. It's possible to use an anonymous expert (sometimes an actor) to deliver information or advice, but most public health organizations opt for survivors or celebrities to carry the message. A survivor has the advantage of being a member of the target audience. The inclusive pronoun *we* is an important cue to help the audience identify with the source. In addition, most designers match sources with the gender, age, ethnicity, and experiences of the target audience to facilitate identification. For example, in a message urging parents to vaccinate their children, a message voiced from the perspective of a mother is probably a safer choice. In two-parent households, mothers are the most likely health monitors of other family members.

Deciding on the Appropriate Color and Cultural Palette

At some point in the process of message design, choices need to be made about what is appropriate visually for an audience. Nondiscursive messages usually take us into the realms of commercial art. Dove personal care products look different than the typical advertisement for Bud Light. The blue and white colors of a Dove campaign could not be successfully transposed into the darker hues of a beer commercial targeting adult men.[13] Contexts and subjects obviously make a difference. Male-oriented messages tend to use darker and more saturated colors: for example, deep blues, red and black. And beer, of course, must look like a golden nectar.

Messages intended to raise concerns about persistent problems (i.e., smoking, drug use, or other forms of risky behavior) frequently drain away bright primary colors in favor of greys and blacks. We will have more to say about these kinds of fear-driven topics at the end of the chapter.

Sandra Moriarty and Lisa Rohe make the vital point that visual design must start with images and colors appropriate to a message's target audience. What are the most appropriate and least appropriate symbols? Does the audience have a preference for particu-

---

The Rhetoric of Hubble's Imagery

The space shuttle *Discovery* launched the Hubble telescope in April 1990; it has had a remarkable run as a celestial observer. Almost everyone has seen images that have transformed the presumed blackness of space into a virtual garden of constellations and stars. For many of us these glorious images are mesmerizing. What many may not know is that NASA colorizes the pictures. (The cover image of the cosmic cloud Orion Nebula, 1,500 light-years from Earth, is an example.)

The original images are functionally black and white. NASA has a strong bias for Photoshopping their images with earth-tone colors. Over 100 years ago, Thomas Moran and Albert Bierstadt painted sweeping landscapes of the mountainous American West. All feature lots of red and ruddy peaks throwing maroon shadows into deep valleys, perhaps inspiring NASA's color palette.

The lesson here is simple. The sciences are not immune from making choices that will sway supporters and stakeholders. We may aspire to present ourselves as hard-headed empiricists. But like NASA, we are all advocates seeking to impress when we offer our work to the world.

lar colors? In short, what's the right *cultural palette* for them? Moriarty and Rohe give us some examples from their research.[14] The best symbols for Mexican Americans often emphasize the family: for example, sitting at the kitchen table, sitting on a porch, or children playing with homemade toys or the family pet. Their research also found that certain elements should *not* be part of this palette: images of the Alamo, the Texas flag, clichés of a daytime siesta, or images of the military or police.[15] Appropriate symbols for an audience of mothers of young children could include a palette of "hearts, flowers, plants, circles, cute animals; shapes that are soft, rounded, and oriented toward feelings"; less appropriate are symbols of "war, violence, sex, starvation, social discontent, and anger."[16] The best *color palette* emphasizes yellow, purple, and pastels, while staying away from black, brown, and neon colors.

Designers need to be cautious about the application of any simple formula, but understanding that there are better and worse mixes of design elements increases the likelihood that they will not blunder into serious missteps. When in doubt, the best a novice designer can do is to spend time examining the web pages and advertising that their target audience routinely uses.

The Visual Image as Persuasion

An important aspect of the cultural palette includes core images: pictures or visual depictions that will immediately be understood as representations of the audience, of the problem that needs to be solved, or a requested action. A message urging teens to wear seat belts when driving might well feature a photo with a group in a car clearly buckled up. In social media campaigns, images often follow this pattern; they *model the behavior* the campaign seeks from the audience. Dynamic images (video), static pictures (print), and effective headlines or supporting text contribute to the impact of messages.[17]

Images can reassure or unsettle us. They are ideal for invoking feelings, familiar associations, and unusual juxtapositions. They give even the most abstract ideas a context—a grounding in the material world that links it to something we already know. Visual references offer shorthand representations of feelings and moods sometimes not easily matched by verbal descriptions. The facial expressions of happiness, anger, and fear are universal—learned very early in life. Unlike learning a foreign language or a specialized field of knowledge, we do not need to master special access codes to understand many forms of aural and visual information.[18] Every culture and subculture has its own mental repository of images that are likely to have well-defined and even sacred meanings. In many cases, these are curated by opinion-leading media with the care of an art historian planning a major exhibition. We know these touchstones when we see them: photos of dust-bowl migrants in 1930s America or refugees fleeing by land or boat from civil wars in Syria or Libya.

Images provide effective analogues to complex ideas or feelings.[19] They can easily represent the essence of a message. Thus, a campaign that urges parents to take greater responsibility for some aspect of their children's health might include a photograph of a child's small fingers firmly in the grasp of an adult's hand. The dependency on adults is thus illustrated poignantly. Pictures also function as commentary. They may be visual memes tied to a product (i.e., Budweiser's Clydesdales, GEICO's gecko) or representations of values more easily shown than discussed (the use of multiethnic actors in Coke ads). All have branded their products in contexts that are intended to make these images instant stand-ins for their message. With sufficient repetition—and without scandals or bad news—certain images trigger reliable attitudes. Add in representations of human faces, and a flood of feelings and associations can be evoked.

Images can also function as icons. *Icons* are graphic or pictorial representations that are instantly recognizable to members of a culture. Their significance is usually highly proscribed; we know what we are supposed to feel when we see them. The audience recognizes golden arches as McDonald's, white on red cursive script as Coca-Cola, and Smokey Bear in cautionary warnings about fire safety. Smokey's message is assured; these images are—pardon the pun—burned into our consciousness. Commercial art relies on the iconic image to enhance recall and favorable recognition for a product or service. It is little wonder that few professionals are more honored in the film business than those who are scenic designers, costumers, and directors of photography. Film actors may get most of the popular acclaim, but the look of a film is often what makes a story compelling.

Some icons trigger strong feelings and emotions out of their time frame, and that can be a problem. Before September 11, 2001, directors of films like *Working Girl* (1988) and *Town and Country* (2001) used the lower Manhattan skyline as a romantic backdrop, with helicopter shots sweeping past the dense skyscrapers of Midtown southward to the slender towers of the financial district. Among the images intended to convey the city's energy and vitality were the twin towers of the World Trade Center. But no more. Their outlines have become public property. The towers were iconic before the tragedy, but the symbolism has completely changed. A picture of them carries too much meaning to be used for anything less than a statement affirming a sense of loss.

Fonts, Pull Quotes, and Headlines

Thinking visually means questioning everything that appears on a page or in one frame. That includes *fonts*, the typeface that will carry the verbal elements of a message. Most publishing programs provide a wealth of options, requiring a message designer to tap into their instincts to figure out what is right for a given topic and audience.

Graphic design experts are quick to note that there are few hard rules on choosing fonts.[20] But there are some useful guidelines and terms that help us see what the best options might include, among them: be careful not to mix too many font styles in the same message; consider other media the target audience reads, duplicating the general style of fonts found in them. For example, content for children or adolescents may feature larger and often rounded font styles, such as Goudy Stout (See the examples in figure 9.2 on p. 196). Goudy Stout suggests a lighter, upbeat, or playful approach to its subject. As a rule, avoid office fonts such as New Times Roman that often look old fashioned and formal; consider choices that are more contemporary, like the ever- popular Helvetica. Helvetica is a *sans-serif font*, omitting the serifs, short lines extending out at an angle from an individual letter. Freestyle Script is the reverse: a *serif font* commonly used in invitations and announcements. Note that script generally lacks the assertive boldness an advocate may want.

Visual Monuments to Loss

Public memorials give form to the nation's preferred narratives of loss and the resolve not to forget. The most visited location in New York is the 9/11 Memorial Park, created on the site of the twin towers of the World Trade Center felled by terrorist attacks in 2001.

The park in the dense downtown area covers sixteen acres with rows of swamp white oak trees bridging two memorial pools. The vast pools (each side measures 176 feet, and the depth is 30 feet) occupy the exact footprints of the towers that used to dominate the lower Manhattan skyline. The walls are black granite over which water cascades before disappearing into the 30-foot square holes at the center of the pools. The impression is both soothing and a bit unsettling as the water seemingly disappears into the square voids. The pools are framed at the top by waist-high bronze borders naming the 2,983 victims who died in and around the towers, as well as at the Pentagon, in the fields of Western Pennsylvania, and the 6 who died in the 1993 World Trade Center bombing. Each pool is ringed by rows of trees measuring 212 feet, marking the outer edge of the original towers. The design, *Reflecting Absence*, attempts to visually represent the feelings of emptiness and loss.

Memorials are visual representations of narratives. The usual vocabulary of memorials includes the use of height and visual dominance to represent remembrance and renewal. War memorials in most town centers are shafts of stone rising into the air from sturdy plinths. The pools are different; they are dark chasms that memorialize and metaphorically allude to the disaster. The September 11 Memorial has the difficult task of accommodating the jumble of emotions associated with the violation of our national invincibility while also honoring the men and women who lost their lives.

Maya Lin was a student at Yale University when she won the competition to design the Vietnam Veterans Memorial at the western end of the Mall in Washington DC. The names of over 58,000 soldiers who died in the long war that tore the nation apart in 1968 are inscribed on the black granite wall. The design was initially disparaged as a "gash of shame" because the memorial recedes into the ground rather than rising above it. But for many, the memorial has become a potent emblem of the sacrifices of that war. Lin was one of the members of the committee that selected the design of architect Michael Arad for the 9/11 memorial (Peter Walker was the landscape architect). Both memorials can be read as a national acknowledgment of the enormous human costs of a national tragedy.

GOUDY STOUT

Times New Roman

Helvetica

Freestyle Script

Figure 9.2   Font examples

Since we are emphasizing messages that will mostly likely be read at a glance, consider a font that *scans* easily. Most sans-serif fonts are designed to be easy on the eyes. Also, avoid abrupt changes in font colors, **point** size (how big the font is) and **weight** (how thick the font is). Bolding any font adds weight, a plus for headlines that should command attention. Smaller supporting text should still be big enough to be easily scanned. It is risky to design anything that requires excessive concentration from the target to scan images and text.[21]

Many web pages that include more text than readers generally will tackle structure the text to catch the eye. One layout tool is the **pull quote** that lifts a few lines from the text, set in larger type, to attract the reader's attention. If the text runs more than a thousand words, the pull quote may use just 15 to 20 as a summary. Pull quotes are often at the front or to the side of the longer text section. Glance at any hardcopy or online version of a news organization to see examples. A short video segment on a website sometimes serves the same function.

In a single page, it is vital that assertive **headlines** appear to attract attention and to declare the attitude and behavior change that is sought. Headlines as assertions frequently take the form of injunctive norms, communicating a message that implies an action that carries the weight of community approval. These are usually better at getting compliance than less assertive forms of headlines.[22] Headlines generally should be full assertions of a point of view rather than topic fragments: not "smoking and children," but "Smoking around children risks their health;" not "vaccination," but "Be sure your children get all of their vaccines."

Most of the supporting text should also be assertive. Many of us default to information giving when writing materials. But an advocate needs to be more emphatic. Recent research suggests that a persuader should be careful not to include too much neutral information. A message may be weakened if overloaded with too many informative, unpersuasive elements. The persuader who lists a series of facts, assuming that they speak for themselves, will often be ineffective in changing attitudes.[23]

Honoring Gestalt Values in Visual Design

Design choices that are made about fonts, graphics, images, copy and sequencing are important, but they are only pieces of a larger whole. There are also several core design values to keep in mind that guide how they fit together. Several *Gestalt values* are especially helpful.

Gestalt theory was a complete psychological system that arose at the end of the 1800s. Its theorists believed that individuals and their creative work had to be understood in the specific context of their lives not as isolated agents. Much of the Gestaltists' psychological work has been discredited, but their descriptions of how we perceive relationships between elements of a visual field have provided a useful set of tools for design. "To the Gestaltists," notes Roy Behrens, "things are affected by where they are and by what surrounds them ... so that things are better described as 'more than the sum of their parts.'"[24] A Gestalt approach to the layout of images and text assumes that good choices create messages that are unified and perceptually satisfying. As Kenneth Burke notes at the beginning of this chapter, specific forms trigger expectations. We are hardwired to process visual information in certain ways. Listed below are five key Gestalt values to consider when making design choices to stimulate and to satisfy audience expectations.

- *Figure and ground.* *We perceive objects against the context of their surroundings.* We expect any background to provide a fitting and appropriate setting for the foreground action. A given *ground* should not dominate the images or words in front of it. It should help make the foreground material more vivid. A film director, for example, needs to be careful that extras in a wide outdoor shot aren't more interesting than the actors who are front and center and meant to be the focus of our attention. We sense this same need when we are taking a photograph, often looking for high contrast between people in the foreground and what is often a suitably neutral background. An art director planning a photo shoot may spend more time working on the background and lighting than on the person or material that will appear in front of it. We see this worked out in the buzzed driving PSA (figure 9.3 on p. 198). Both the note on the windshield and the supporting action step for the campaign are on clean and uncluttered backgrounds.

  A ground should dominate only when the message intends to suggest the vulnerability of a *figure*, as when a single surfer is photographed against an enormous wave. In the two schematic images below the grey provides a suitable ground for the word. The darker shading in the second illustration competes with the word, violating what should be a complementary figure/ground relationship.

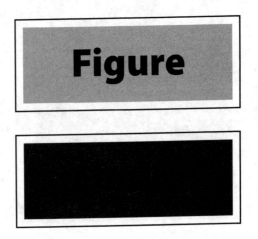

Figure 9.3

- *Similarity.* *We group similar things in the same frame together.* Images should have obvious and predictable connections to each other. Everything in the same frame should belong physically or psychologically together. Text (headlines as well as amplification) should use consistent fonts, rhetoric, and syntax within the same message or frame. Images should look natural and complete rather than odd or disjointed. This relationship is illustrated below in the schematic diagram by the insertion of an X in a field of plus signs. The X breaks the pattern established in the top box. For example, we can easily warm to an image of a three-year-old sitting on the grass under a tree. But a photograph of the child sitting on the curb next to a busy road would be alarming. Young children at the edges of traffic would unsettle viewers. This kind of awareness of composition means a designer of a visual message must formally consider whether all of the elements in a single frame are appropriate. The audience should not have to puzzle out connections that seem odd or confusing. Of course, if the misalignment of two elements is intentional and an integral part of the message, the effect can be positive. A child photographed near a table on which a handgun appears might work *if* the message is a reminder to keep guns locked up.

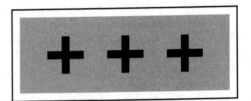

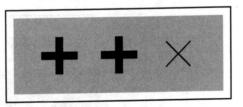

- *Proximity.* *If positioned near each other, we assume a close relationship between the things or people pictured.* The nearer individuals are to each other, the more we seek to interpret their presumed connections. Their status as coworkers, friends, relatives, or intimate partners becomes a significant part of what we are reading into the message. In Damien Chazelle's popular film *La La Land* (2016) future lovers Sebastian and Mia first encounter each other in separate cars on a freeway. We later see them at the same party, but not with each other. Soon enough they are sharing the same park bench and on their way to becoming a couple. As the story evolves, their distance from each other grows smaller. In our schematic below, when the two hearts in the first image are separated by more space, the message of closeness or connection is undermined.

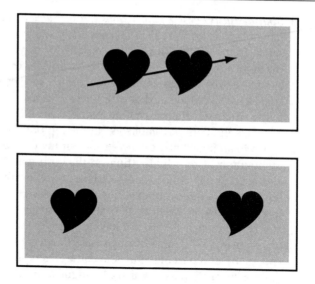

- *Continuation. The visual layout of a message should create a line or natural curve for the eye to follow.* The delicate business of composing representational images in all media must take care to lead the viewer's eyes to the central point of the message. Most visual forms encourage a consumer to follow a natural progression through an image.[25] In Leonardo de Vinci's *The Last Supper*, our eyes track to Jesus rather than to the apostles. Similarly, in Michelangelo's Sistine Chapel fresco, we follow Adam's outstretched arm and hand reaching toward the hand of God. In our example below, the top image fulfills this continuation function better than the bottom image. The addition of a path leads our eye to

the tree and completes the image. While this is a somewhat subjective process, researchers have successfully used software that allows the tracking of eye movement across a message.[26] A designer can often do the same by asking a subject looking at a proposed message several basic questions: What did you notice first? How long did it take you to understand what the message was about? And what, if anything, is distracting in the message?

- *Closure. We have a natural urge to complete what has been started.* Within the frame of a message, elements that raise questions must be answered. In art, music, and rhetoric, elements that are implied or partly concealed are often finished psychologically by the audience.[27] Leave off the last segment of a well-known song, and we will mentally complete the final few measures. Show us the first two acts of a play, and we will feel cheated if we cannot see the third. Give someone the setup line for a joke, and they will insert a plausible punch line. In our model below, two opposing arrows in the first frame suggest impasse or conflict. Their agreement in the second suggests closure, with movement in the same direction. A good rule of thumb is to make *everything in a single frame understandable in their own terms.* An effective piece of visual persuasion answers the questions that it raises. For example, a photograph of an individual should include a facial expression that is understandable by reference to other details in the image. In contrast, a photograph of a person who looks alarmed by what she is seeing *beyond* the frame would—in most cases—violate the principle. We would want to know what has provoked her alarm. The principle applies in other ways as well. A color palette used in one message should carry over to others in the campaign. Voicing and various thematic elements usually remain consistent across messages within the same campaign.

These Gestalt values can be seen in two public service announcements on the following pages. The American Diabetes Association image of the bride who will be married without the presence of her mother (figure 9.4) sets up an obvious short narrative that is explained in the copy that follows. Amplification about the risks and

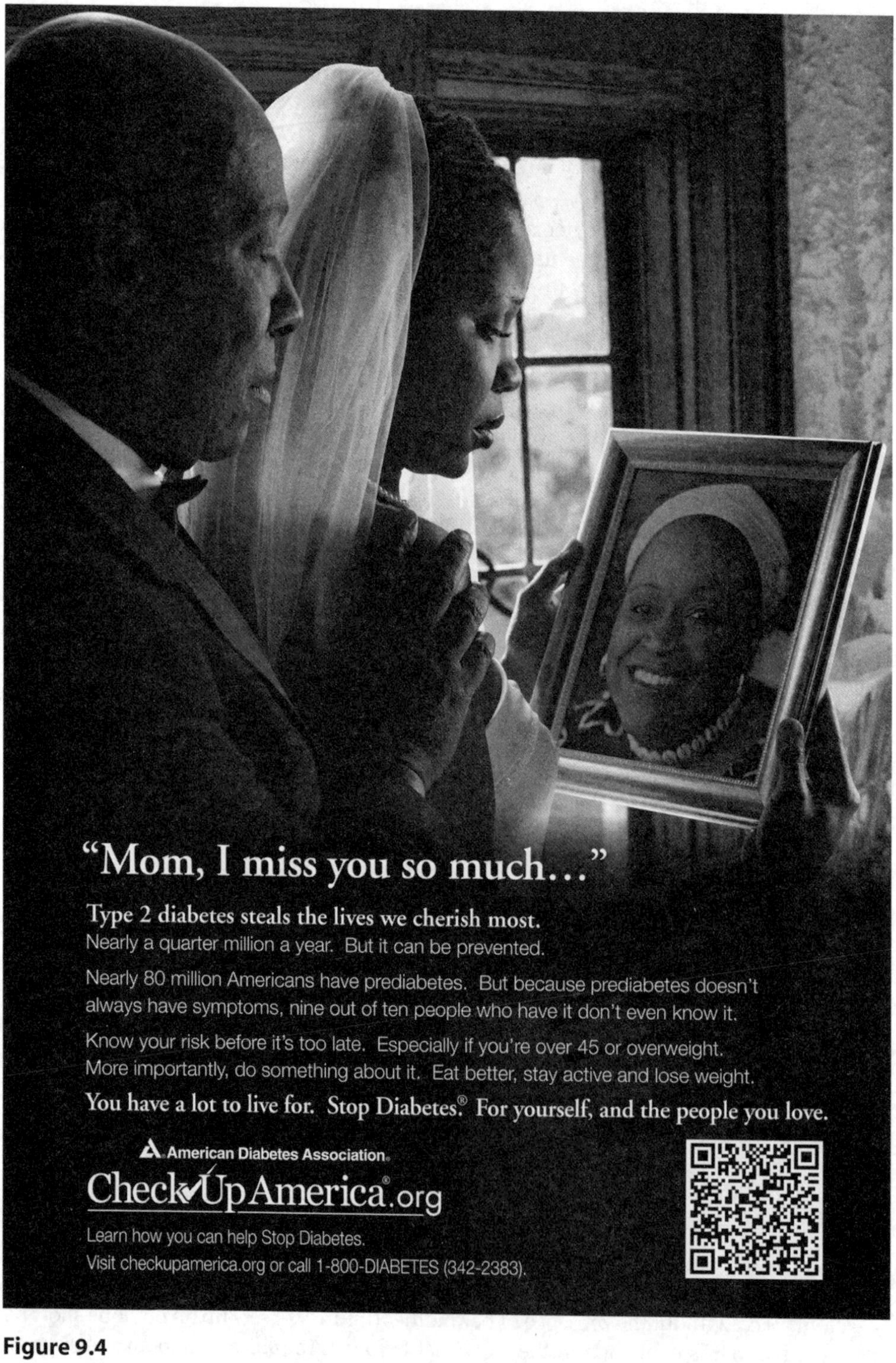
"Mom, I miss you so much..."
Type 2 diabetes steals the lives we cherish most.
Nearly a quarter million a year. But it can be prevented.
Nearly 80 million Americans have prediabetes. But because prediabetes doesn't always have symptoms, nine out of ten people who have it don't even know it.
Know your risk before it's too late. Especially if you're over 45 or overweight. More importantly, do something about it. Eat better, stay active and lose weight.
You have a lot to live for. Stop Diabetes.® For yourself, and the people you love.
American Diabetes Association.
CheckUpAmerica®.org
Learn how you can help Stop Diabetes.
Visit checkupamerica.org or call 1-800-DIABETES (342-2383).

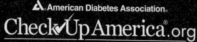

Figure 9.4

prevalence of diabetes features white text made clearer because it is set off against a dark *ground*. The eye goes first to the image of the daughter and photograph of her mother, but the message gains *closure* by essentially answering what has been set up in the visual tableau. We can also see the strength of a monochrome color scheme. In color, the text box and photo could feature too many dissimilar colors. In black and white, the shading adds a degree of *similarity*. The darkness of the father's suit coat functions as a pathway of *continuation* to the dark ground and its copy, enabling the reader to take in the message as a single and unified Gestalt. Even though the public service ad is trying to persuade by nudging the reader's awareness of a violated expectation—weddings are supposed to be cherished family events, especially for parents—the message itself avoids violations of our visual expectations.

The second PSA, "OMG" is a public service announcement to discourage texting and driving; it is part of the "Decide to Drive" campaign sponsored by the American Academy of Orthopedic Surgeons (figure 9.5 on p. 204). This PSA works somewhat differently from the previous example. Color versions of this ad have appeared in magazines, on websites, and as graphics on city buses. The ad is simple and direct. All the copy is set out against a contrasting white *ground:* black text and red splotches of blood stand out against the background of a broken windshield. The answer to the problem of the broken glass and urgent text appears in the simple statements that appear at the bottom: "TEXTING WHILE DRIVING IS A DEADLY DISTRACTION." In Gestalt terms, the message is all of a piece. Each visual element gains meaning and clarity from what is in the rest of the frame. The calculated proximity of these elements adds urgency to the claim that texting is deadly. Perhaps the only weakness in the message is the less unified bottom, with too many sponsor logos and a "Spread the word" line that is not well integrated into the rest of the message.

We have only scratched the surface in offering suggestions for the design of messages when time is short and the possibility for distraction is very high. The process of thinking in terms of color palettes, images, suitable fonts and Gestalt values can help the persuader in designing visual messages to satisfy audience expectations. We conclude our discussion of visual and nondiscursive persuasion with two additional design considerations that often arise in social marketing campaigns using visual appeals.

When Less Is More

Novices designing messages often add too many complications to what must remain a unified and simple form. When too much is happening in the same space—lots of text boxes, images, and font styles—it creates *visual noise*. Noise of any kind refers to elements surrounding a message that distract audiences, weakening the overall impact. Visual noise happens when there is too much going on in the ground of the message. Imagine viewing a 30-second video PSA urging American high school students to stay in school and graduate: a significant problem in many counties with low levels of household income. Imagine seeing a visual montage of twenty images of school life and employment training. Add in sound bites from different kids, an announcer reading copy and a rapper's lament about not getting ahead in a "cruel world." The effect is overload, even for the targeted youthful

Figure 9.5

audience accustomed to a circus of rapidly accumulating impressions. The message drowns in a din of sounds and images. Less would do more. A better approach might focus on the rapper delivering the message, with perhaps some of his words splashed under his image. What was to be the announcer's final reminder, "Stay in school," can be delivered by the rapper straight to the camera as the final shot.

Nondiscursive messages stand out when they are relatively simple. Direct descriptive text and a simple image can combine to communicate a great deal in a relatively short space. Consider the antismoking ad (figure 9.6 on p. 206). It is thematically unified. Everything in the message works to a single persuasive end. Note the reversal of conventional figure and ground colors. The plain text stands out as white-on-black. The eye is drawn first to the uncomplicated image of the smoker and his limp cigarette, and then to its explanation in the 13-word sentence. The use of the word *impotence* and the visual pun of the cigarette work together to provide unambiguous closure to the message. Smoke as a young man, the ad claims, and you risk the loss of sexual function. Every element contributes to the warning.

Risks and Advantages of Fear Appeals

One of the important and strategic questions a persuader working on a social marketing campaign must consider is whether it will help to use *fear appeals*. Fear-based *persuasion* depends on alarming or scaring the target with the consequences of not changing a behavior. We are used to seeing antismoking messages that remind current or future smokers that their lives will be shortened, they may get one of several forms of cancer, and that second-hand smoke harms their children. But should similar direct and negative effects be used in other campaigns? For instance, eating too much red meat? Binge drinking while in college? Setting up a credit card account while still in school? Having unprotected sex? A fear approach on these topics would require graphic images of unwanted effects—putting the physical or psychological results of the problem vividly on display.

Messages focusing on fear appeals tend to have their own rules. The color palette is often dark. Color is absent or muted. Warnings are vivid, often in heavy black or red text. And images tend toward the disturbing. The designers of the texting and driving message in figure 9.1 chose a middle ground. The ambulance is a frightening image, but we don't see a bloodied figure slumped over a steering wheel or lying in the street behind a crushed automobile.

Research on the effectiveness of fear appeals is divided. As Charles Atkin noted in a meta-analysis of health campaign studies,

> Fear appeals can be risky because there may be boomerang effects or null effects due to defensive responses by the audience members who attempt to control their fear rather than the danger. The three crucial selective defense mechanisms are selective avoidance of the message itself (due to unpleasant or alarming depictions), selective perception of the information (particularly the perceived likelihood of negative outcomes), and denial of applicability to the self.[28]

On the other hand, messages of warning may benefit from images and effectively represent potential consequences if a person resists changing a problematic behavior. For example, most messages that remind cigarette users that their children

Figure 9.6   (Courtesy of California Department of Health Services)

deserve to breathe clean air can be quite effective, especially when a child is shown through the haze of carcinogenic particulates that make up smoke. Fear appeals represent another area in which predicting persuasive effects is a complex endeavor.

SUMMARY

In this chapter, we pursued two different but related lines of exploration. One goal was to gain a fresh set of eyes for nondiscursive persuasion messages. We reviewed the role of graphics, images, and layout for effective persuasion. Evocative images, color choices, and headlines attract attention.

Our second line of exploration used social marketing campaigns as a representative message form. They are a good category to explore since so many of the most urgent personal and political choices facing Americans are tied to health care, and because these messages offer challenges common to other forms of nondiscursive media. Using important tools such as the five Gestalt values (figure/ground, similarity, proximity, continuation, and closure), careful image selection, consideration of color and cultural palettes, we made a number of tactical suggestions for visually oriented messages.

- Using images, fonts, and icons that thematically enhance your message
- Making every word and image count, with an emphasis on concrete symbols that communicate a clear problem and solution
- Using assertive headlines in place of questions and single-word topics
- Choosing fonts and images that match the topic and the target
- Avoiding designs with distracting visual noise
- Voicing messages from sources that a target can relate to
- Remaining open to the possibility that fear drive images or appeals might boomerang.

Even though we may strategize carefully over the choices of certain communication elements, it pays to be humble about anticipated effects. Even well-intentioned plans can run aground for unexpected reasons. Unanticipated effects can—and have—boomeranged. For example, some antidrug messages actually made drug use more acceptable, and advertisements sometimes leave us cheering for the other brand. A message designer is, in a sense, put to the ultimate test of applying tactics and strategies to affect individuals who are not as predictable as we would wish. Even so, perhaps nothing is quite as satisfying as using our talents as advocates to promote a worthy cause.

QUESTIONS AND PROJECTS FOR FURTHER STUDY

1. Assess sample messages from the Truth Campaign that targets younger Americans to not take up smoking (https://www.thetruth.com/). Make notes on how they have branded the campaign to be thematically consistent. What is the dominant color palette for the campaign? How are the messages voiced? What images do they favor in still photos and online videos? And how well do you think they speak to their target of teens?

2. Research a social marketing campaign you have seen: for example, AT&T's "It Can Wait" campaign. Other campaigns related to HIV prevention, HPV vaccines, and many other problems can be seen at the Center for Disease Control's Gateway to Health Communication & Social Marketing Practice (https://www.cdc.gov/healthcommunication/campaigns/index.html). Write a short critique of the messages presented on one problem, using standards developed in the chapter. In your opinion, what would enhance the messages? How would you rate the chances of the campaign to change attitudes and/or behavior?

3. Using Anthony Pratkanis's "Social Influence Analysis: An Index of Tactics" listed in the Additional Reading section, identify a persuasion tactic that you find especially interesting. In a brief summary to your group, explain the tactic and how it might fit in a given persuasion situation.

4. Develop a single page ad for the Truth campaign or one of the CDC's many health topics. Identify the target audience. Using stock photos from Google Images or another source, design the message, writing your own original headlines and supporting text. Present it to the class and defend the design choices that you made.

5. Working with a partner and using some of the recommendations for constructing nondiscursive forms of persuasion, identify a target audience and design a one-page ad for a social action group that interests you (Greenpeace, Mothers Against Drunk Driving, Planned Parenthood, etc.). Consider the role of photos, headlines, key symbols, and additional persuasive copy.

Additional Reading

Roy Behrens, *Design in the Visual Arts* (Englewood Cliffs, NJ: Prentice-Hall, 1984).

Bruce Gronbeck, "Reconceptualizing the Visual Experience in Media Studies," in Judith Trent (Ed.), *Communication: Views from the Helm for the 21st Century* (Boston: Allyn & Bacon, 1998).

Paul Lester, *Visual Communication: Images with Messages*, 6th ed. (Belmont, CA: Wadsworth, 2014).

Anthony Pratkanis, "Social Influence Analysis: An Index of Tactics," in Anthony Pratkanis (ed.), *The Science of Social Influence: Advances and Future Progress* (New York: Psychology Press, 2007), pp. 17–82.

Lawrence J. Prelli, *Rhetorics of Display* (Columbia: University of South Carolina Press, 2006).

John Rossiter and Larry Percy, "Visual Communication in Advertising," in Richard Jackson Harris (Ed.), *Information Processing Research in Advertising* (Hillsdale, NJ: Lawrence Erlbaum Associates, 1983), pp. 103–109.

Ken Smith, Sandra Moriarty, Gretchen Barbatsis, and Keith Kenney (Eds.), *Handbook of Visual Communication* (Mahwah, NJ: Lawrence Erlbaum, 2005).

David Stewart, ed. *The Handbook of Persuasion and Social Marketing Vol. 3*, (Santa Barbara, CA: Praeger, 2015).

Edward Tufte, *Visual Explanations* (Cheshire, CT: Graphics Press, 1997).

Notes

1. Kenneth Burke, *Counter-Statement* (Berkeley: University of California Press, 1968, p. 31.
2. Chandler Phillips, "Confessions of a Car Salesman," *Edmunds.com*, May 4, 2009, http://www.edmunds.com/car-buying/confessions-of-a-car-salesman-pg2.html
3. See, for example, Daniel J. Levitin, *This Is Your Brain on Music* (New York: Penguin, 2006), pp. 237–240.

4 Bruce Gronbeck, "Reconceptualizing the Visual Experience in Media Studies," in Judith Trent (Ed.), *Communication: Views from the Helm for the 21st Century* (Boston: Allyn & Bacon, 1998), pp. 291–292.

5 Cicero, *De Inventione*, Book 1, Trans. H. M. Hubbell, 1949, (Cambridge MA: Harvard University Press, 1949).

6 David Stewart, "Introduction," in David Stewart (Ed.), *The Handbook of Persuasion and Social Marketing Vol. 3* (Santa Barbara, CA: Praeger, 2015), p. 1–5.

7 For excellent examples of visual presentations of ideas see Edward Tufte, *Visual Explanations* (Cheshire, CT: Graphics Press, 1997).

8 See Nicholas Carr, *The Shallows: What the Internet Is Doing to Our Brains* (New York: Norton, 2010), pp. 135–137.

9 See, for example, Robert E. Burnkrant and Alan Sawyer, "Effects of Involvement and Message Content on Information-Processing Intensity," in Richard Jackson Harris (Ed.), *Information Processing Research in Advertising* (Hillsdale, NJ: Lawrence Erlbaum Associates, 1983), pp. 43–64.

10 Allison Schiff, "Direct Mail Response Rates Beat Digital." June 14, 2012, *DMNnews.com*, http://www.dmnews.com/dma-direct-mail-response-rates-beat-digital/article/245780/

11 Dave Chaffey, "Ecommerce Conversion Rates," *Smart Insights.com*, March 2, 2017, http://www.smartinsights.com/ecommerce/ecommerce-analytics/ecommerce-conversion-rates/

12 Daisuke Wakabayashi, "A Google Gold Mine Below the Search Bar," *The New York Times*, April 24, 2017, pp. B1, B3.

13 Compare messages on their websites at http://www.budlight.com/ and http://www.dove.us/Social-Mission/campaign-for-real-beauty.aspx

14 Sandra Moriarty and Lisa Rohe, "Cultural Palettes in Print Advertising: Formative Research Design Method," in Ken Smith, Sandra Moriarty, Gretchen Barbatsis, and Keith Kenney (Eds.), *Handbook of Visual Communication* (Mahwah, NJ: Lawrence Erlbaum, 2005), pp. 117, 120.

15 Ibid, p. 124.

16 Ibid., p. 125.

17 John Rossiter and Larry Percy, "Visual Communication in Advertising," in Harris, pp. 103–109.

18 Joshua Meyrowitz, *No Sense of Place* (New York: Oxford, 1985), pp. 93–99.

19 See, for example, Robert Hariman and John Louis Lucaites, "Liberal Representation and Global Order: the Iconic Photograph from Tiananmen Square," in Lawrence J. Prelli (Ed.), *Rhetorics of Display* (Columbia: University of South Carolina Press, 2006), pp. 121–138.

20 Dan Mayer, "What Font Shall I Use?" *Smashing Magazine*, December 14, 2010, https://www.smashingmagazine.com/2010/12/what-font-should-i-use-five-principles-for-choosing-and-using-typefaces/

21 Ibid., to see more useful guidelines.

22 Robert Cialdini, Linda Demaine, Brad Sagarin, Daniel Barrett, Kelton Rhoads, and Patricia Winter, "Managing Social Norms for Persuasive Impact," *Social Influence*, March, 2006, 3–15.

23 Anthony Pratkanis, "Social Influence Analysis: An Index of Tactics," in Anthony Pratkanis (Ed.), *The Science of Social Influence: Advances and Future Progress* (New York: Psychology Press, 2007), p. 45. Readers may find this article useful as a survey of message design concepts and tactics.

24 Roy Behrens, *Design in the Visual Arts* (Englewood Cliffs, NJ: Prentice-Hall, 1984), p. 49.

25 For an overview of eye-tracking research and technology see Sheree Josephson, "Eye Tracking Methodology and the Internet," in Ken Smith, Barbatsis, and Kenney, pp. 63–80.

26 Tarun Wadhwa, "Eye-Tracking Technologies Are About To Make Advertising Even More Invasive," *Forbes*, May, 2013, https://www.forbes.com/sites/tarunwadhwa/2013/05/08/with-recent-advances-in-eye-tracking-advertising-set-to-become-even-more-invasive/#6316c9f22a0c

27 See, for example, Paul Lester, *Visual Communication: Images with Messages*, 4th ed. (Belmont, CA: Wadsworth, 2006), pp. 3–28; Ralph Haber and Maurice Hershenson, *The Psychology of Visual Perception*, 2nd ed. (New York: Holt, Rinehart and Winston, 1980), pp. 315–316.

28 Charles Atkin, "Promising Strategies for Media Health Campaigns" in William Crano and Michael Burgoon (Eds.), *Mass Media and Drug Prevention* (Mahwah, NJ: Erlbaum, 2002), pp. 45–46.

Index

Acceptance, latitude of, 116
Adams, John, 31–32
Adaptation, ethics of, 149
Ad hominem, 70–71
Administrative persuasion, 172–174
Adorno, T. W., 95–96
Advertising
  advertising campaigns, 166–170, 182
  assessing ads, 168–170
  clutter in, 15, 170, 189–190
  costs, 138
  demand created through, 167–168
  evolving strategies, 167
  fake news site for, 82–83
  four basic functions of, 167–168
  Gestalt elements in, 201–204
  inbound/outbound marketing, 164
  individualized persuasive appeal of, 75, 76
  Internet, 33, 136
  persuasion function, 167
  political, 135, 146, 176–177, 179
  positioning approach, 167, 169
  precipitation function, 167
  public service ads, 201–204
  rational reasons approach, 167

  reinforcement function, 167
  reminder function, 167
  social norms marketing, 132
  unanticipated effects of, 5–6
Advocacy
  authoritarian states and, 27
  believing in what we want others to accept, 145
  language of, 44–56
  manipulation and, 16
  in open society, 26–41
  reality shaping, 46
  self-perceptions and, 46
  subduing in a one-party state, 26–28
Agency, assigning, 92, 111, 113
Agenda setting, 180
Alien and Sedition Acts, 32
Alpha Dogs (Harding), 179
American Library Association, 35
Amnesty International, 27
Analytic arguments, 62–64
Anchor position, 115
Andersen, Peter, 161
Anonymity/identity concealment, 71, 92–93
Apple, 36, 168–169
Arad, Michael, 195
Arguments/argumentation
  analytic arguments, 62–64
  appeals vs. argumentative good reasons, 75

  circular, 72–73
  demonstration and, 65
  fallacious, 70–73
  implied and stated components of, 67–68
  persuasion vs., 73–76
  political debates as, 61
  practical enthymemes, 60, 62, 64–65, 67, 74, 76
  understanding, 61–65
Aristotle
  on arguments as form of demonstration, 65
  on audience-specific norms, 141
  on character/ethos of rhetors, 13, 84
  on commonplaces, 140
  on credibility, 13, 84
  on enthymemes, 62, 64–65, 76
  on human communication, 6
  on practical reasoning, 60, 62, 64–65
  on resistance, 14
  on three forms of proof, 69
  on truth in persuasion, 30
Artifactual communication, 161
Assange, Julian, 134
Assimilation effect, 116
AT&T, 33
Atkins, Charles, 15